Crossing Bridges

Crossing Bridges

Training resources for working with mentally ill parents and their children

Reader – for managers, practitioners and trainers

Edited by Adrian Falkov, Consultant Child Psychiatrist

A joint project supported by:

The Department of Health

Lambeth Healthcare (NHS) Trust

Lewisham Social Services Department

Lewisham and Guy's Mental Health (NHS) Trust

Southwark Social Services Department

Guy's, King's and St Thomas' Schools of Medicine, Dentistry and Biomedical Science

Crossing Bridges

Training resources for working with
mentally ill parents and their children

Reader – for managers, practitioners and trainers

Edited by Dr Adrian Falkov

Published by:

The Department of Health

Produced for the Department of Health by:

Pavilion Publishing (Brighton) Limited
The Ironworks
Cheapside
Brighton
East Sussex BN1 4GD

Telephone: 01273 623222

Fax: 01273 625526

Email: info@pavpub.com
Web: www.pavpub.com

First published 1998. Reprinted 1999, 2000, 2001.

ISBN 1 900600 48 X

Pavilion Editor: Anna McGrail

Cover design: Métier Design Consultancy

Page design and typesetting: Stanford Douglas

Printed by: Ashford Press (Southampton)

When someone is ill it can be scary....

When it is someone you love it can be very, very, upsetting and maybe you feel very sad inside.

IF IT IS THE PERSON WHO LOOKS AFTER YOU MOST YOU MAY FEEL ANGRY WITH THEM you may feel so cross that you want to shout or stamp or break something.

IF IT IS YOUR MUMMY OR DADDY OR ANOTHER SPECIAL PERSON IN YOUR LIFE YOU MAY EVEN THINK THEY DON'T LOVE YOU ANY MORE AND YOU may even think that it is all your fault.

A mother with a long-standing mental illness talks about her hopes and fears regarding her daughter:

> *'I don't think I'm strong enough... If I'd known [about my psychosis] I wouldn't have had her... It was selfish ... because I thought I might be lonely. She's always saying she loves me, but I know I've failed her.'*

Mother goes on to describe how:

> *'...because Sally is bright, she dominates me – my brain is dead – it's not like it used to be – so I ask her to change the Hoover bag, the Teletext. If we get a new phone – she does it – you know, Doctor – she's like the man about the house. So that person's going to take control – they're the superior brain, but then I resent it because I'm the elder... I hope she finds a good man and a happy life – that this business with me won't affect her future.'*

The words and drawings on the previous page are taken from *Children have feelings*, a booklet for working with children whose parents have a mental illness. It is important to listen to the voices of children and parents. By providing opportunities for children to talk and by listening to what they have to say, we can begin to help them and their families.

The full version of *Children have feelings* is included in **Appendix vi**. You may wish to photocopy this, along with *Coping at home*, a booklet providing advice for parents (see **Appendix vii**).

Contents

Introduction to the training materials 1

Participants 4

Chapter One   Overview 7

Identifying need 7

Conceptualising need 12

Meeting need 18

Chapter Two   Impacts on children and parents 27

A conceptual framework 27

1   Adult mental health 30

Depression 37

Anxiety disorders 44

Schizophrenia 47

Personality disorders 51

2   Child mental health and development 55

3   Parenting and the parent-child relationship 60

4   Protective factors, stressors and resources 69

Implications for practice 73

Chapter Three   Legal and policy frameworks 81

Adult mental health legislation and policy 82

Childcare support and protection systems 94

Confidentiality and information sharing 106

Chapter Four   Systems and organisational frameworks 109

The organisational context 109

Needs-led services 112

Framework of services 112

The way forward 115

Chapter Five   Service user perspectives 117

Young carers 117

Involving users in service development 124

Chapter Six   Access to services. 129

Culture and mental illness 131

Women and mental illness. 133

Family violence and mental illness. 136

Key points for practice 137

Chapter Seven   Inter-agency service responses 139

Developing integrated services 140

A service protocol 140

Joint work. 143

Engaging parents and children 145

Parental self-harm. 149

Chapter Eight   Preventive interventions 151

Aims and principles of prevention. 151

Preventive strategies 152

Communicating with families 154

Intervention for individual families 158

Specialist intervention programmes 160

Appendices   Appendix i: Key documents 164

Appendix ii: Glossary 166

Appendix iii: Developmental indicators 167

Appendix iv: 'What's Wrong With Mum?' 172

Appendix v: Resources and further reading 174

Appendix vi: 'Children have feelings' 181

Appendix vii: *Coping at home: A booklet for parents* 189

Introduction to the training materials

'The training materials are a tool for managers and practitioners. Consequently, they can be used in any way which suits local circumstances. Ideally, they should be part of a planned approach to improving services within a jointly agreed policy and resource framework. Realistically, very few organisations will have resolved all the issues before using the pack. The materials themselves can be a good way of raising awareness and building up momentum for tackling the problems of joint working in this area. It is likely that one or more people will need to "champion" the issue in order to overcome the inertia that is present in most organisations when a new issue is discovered. Top-down or bottom-up, it doesn't really matter, so long as practice and policy are integrated in the end.'

Paul Curran, Assistant Director of Social Services, London Borough of Lewisham

Between one in four and one in five adults will experience a mental illness during their lifetime. At the time of their illness, at least a quarter to a half of these will be parents. Their children have an increased rate of mental health problems, indicating a strong link between adult and child mental health. Parental mental illness has an adverse effect on child mental health and development, while child psychological and psychiatric disorders and the stress of parenting impinge on adult mental health. Furthermore, the mental health of children is a strong predictor of their mental health in adulthood. Although these links have been recognised for many years, it is not generally reflected in effective, co-ordinated service provision that meets the needs of *all* family members.

This Reader is part of *Crossing Bridges*, a training pack funded by the Department of Health to enhance practice and improve services for families in which mentally ill adults live together with dependent children. The training materials have been developed around an integrated, ecological model for practice in which mental illness is set firmly within a social, family and child development context. Genetic factors, individual qualities and experience, relationships, life events and daily living circumstances are all essential to consider in any attempt to address the needs of children and their families.

The pack is intended for use by trainers in all agencies to promote good practice (raising awareness, knowledge and skills) amongst staff in adult mental health and children's services, as well as within primary care and voluntary sector services. Improving inter-agency collaboration is a core aim.

The pack consists of a **Reader** and a **Trainer** which have been designed to complement each other.

The Reader

The Reader introduces and supports the training materials by providing information on:

- key topics in adult mental health
- parenting and parent-child relationships
- child development and mental health
- legislation
- implications for practice.

There are:

- examples of good practice (including work involving users, parents and children)
- conceptual frameworks and suggested models and protocols to improve understanding and practice
- references and recommendations for further reading and sources of information on good practice.

The Reader provides essential background information for trainers and is a further reference for participants. The Reader can stand alone and this will help those who have been unable to participate in training.

There are eight chapters, each of which has been included on the basis of feedback from focus groups and evaluation of the pilot training as well as relevance to the core themes.

Chapter One summarises the evidence about the extent of links between the needs of children and their mentally ill parents/carers and highlights opportunities for identifying and meeting those needs.

Chapter Two provides the conceptual framework which links together the core components – adult and child mental health, parenting and child development – which this pack sets out to address. Each component is examined in some detail by presenting selected information from much larger bodies of knowledge. Relationships between the key components – for example, the interplay and mutual influences between parenting and parental mental illness – are emphasised throughout. The dynamic involvement of a broad range of protective factors and stressors is also emphasised.

Information on relevant mental health and childcare legislation and policy is provided in **Chapter Three**.

Chapter Four introduces the organisational systems and frameworks within which current practice occurs. The importance of support for staff from all management tiers is emphasised, as is the prerequisite for improving practice and creating opportunities for collaboration within and between services and agencies.

Chapter Five provides a user perspective, including a focus on young carers and an example of good practice in user involvement to develop services.

Information about access to services is presented in **Chapter Six**. This covers needs assessment, the components of access and barriers to effective service use due to race, culture, ethnicity, gender and disability.

Referral pathways, information gathering, joint assessment and care planning are discussed in **Chapter Seven**. The core theme of improving communication within families and between practitioners and family members is described.

Chapter Eight provides an overview on prevention, including practical strategies. Examples illustrate the possibilities for improving practice by responding to the needs of all family members where a parent has mental illness.

The Trainer

The Trainer consists of four modules:

- Module for Managers

- Foundation Knowledge

- Working Together

- Assessment, Planning and Intervention.

It provides:

- a detailed guide for trainers on the use of materials, including how to involve service users and how to ensure that managers at all levels are an integral part of the training

- a guide on individual sessions within each of the modules, together with learning objectives and outcomes

- materials to support the training including exercises, case studies and handouts.

The aim is to ensure that training is linked and integrated into individual practice and service provision at all stages.

Participants

The project group

Antony Cox (*Chair*)	Emeritus Professor of Child and Adolescent Psychiatry	Lewisham & Guy's (NHS) Trust
Marie Diggins	Social Worker and Lead Officer	Lewisham Social Services Department
Adrian Falkov (*Co-ordinator*)	Consultant Child Psychiatrist	Lambeth Healthcare (NHS) Trust
Jenny Gray	Social Services Inspector	Department of Health
Geraldine Holt	Consultant Psychiatrist	Lewisham & Guy's (NHS) Trust
Kate Mayes	Training Officer	Southwark Social Services Department
Natalie Silverdale	Researcher	Lambeth Healthcare (NHS) Trust
Geraldine Xiberras	Administrator	Lambeth Healthcare (NHS) Trust

The steering group

Reba Bhaduri	Lead Inspector	Department of Health
Nick Bouras	Senior Lecturer	Lewisham & Guy's (NHS) Trust
Ann Buchanan	Lecturer in Applied Social Studies	University of Oxford
Antony Cox (*Chair*)	Emeritus Professor of Child and Adolescent Psychiatry	Lewisham & Guy's (NHS) Trust
Tom Craig	Professor of Community Psychiatry	Lambeth Healthcare (NHS) Trust
Paul Curran	Assistant Director	Lewisham Social Services Department
Adrian Falkov (*Co-ordinator*)	Consultant Child Psychiatrist	Lambeth Healthcare (NHS) Trust
Judith Harwin	Professor of Social Welfare Studies	University of Sussex, Brighton
Dele Olajide	Consultant Psychiatrist	Woodside CMHC
Clive Marritt	Social Care Group 6	Department of Health

Contributors

Ruth Dixon	Policy Officer, Mental Health	Southampton City Social Services Department
Kevin Gournay	Professor of Psychiatric Nursing	Institute of Psychiatry
Richard Green	Evaluation Officer	NSPCC
Hilary Griggs	Principal Clinical Psychologist	Shropshire Community/ Mental Health Trust
Dora Jonathan	Director	Jonathan Associates
Ilan Katz	Practice Development Unit	NSPCC
Heide Lloyd	Research Contributor	
Omilade Oladele	Freelance Trainer	
Melanie Phillips	Training Consultant	
Briege Rooney	Senior Social Worker	Newbury Social Services Department
Jo Salter	Training Officer	Lewisham Social Services Department
Lin Slater	Designated Nurse Child Protection	Lambeth Healthcare (NHS) Trust
Steve Walker	Training Officer	Kingston Social Services Department
Joanne Warner	Lecturer in Applied Social Studies	University of Oxford
Amy Weir	Principal Manager	Camden Social Services Department
Jane Wonnacott	Freelance Trainer and Consultant	

We are also grateful for the support provided by:

- London Borough of Lewisham Social Services Department in piloting materials, together with Lewisham & Guy's Mental Health Trust
- Participants, trainers and users for their commitment and feedback during the piloting phase
- London Borough of Southwark Social Services Department
- Lambeth Healthcare (NHS) Trust (Department of Child and Family Psychiatry).

Chapter One

Overview

Identifying need

The link between mentally ill parents and their children

For much of this century, there has been awareness of the strong association between parental mental illness and difficulties in the development and psychosocial adaptation of their children.[1-9] The association has been reported for a wide range of parental psychiatric disorders,[10-23] and a wide variety of problems in their children have been described. Furthermore, strong continuities exist between psychiatric disorders in childhood and adulthood[24, 25] and across generations,[26-28] but **not all children whose parents are mentally ill will inevitably experience difficulties**.[29, 30]

Increasingly, researchers have addressed interactions between various child, family and environmental variables to discover why problems in mentally ill parents and their children are linked. The circumstances associated with positive adaptation in children and good outcomes for families have also become a focus for research and clinical activity.[31] Interest in genetic inheritance of mental illness and children's development and mental health has not been matched by similar efforts and achievements in service development for family members whose needs have been variously described as hidden, lost or neglected.[32-34]

In particular, there has been a **failure to integrate research findings into practice**. A disparity exists therefore, between the extensive identification of emotional and behavioural problems in children, and a scarcity of initiatives in service development and training to address needs of *both* mentally ill parents and their children, especially in relation to parental mental illness and its impact on childcare, parenting, significant harm and maltreatment.[35-38]

Issues for working together

Supporting parents and children living together

Since the 1950s, there have been substantial bed reductions in psychiatric hospitals as part of the deinstitutionalisation process.[39,40] **Care in the Community means that mentally ill parents and their dependent children will be spending more time together.** This creates the dual burden of increased childcare responsibilities for parents and greater exposure of children to problematic parental symptoms and behaviours when they arise.

Parental hospitalisation

For those parents with severe, enduring mental illness, repeated hospitalisation for variable lengths of time can seriously disrupt the continuity of care provided for children and the formation of stable, harmonious relationships. Psychiatric admission rates for England (1991–1992) indicated that women in the 20–44 age-band accounted for nearly 20% of all in-patient episodes.[41] Given that women continue to provide the bulk of childcare, the **crisis of parental hospitalisation provides important opportunities for assessing the needs of all family members.**[42–45] Particular effort is required to improve co-ordination between mental health services and provision of childcare support during and after episodes of parental mental illness.[35]

Separation, reintegration and consequences of loss

A lucid moment

> '*I lost my mind,*
> *And then my partner,*
> *And then my child.*
> *What's left but me?*
> *An empty shell of what I once hoped to be.*'

The consequences of parental mental illness have major implications for the quality of life and relationships for all family members.[46,47] When parents are hospitalised, children need support to adapt to their absence.[48] Their return may be even more difficult, especially if separation has been prolonged and there has been little contact and preparation for being re-united. For some children of mentally ill parents, accommodation away from natural parents, or their adoption, occurs because parents are severely and persistently mentally ill or have committed suicide. These are some of the circumstances in which adults and children experience distress, uncertainty, confusion and despair.

There is a complex interplay between mental illness and loss, both physical and emotional. Losses range from short-term, crisis-related losses to permanent changes in family composition and children's carers as a direct or indirect consequence of mental illness. They range from loss of resources to loss or distortion of relationships. Failed hopes, aspirations and expectations involving both parents and children can have lifelong implications within and between generations, highlighting the need to address consequences of loss in a variety of practical and therapeutic ways.

Identifying the number of families with mentally ill adults/carers and dependent children

At any one time, at least 10% of the general (adult) population experiences some form of mental illness,[49,50] and throughout a person's lifetime there is a one in four chance of experiencing a period of mental illness.

Zuravin,[51] quoting Myers *et al.* regarding depression, states:

> *'Ironically, at highest risk for this socially devastating illness are those with the most responsibilities for others, 25–44 year-old females, women in the very midst of caring for families and rearing children.'*

Specialisation in training and service development has meant that the core focus for Adult Mental Health (AMH) services is on the affected adult whilst in children's services the emphasis is on children and parents, but not adult mental health. It is therefore not surprising that the overlap between adult mental illness, parental status and child development has not been addressed and that very little systematic data is currently available on the number of mentally ill adults who are parents and on the number of referred children whose parents are mentally ill.[52–55]

Various studies have attempted to estimate the number of families who would be eligible for services. These have occurred in a range of settings across various tiers of service provision including:

1 *General population and primary care sector*

2 *Secondary/tertiary (specialist) services*

   – Adults known to mental health (AMH) services who are parents
   – Parents of children referred to local authority children's services and Child Protection Services
   – Parents of children referred to child and adolescent mental health services (CAMHS)
   – Children of parents subject to childcare court proceedings (and/or referred to specialist treatment programmes)

3 *Services involved with child fatalities.*

1 *General population and primary care sector*

● The National Household Survey of Psychiatric Morbidity in Great Britain revealed that the prevalence of any neurotic disorder (especially depression, mixed anxiety-depression and alcoholism) was highest among lone parents.[56]

● In a metropolitan area, Richman *et al.*[57] found that amongst mothers with responsibility for young children, the prevalence of depression was 30–40%.

● In their seminal work, Brown & Harris[58] found about a quarter of inner-city women with young children in their sample experienced depression following a significant life event.

Working-class women with children were more than four times as likely as middle-class women to become depressed in the presence of an adverse life event. The presence of three or more children in the home, the absence of a close confiding relationship and absence of paid employment increased the risk, as did the 'vulnerability factor' of having lost a mother before the age of eleven.

The studies undertaken in primary care settings highlight the widespread prevalence and important interplay between mental health problems, childcare burden and social adversity. **Given the number of mentally ill adults of child-bearing and child-rearing age, and the adverse impact on children's psychosocial adaptation, there are substantial public health implications for better detection, intervention and prevention of parental mental illness.**

2 Secondary/tertiary (specialist) services

Adults known to AMH services who are parents

- Blanch *et al.*[52] reported that in New York State a quarter of all clients identified as having a serious and persistent mental illness had children. Amongst females under 35 years needing intensive case management, 45% were mothers.

- In a preliminary audit of a sectorised community AMH service[59] regarding AMH professionals' awareness of their patients' children, 28% of 157 patients (CPA Level 2 and supervision register patients included) were parents. More than 95% of children were over one year old.

- A casenote audit of 124 consecutive female admissions to three acute psychiatric in-patient units[60] revealed a minimum of 20% were parents of dependent children. Very limited details about children were found in case notes.

- An adult in-patient study[45] indicated that 26% of 193 consecutive referrals had dependent children. Interviews with ill parents highlighted parental concerns about childcare arrangements, separation, their children's needs and the difficulties encountered in talking with their children about their illness.

- A census of professionals working in mental health and social care settings revealed that one-fifth of clients in a defined area of a deprived Inner London Borough had a severe mental illness and dependent children. Nearly two-thirds of ill parents were women, 37% of whom were recorded as having a current diagnosis of psychosis. In a quarter there was a history of known self-harm and in 31% there was a history of compulsory admission requiring use of the *Mental Health Act, 1983*. Responses to various socio-economic indicators suggested a multiply-disadvantaged group with severe mental health problems.[61]

- The parental status of adults assessed in crisis by Approved Social Workers in seven local authorities over a three-year period revealed that parents of dependent children were under-represented, and that of the 551 assessments involving parents living with their dependent children, 72% involved women. Where the diagnosis was known, 70% of parents had a diagnosis of a psychotic illness, especially affective (depressive) psychosis.

Those from ethnic minority groups were over-represented and parents were less likely to be detained under the Mental Health Act.[62]

Studies undertaken in AMH services suggest that a substantial proportion (at least 20%, probably one-third and in some cases up to 50%) of adults known to mental health services have children but that much less is known about the extent and nature of children's needs, including their needs for safety and protection.

Their children's high risk for psychiatric morbidity provides an opportunity for earlier intervention – reducing morbidity and distress in the short term and preventing future difficulties with mental health and parenting in the long term. This is an issue of particular relevance given the enduring nature of mental illness and because of the strong continuities that have been demonstrated between the experience of early adversity and later difficulties in adulthood.[24]

Parents of children referred to local authority children's services and Child Protection Services

- In an English study of local authority child protection agencies, Bell *et al.*[63] reported that of children referred due to child protection concerns, mental illness in a parent (including a suicide attempt) was recorded in 13% of 1,771 families and substance abuse in 20%.

- In the New York State study,[52] approximately 16% of children in foster care and 21% of children receiving preventive services had at least one parent with a diagnosed serious mental illness.

- Prior, Glaser & Lynch[64] found that amongst children on the child protection register for emotional abuse in four geographically representative local authorities, mental health problems and/or substance misuse (as described in case conference minutes) were evident in nearly half (46%) of the sample of 56 families (mental illness alone in 31% and alcohol and drug misuse alone in 26%).

- Isaacs, Minty & Morrison[37] found parental mental illness to be an important cause of children entering the care system and an important contributor to some children remaining in care for long periods.

- Sheppard,[65] investigating depression amongst the mothers of children on social worker caseloads, found more than one-third were moderately to severely depressed.

- A city-wide postal survey conducted by Leeds social services department,[66] which asked 800 workers from various agencies to identify parents with schizophrenia who had children under the age of 18, generated a 36% return rate and identified 207 parents and 321 children.

- The FAMILI (Families And Mental Illness Initiative) survey[61] indicated that nearly 30% of parents of referred children who had been allocated a social worker had parents with a significant mental health problem.

Parents of children referred to child and adolescent mental health services (CAMHS)

About one-third of parents of children known to CAMHS have been shown to be suffering from concurrent psychiatric disorder.[67]

Children of parents subject to Childcare Court proceedings (and/or referred to specialist treatment programmes)

● Studies based on (small) samples of parents subject to childcare court proceedings demonstrate substantial numbers of parents with mental health problems and substance dependence.[68–70]

● Amongst those referred to child abuse treatment programs, severe parental personality problems, persistent substance misuse and parental psychosis with delusions involving a child have all been implicated as poor prognostic factors.[71]

All these surveys highlight the importance of considering childcare and protection issues amongst mental health services and the development of a mental health perspective amongst child protection agencies.

3 Services involved with child fatalities

Studies of selected samples of children and mentally ill adults where fatal child abuse and homicide have occurred highlight links between parental mental illness and severe maltreatment. These studies emphasise the importance of ensuring effective communication and collaboration at all levels between staff within services to support parents who are struggling to meet the needs of their children including ensuring their safety.[72–77]

Conceptualising need

Mental health and *social care needs of children* and *parents*

Between a quarter and a half of the one in four adults who will experience a mental illness during their lifetime are parents. Their dependent children are at greater risk compared to the general population, of experiencing a range of problems in psycho-social adaptation. Some of the areas in which difficulties have been documented in clinic and community samples are: attachment problems, cognitive delays, psychiatric disorders, academic under-achievement and poor peer and family relationships.[78–85] Their needs for protection have also been noted,[86] including anecdotal reports of suicide in adolescents.[87] **It is the combination of bio-genetic inheritance and psycho-social adversities associated with mentally ill adults (impact of illness on parenting; family discord and disorganisation; poverty and housing problems; disruption in childcare and schooling) which increases the likelihood that children will experience difficulties.**

Current estimates suggest that amongst children whose parents are known to AMH services between one-third and two-thirds of children will experience difficulties, dysfunction or disorder, depending on the nature of the sample and criteria used for determining morbidity.[88] A child whose parent is mentally ill has a 70% chance of developing at least a minor adjustment problem by adolescence.[89] A child with two mentally ill parents will have at least a 30% chance of developing a more serious mental health problem; the proportion rises depending upon the extent of associated psycho-social adversities. Amongst referred children (those known to children's services, especially child protection services) the proportion with severe and multiple difficulties will be substantially higher.

Amongst families with a mentally ill member, various studies have reported:

- **financial difficulties** due to limited work opportunities (particularly if the mentally ill parent was previously the main earner)

- lack of **knowledge about welfare and benefits** [90]

- **high rates of divorce, separation and comorbidity in partnerships.** The links between mental illness and relationship difficulties are complex, and difficulties can occur due to co-occurrence of mental illness in both partners or as a response to the stress of living with a partner who is mentally ill. Higher than average rates of mental illness have consistently been found in partners of mentally ill individuals. [80,81,91–93]

Parental mental illness and child maltreatment

A range in the quality of parent-child relationships

The spectrum of parent-child interactions has been shown to include child fatalities and serious abuse and neglect at one extreme, through to impressive coping and caring despite the presence of severe mental illness in a parent/carer at the other extreme. [72,86,94]

Within the population of families with mentally ill parents and dependent children, there are several subgroups which can be identified. For example, children who are:

A   'well'
B   resilient but in need of support
C   vulnerable and in need of services
D   vulnerable and in need of services and protection
E   children who have been killed.

Children and young people who appear 'well' (group A) may include those who are doing well but also those whose needs are unmet because they are not in contact with services (hidden morbidity associated with poor access to services).

Table 1 A range of need amongst children of mentally ill parents				
A 'Well'	**B** Resilient but in need of support	**C** Vulnerable and in need of services	**D** Vulnerable and in need of services and protection	**E** Child fatalities
Increasing needs of children → → → →				
Decreasing number of children → → → →				

Young people who have responsibility for a mentally ill parent could appear to be coping but still need support (group A or B). They are capable young people whose needs are frequently not recognised (see **Chapter Five**).

The bulk of families known to mainstream and statutory services for children (groups C and D) will require a range of supports from various services, and at times, protection. Although the actual numbers of families where parents are struggling to meet children's needs and ensure their safety may be small in comparison to the overall population of children whose parents are mentally ill, their needs will be substantial, diverse and disproportionate to their numbers. Amongst these families lie the greatest challenges for inter-agency collaboration to ensure children's safety and provide support that is relevant to the needs of individual family members.

Whilst a child's death (group E) can highlight poor practice, it is debatable as to how many fatalities of individual children can be prevented. The importance of 'lesson learning' lies less in the prevention of individual deaths and more in the positive impact on procedures and practices. Promoting good practice can help the much larger group of children who are abused, but not killed and constitute the 'at risk' population from which many of the fatalities will arise. The recommendations from both adult homicide inquiries and child death reviews are remarkably similar – **improving communication, co-ordination and collaboration within and between all services and agencies.**[72,74,75]

Child protection

Studies conducted over the past 15 years document high rates of psychiatric disorder in parents of maltreated children. The strongest associations occur in court and clinically referred samples where families are known to child protection services (CPS).[86] These studies rightly emphasise the non-causal nature of the relationship. Psychiatric disorder could be a consequence of being known to CPS or the presence of psychiatric disorder may make such parents more likely to be referred to CPS.

Parental mental illness may influence child protection enquiries in several ways:[95]

● Parents may be reluctant to divulge past experience of mental illness (stigma of mental illness associated with being 'unfit' to parent).

● Social workers may interpret parental reluctance to provide information as related to child maltreatment.

● When dealing with parents/carers who behave in unusual, bizarre or threatening ways, staff may be reluctant to raise suspicions of child abuse.

● Professionals may have insufficient awareness, knowledge and skills about the impact of parental symptoms and behaviours on children's development and mental health which impedes assessment and treatment.

Much less is known about overall maltreatment rates and patterns amongst parents in contact with adult mental health services.

Psychiatric diagnosis and comorbidity (dual/triple diagnoses)

The main adult psychiatric disorders implicated in substantiated physical abuse and neglect of children are depression, substance dependence and personality disorder occurring individually or in various combinations. The triad of **episodic parental depression** and **underlying personality disorder** complicated by substance misuse appears to carry a particularly poor prognosis for parent-child relationships.

The combination of two parents with psychiatric disorders, especially depressed female partner/mother and personality disordered male partner/father can lead to serious difficulties in meeting children's needs and ensuring their safety. Although psychotic illnesses are less common than depression or anxiety disorders and substance abuse, they afflict a substantial proportion of parents who kill their children.[72]

Types of maltreatment

Most studies have focused on physical abuse and neglect, but subtypes of abuse are increasingly being delineated. A few studies have described specific associations between parental disorder and child maltreatment. For example, between parental alcoholism and child abuse and neglect; depression or anxiety and child neglect;[96] cocaine abuse and child sexual abuse; alcohol dependence and physical maltreatment of children.[70] Emotional abuse and neglect remains the least studied but perhaps most relevant and potentially problematic type of maltreatment. It does not present in the readily observable way that physical abuse and neglect manifest but, if actively sought, is certainly evident in families whose children are known to CPS.[64]

Amongst children known to social services, especially CPS, high rates of undiagnosed psychiatric disorder and low referral rates to mental health services have been demonstrated.[51] It is also likely that undiagnosed/untreated psychiatric disorder contributes both to the severity of the maltreatment and to parental resistance to the usual regimen of agency support. A study by Glaser *et al.*[64] of children registered for emotional abuse found that 61% of families/children had been referred to child mental health services, and 43% were either known to or later referred to AMH services.

Unintended emotional neglect of children by parents

In some circumstances, the neglect of children's emotional needs is unintentional. A parent/carer may be doing her/his best whilst also struggling with a devastating illness. It is perhaps not surprising that adult workers may feel the need to defend their client whom they perceive as being unfairly victimised if their capacity to care for their child is called into question. These competing needs can become the basis for polarised views which block effective joint working. Balanced consideration of all family members' needs by staff in *all* services is crucial.

User perspectives

Discrimination – Tackling myths, stigma and polarised perceptions

The number of children born to parents with schizophrenia doubled from 1935 to 1955 and the conception rate (for adults with schizophrenia or depression, is now believed to be quite close to that of the general population.[97–99]

The combination of 'madness', parenting and vulnerable children creates a danger of active and covert discrimination and reduction of opportunities for affected families. Taken individually, gender, race, mental illness and parenthood each carry the risk of discrimination and oppression. However, the adversities are greatly magnified when they occur together within individual families – **mentally ill women from ethnic minority groups who are parents repeatedly appear as the most vulnerable group – socially alienated, materially deprived with least access to support.**[100–102]

Polarised perceptions about the parenting capabilities of those who are mentally ill simply serve to perpetuate unhelpful myths and stigma – for example, the view that mental illness precludes being able to be a good parent or the converse, that a parent with mental illness must be allowed to look after her/his children (whatever the consequences for the child).

The fear of children being removed from their families continues to affect the quality of child, parent and practitioner relationships. **There is evidence that some parents who are severely mentally ill are at greater risk of their children being removed from their care but child maltreatment is not inevitably linked to parental mental illness.**[103–105]

Listening to users[106–109]

For *themselves*, parents want:

- good quality care and support to meet the needs of their children
- more understanding and less stigma and discrimination by communities and society in general about mental illness
- parent support groups
- support in looking after their children
- ongoing support from services beyond the acute crisis so that continuity in relationships with keyworkers can occur.

For *their children*, parents want:

- opportunities for children to talk about fears, confusion and guilt
- opportunities for children to meet people (adults whom they can trust) and to participate in activities where they can meet other children
- provision of explanations about events and circumstances surrounding parental illness
- continuity of care and minimal disruption of routines during crises, including hospitalisation of parent/carer.

Children want:

- information about the illness and prognosis

- recognition of their role in the family

- practical and domestic help

- a contact person in the event of a crisis regarding parent

- someone to talk with – not necessarily formal counselling.

A substantial obstacle to addressing the needs and concerns of children and young carers whose parents are mentally ill has been a lack of awareness about their existence.[110,111] The situation for those young people caring for adults with mental illness is further compounded by the stigma associated with mental illness and the absence of physical evidence of the 'illness'. Their needs are often hidden by their resilient capabilities and they are at times 'rewarded' with ongoing (practical and emotional) responsibilities for their parents. Finding this 'hidden' group is an inter-agency challenge requiring improved co-ordination and accessibility of services so that realistic opportunities are created for children to be appropriately supported and for young carers to come forward and talk.[112]

Practitioners must ensure that the positive aspects of caring for a mentally ill parent are not outweighed by overwhelming responsibilities which affect the opportunities and well-being of the child or young person. Resilience (the absence of emotional or behavioural disturbance in the face of stressors) should not be interpreted as indicating absence of need.

For children of all ages, increased understanding of their adaptation to the adversities of growing up with a mentally ill parent would improve opportunities for intervention and reduction of distress and morbidity in the short term. This approach would also facilitate implementation of longer-term preventive strategies with the potential to reduce the proportion of children who grow up and require mental health and other services as adults.

Grown-up 'survivors'

There are poignant anecdotal accounts by those adults who grew up with a mentally ill parent.[113–115] These descriptions reveal common themes such as isolation and loneliness, guilt and loyalty, abuse and neglect, grievances about mental health services and the importance of social supports throughout life.[116]

> *'People tend to protect children and young people. For me, this translated into ignoring my need to be informed and involved. My life was affected anyway and if I had had guidance it might have made the experience more positive. I needed good, age specific information about my mother's condition and its consequences. And I needed someone to talk to who would listen in confidence and help me to express and explore the complex feelings and situations I was dealing with.'* [115]

The long-term impact of burdensome early caring experiences includes:

- the development of premature self-reliance with difficulties in adulthood asking for help, relying on others, and developing trust and intimacy in relationships

- the emergence of symptoms requiring treatment, grief over loss of a balanced childhood, and diminished quality of life

- the effects of earlier experiences making caregiving in adult life (for the elderly parent or the transition to parenthood) too daunting.

These difficulties highlight the lifelong implications of mental illness in families and provide further evidence for the importance of support for children and young carers as part of a longer-term preventive strategy.

Meeting need

Mental illness is common and can be enduring and debilitating for affected individuals and all those living in the same household. It is an important public health issue with both current and long-term implications for family members, service providers and policy makers. A Task Force established in New York State[52] looking at barriers to collaboration noted:

> '...*Testimony suggested that mental health providers generally view people as patients rather than as family members or parents...Assessment...rarely includes questions about parental status or child care responsibilities, nor do providers see it as their responsibility to assist family with problems caused by the mental health admission...or to communicate with family members (especially children) about a parent's mental illness. Discharge plans do not routinely attend to needed parental supports, nor do mental health providers reach out to DSS [Social Services Departments] at the point of discharge. Few, if any, hospitals make special arrange-ments to accommodate visitation between parent and child during a parent's in-patient stay.*'

The feedback from focus groups undertaken as part of the development of this training pack, together with information from other sources,[117-120] generated a number of repeating themes from practitioners and managers across adult and children's services in various agencies:

- lack of training – a need and wish for multidisciplinary, inter-agency training to improve practice and overcome barriers to collaboration

- the need for active support by managers across all service tiers to promote more effective working together

- cultural, ethnic and discrimination issues to be seen as an integral part of training, policy and practice.

- recognition of the adverse impact on families of specialisation in services (adult *vs* child; mental health *vs* social care) and exclusive focus on core client groups

- lack of understanding about other services and 'specialisms' creating a significant barrier to positive relationships between staff in different teams and settings; all practitioners wished to understand more about others' roles and procedures, but stressed that ongoing contact was a primary requirement for effective working together

- current provision for adults and children was service-led and not needs-led, reinforced by a growing culture of 'purchasing and contracting'; front-line workers felt particularly helpless in promoting the needs of families within this context

- support for the development of 'family-based care', especially services which were non-statutory, accessible, flexible and involving user groups throughout

- the need to make efficient and effective use of limited resources was a prominent feature of all feedback

- there was much support for the provision of age-appropriate information directly to children.

General approaches

This is a summary of the key points which will be looked at in more detail in subsequent chapters.

- Mental illness should be seen as **one of a number of adversities** that influence the quality of life of many families.

- The **health and social care needs of children and parents** should be considered jointly.

- A **life-span perspective** emphasises children's changing developmental needs over time and recognises the lifelong implications of severe mental illness for all family members. It points to the need for proactive, preventive interventions and user wishes for continuity of support beyond crises.

- Promoting children's understanding and **improving family communication** about mental illness can help to maximise family resources and mutual support.

- **Early intervention** can benefit all family members in the short term as well as reducing the manifestation and/or severity of future problems in children and parents.

Identification

- Systematic mechanisms are needed for **recording which adults known to services have dependent children** and which parents have mental health problems.

- Staff in adult mental health services are well placed **to identify those patients who are parents and to initiate assessment and intervention where necessary.** Whilst not all children will need formal treatment, parents' childcare burden should be recognised and their children should have the best chance for optimal development.

- **Parents of children referred to children's services, especially CPS, are at particular risk for mental health problems.** Improved access to adult mental health services is needed.

Training

● **Support for training** is required to improve practitioners' recognition of and responses to the needs of children and parents.

● For adult mental health practitioners, this requires consideration of the interpersonal context of their clients/patients, in particular their role as parents, their childcare responsibilities and the nature of their children's experiences and needs within the parent-child relationship.

● For practitioners in children's services, a mental health perspective is essential so that the impact on parenting, on parent-child relationships and on child development is routinely considered and appropriate intervention planned. Sheppard has documented the poor recognition of maternal depression by social work practitioners and the incorrect diagnosis of depression.[65] The FAMILI survey[61] provided evidence on the extensive lack of even basic information (age, gender, number, whereabouts, key carer identity) concerning children amongst all services.

● The use of screening tools has been discussed by Dore *et al.*[121] Various validated and brief screening instruments / questionnaires are now available to facilitate the assessment of adult mental health, child mental health and parenting and some have been used in various ways for prevention and early intervention.[122, 123] The 'Orange Book'[124] revision, currently in progress, will include a selection of assessment instruments.

Management

● **Active support and supervision** for front-line staff are essential requirements for good practice. This investment can facilitate implementation of relevant protocols and policies by operational managers and the monitoring of progress and strategic direction by senior managers.

● When adversities are overwhelming and co-ordinated attempts to help parents meet their children's needs and ensure their safety have been unsuccessful, further disruption, discontinuity and confusion for children should be minimised by assertive decisions and actions to provide alternative, stable care.[103]

● **Working together** can create opportunities for discussion within teams, across services and agencies to promote shared understanding about ways of working. Various models of joint working are being tried such as integrated multidisciplinary teams, secondment placements and interagency options.

● Such activities could facilitate good practice by initiating **earlier communication between agencies** which could reduce the need for traumatic separations and enhance quality of life for all family members. Pre-discharge planning meetings, joint children's services and community care plans, joint commissioning and sharing of resources and provision are areas in which greater collaboration can occur.

- **Making the best use of inevitably limited resources** must involve more joint but focused discussion to clarify the nature of needs, thresholds and combined capabilities within adult and children's services across agencies.

References

1 Canavan & Clark (1923) The mental health of 463 children from Dementia Praecox stock. *Mental Hygiene*, **7**, 137.

2 Clausen, J. & Radke Yarrow, M. (Issue Eds.) (1955) The impact of mental illness on the family. *Journal of Social Issues*, **11** (4).

3 Buck, C. & Laughton, K. (1959) Family patterns of illness: The effect of psychoneurosis in the parent upon illness in the child. *Acta Psychiatrica Neurologica Scandanavica*, **34**, 165–175.

4 Rutter, M. (1966) Children of Sick Parents: An Environmental and Psychiatric Study. *Institute of Psychiatry Maudsley Monographs* No. 16. Oxford University Press.

5 Rieder, R. O. (1973) The offspring of Schizophrenic parents: A review. *Journal of Nervous & Mental Disorders*, **157**, 179–190.

6 Weissman, M. M. & Paykel, E. S. (1974) *The depressed woman: A study in social relationships*. University of Chicago Press.

7 Morrison, H. (Ed). (1983) *Children of Depressed Parents: Risk, Identification and Intervention*. New York: Grune & Stratton.

8 Watt, N., Anthony, E. J., Wynne, L. C. & Rolf, J. E. (Eds.) (1984) *Children At Risk For Schizophrenia: A Longitudinal Perspective*. Cambridge University Press.

9 Downey, G., & Coyne, J. C. (1990) Children of depressed parents: An integrative review. *Psychological Bulletin*, **108**, 50–76.

10 Beardslee R., Bemporad, J., Keller, M. & Klerman, G. (1983) Children of parents with major affective disorder: A review. *American Journal of Psychiatry*, **140**, 825–832.

11 Weissman, M. M., Leckman, J., Merikangas, K., *et al.* (1984) Depression and anxiety disorders in parents and children: Results from the Yale family study. *Archive of General Psychiatry*, **41**, 845–852.

12 Barnett, B., Schaafsma, M., Guzman, A. & Parker, G. (1991) Maternal anxiety: A 5 year review of an intervention study. *Journal of Child Psychology & Psychiatry*, **32** (3) 423–438.

13 McNeil, T., Kaij, L., Malmquist-Larsson, A. *et al.* (1983) Offspring of women with non-organic psychoses. *Acta Psychiatrica Scandinavia*, **68**, 234–250.

14 Hammen, C., Burge D., Burney, E. & Adrian, C. (1990) Longitudinal study of diagnoses in children of women with Unipolar and Bipolar Affective disorder. *Archive of General Psychiatry*, **47**, 1112–1117.

15 Cytryn, L., McKnew, D., Zahn-Waxler, C. *et al.* (1984) Special section: Infants of parents with Bipolar Illness. *American Journal of Psychiatry*, **141** (2) 219–242.

16 Livingstone, R. (1993) Children of people with somatisation disorder. *Journal of the American Academy of Child and Adolescent Psychiatry*, **32**, 536–544.

17 Derrin, S. (1986) Children of substance abusers: A review of the literature. *Journal of Substance Abuse Treatment*, **3**, 77–94.

18 Owings West, M. & Prinz, R. (1987) Parental alcoholism and childhood psychopathology. *Psychological Bulletin*, **102** (2) 204–218.

19 Rydelius, P. (1997) Annotation: Are children of alcoholics a clinical concern for child and adolescent psychiatrists of today? *Journal of Child Psychology & Psychiatry*, **38**, 615–624.

20 Hogan, D. (1998) Annotation: The psychological development and welfare of children of opiate and cocaine users: Review and research needs. *Journal of Child Psychology & Psychiatry*, **39** (5) 609–620.

21 Stein, A. & Fairburn, C. (1989) Children of mothers with bulimia nervosa. *British Medical Journal*, **299**, 777–8.

22   Feldman, R. *et al.* (1995) A comparison of the families of mothers with borderline and nonborderline personality disorders. *Comprehensive Psychiatry*, **36**, 157–163.

23   Bools, C., Neale, B. & Meadow, R. (1994) Munchhausen Syndrome By Proxy: A study of psychopathology. *Child Abuse & Neglect*, **18**, 773–788.

24   Quinton, D., Rutter, M. & Gulliver, L. (1990) Continuities in psychiatric disorders from childhood to adulthood in the children of psychiatric patients. In: L. Robins and M. Rutter (Eds.) *Straight and Devious Pathways from Childhood to Adulthood*. New York: Cambridge University Press.

25   Landerman, R., George, L. & Blazer, D. (1991) Adult vulnerability for psychiatric disorders: Interactive effects of negative childhood experiences and recent stress. *Journal of Nervous & Mental Disease*, **179** (11) 656–663.

26   Oliver, J. E. (1985) Successive Generations of Child Maltreatment: Social and medical disorders in the parents. *British Journal of Psychiatry*, **147**, 484–490.

27   Oliver, J. E. (1988) Successive Generations of Child Maltreatment: The Children. *British Journal of Psychiatry*, **153**, 543–553.

28   Andrews, B., Brown, G. & Creasey, L. (1990) Intergenerational links between psychiatric disorder in mothers and daughters: The role of parenting experiences. *Journal of Child Psychology & Psychiatry*, **31** (7) 1115–1129.

29   Kauffman, C., Grunebaum, H., Cohler, B. & Gamer, E. (1979) Superkids: Competent children of psychotic mothers. *American Journal of Psychiatry*, **136** (11) 1398–1402.

30   Anthony, E. J. & Cohler, B. J. (Eds.) (1987) *The Invulnerable Child*. New York: Guilford Press.

31   Rolf, J., Masten, A. S., Cicchetti, D. *et al.* (Eds.) (1990) *Risk and protector factors in the development of psychopathology*. New York: Cambridge University Press.

32   Elliot, A. (1992) *Hidden Children: A study of ex-young carers of parents with mental health problems in Leeds*.

33   Bower, M. & Taylor, J. (1996) *Forgotten families, Young Minds*. London: Young Minds (in-house publication).

34   Nicholson, J., Geller, J., Fisher, W. & Dion, G. (1993) State policies and programs that address the needs of mentally ill mothers in the public sector. *Hospital & Community Psychiatry*, **44** (5) 484–489.

35   Ekdahl, M., Rice, E. & Schmidt, W. (1962) Children of parents hospitalised for mental illness. *American Journal of Public Health*, **52** (3) 428–435.

36   Brown, G. & Davidson, S. (1978) Social class, psychiatric disorder of mother & accidents to children. *The Lancet* (Feb 18) 378–380.

37   Isaac, B., Minty, E. B. & Morrison, R. M. (1986) Children in care: The association with mental disorder in parents. *British Journal of Social Work*, **16**, 325–329.

38   Sheppard, M. (1993) Maternal depression and child care: The significance for social work research. *Adoption and Fostering*, **17**, 10–15.

39   O'Driscoll, C. *et al.* (1993) The TAPS project 7: Mental hospital closure – A literature review on outcome studies and evaluative techniques. *British Journal of Psychiatry*, **162** (supplement 19) 7–17.

40   Goldman, H. (1982) Mental illness and family burden: A public health perspective. *Hospital & Community Psychiatry*, **33** (7) 557–560.

41   Department of Health (1995) *Mental Health in England: 1982–1992*. Government statistical service.

42   Shachnow, J. (1987) Preventive intervention with children of hospitalised psychiatric patients. *American Journal of Orthopsychiatry*, **57**, 66–77.

43   Oppenheimer, R. (1981) At risk: Children of female psychiatric inpatients. *Child Abuse and Neglect*, **5**, 117–122.

44   El-Guebaly, N., Offord, D., Sullivan, K., & Lynch, K. (1978) Psychosocial adjustment of the offspring of psychiatric inpatients: The effect of alcoholic, depressive and schizophrenic parentage. *Canadian Psychiatric Association Journal*, **23**, 281–289.

45   Stormont, F., Craig, T., Atakan, Z., *et al.* (1997) Concerns about the children of psychiatric in-patients – what the parents say. *Psychiatric Bulletin*, **21**, 495–497.

46   Webster, J. (1990) Parenting for children of schizophrenic mothers. *Adoption & Fostering*, **14** (2) 37–43.

47   Miller, F., Dworkin, J., Ward, M. & Barone, D. (1990) A preliminary study of unresolved grief in families of seriously mentally ill patients. *Hospital and Community Psychiatry*, **41** (12) 1321–1325.

48   Castleberry, K. (1988) Helping children adapt to the psychiatric hospitalisation of a parent. *The Psychiatric Hospital*, **19** (4) 155–160.

49   Thompson, D. & Pudney, M. (1990). *Mental illness: The fundamental facts.* London: Mental Health Foundation.

50   Mind (1997) *Mental health statistics.* London.

51   Zuravin, S. (1988) Child abuse, child neglect, and maternal depression: Is there a connection? In: National Centre on Child Abuse and Neglect, *Child Neglect Monograph: Proceedings from a symposium Office of Human Development Services.* Washington DC.

52   Blanch, A. K., Nicholson, J. & Purcell, J. (1994) Parents with severe mental illness and their children: The need for human services integration. *The Journal of Mental Health Administration*, **21** (4) 388–396.

53   Wang, A. & Goldschmidt, V. (1994) Interviews of psychiatric inpatients about their family situation and young children. *Acta Psychiatrica Scandinavica*, **90**, 459–465.

54   Poole, R. (1996) General adult psychiatrists and their patients children. In: M. Gopfert, J. Webster & M. V. Seeman, *Parental Psychiatric Disorder: Distressed Parents and Their Families.* Cambridge University Press.

55   Kaplan, S. (1983) Psychiatrists and child abuse. I. Case assessment by child protective services. *Journal of the American Academy of Child Psychiatry*, **22**, 253–256.

56   Meltzer, H., Gill, B., Petticrew, N., Hinds, K. (1995) *The prevalence of psychiatric morbidity among adults aged 16–64 living in private households in Great Britain.* OPCS Surveys: Report 1. London: OPCS.

57   Richman, N., Stevenson, J. & Graham, P. (1982) *Pre-school to School: A Behavioural Study.* London: Academic Press.

58   Brown, G. W. & Harris, T. (1978) *Social Origins of Depression: A study of psychiatric disorders in women.* London: Tavistock.

59   M. Oates, personal communication.

60   Montoliou-Tamarit, L. & Lau, A. (accepted Nov. 1997) Children's needs when their mothers are admitted to psychiatric units. *Psychiatric Bulletin.*

61   Falkov, A., Murphy, M. & Antweiler, U. (as yet unpublished) *The 'Families And Mental Illness Initiative' (FAMILI), an interagency survey.*

62   Hatfield, B., Webster, J. & Mohamad, H. (1997) Psychiatric emergencies: Assessing parents of dependent children. *Psychiatric Bulletin*, **21**, 19–22.

63   Bell, C., Conroy, S. & Gibbons J. (1995) *Operating the child protection system: A study of child protection practices in English local authorities.* London: HMSO.

64   Glaser, D. & Prior, V. (1997) Is the term child protection applicable to emotional abuse? *Child Abuse Review*, **6**, 315–329.

65   Sheppard, M. (1997) Social work practice in child and family care: A study of maternal depression. *British Journal of Social Work*, **27**, 815–845.

66   Wood, L., Landells, S. & Pritlove, J. (1994) *Young carers of a parent with schizophrenia: A Leeds survey.* City of Leeds: Department of Social Services.

67   Dover, S., Leahy, A. & Foreman, D. (1994) Parental psychiatric disorder: Clinical prevalence and effects on default from treatment. *Child care, health and development*, **20**, 137–143.

68   Famularo, R., Barnum, R. & Stone, K. (1986) Court-ordered removal in severe child maltreatment: An association to parental major affective disorder. *Child Abuse and Neglect*, **10**, 487–492.

69   Murphy, J., Jellinek, M., Quinn, D. *et al.* (1991) Substance abuse and serious child maltreatment: Prevalence, risk and outcome in a court sample. *Child Abuse and Neglect*, **15**, 197–211.

70   Famularo, R., Kinscherff, R. & Fenton, T. (1992) Parental substance abuse and the nature of child maltreatment. *Child Abuse and Neglect,* **16** (4) 475–483.

71   Jones, D. (1991) The effectiveness of intervention. In: M. Adcock, R. White & A. Hollows, *Significant Harm.* Croydon: Significant Publications.

72   Falkov, A. (1996) Department of Health Study of Working Together 'Part 8' Reports: Fatal child abuse and

parental psychiatric disorder. *Department of Health Social Care Group*, ACPC Series, Report No. 1.

73   Wilczynski, A. (1994) The incidence of child homicide: How accurate are the official statistics? *Journal of Clinical Forensic Medicine*, **1**, 61–66.

74   Boyd, W. (1996) *Report of the Confidential Inquiry into Homicides and Suicides by Mentally Ill People.* Royal College of Psychiatrists.

75   The Woodley Team Report (1995) *Report of the Independent Review Panel to East London and the City Health Authority and Newham Council, following a homicide in July 1994 by a person suffering with a severe mental illness.* London: East London & City Health Authority.

76   Special issue on fatal child abuse. *Child Abuse Review*, **4** (1995) 309–92.

77   Spotlight on practice on child maltreatment fatalities. *Child Abuse and Neglect*, **19** (1995) 843–83.

78   Radke-Yarrow, M., Cummings, E. S., Kuczynski, L., & Chapman, M. (1985) Patterns of attachment in two-and three-year olds in normal families and families with parental depression. *Child Development*, **56**, 884–893.

79   Laucht, M., Esser, G. & Schmidt, M. (1994) Parental mental disorder and early child development. *European Child and Adolescent Psychiatry*, **3**, 125–137.

80   Rutter, M., & Quinton, D. (1984) Parental psychiatric disorder: Effects on children. *Psychological Medicine*, **14**, 853–880.

81   Emery, R. E., Weintraub, S., Neal, J. N. (1982) Effects of marital discord on the school behaviour of children of schizophrenic, affectively disordered and normal parents. *Journal of Abnormal Child Psychology*, **10**, 215–228.

82   Asarnow, J. R. (1988) Children at risk for schizophrenia: Converging lines of evidence. *Schizophrenia Bulletin*, **14**, 613–631.

83   Murray, L. J. (1992) The impact of postnatal depression on infant development. *Journal of Child Psychology and Psychiatry*, **33**, 543–561.

84   Orvaschel, H., Weissman, M. N., Padian, N. & Lowe, E. T. L. (1981) Assessing psychopathology in children with psychiatrically disturbed parents. *Journal of the American Academy of Child and Adolescent Psychiatry*, **20**, 112–122.

85   Canino, G., Bird, H., Rubio-Stipec, M., *et al.* (1990) Children of parents with psychiatric disorder in the community. *Journal of the American Academy of Child and Adolescent Psychiatry*, **29**, 398–406.

86   Falkov, A. (1997) *Parental Psychiatric disorder and child maltreatment – Part II: Extent and nature of the association.* Highlight Series No. 149. London: National Children's Bureau.

87   Drake, R., Racusin, R. & Murphy, T. (1990) Suicide among adolescents with mentally ill parents. *Hospital & Community Psychiatry*, **41** (8) 921–922.

88   Silverman, M. (1989) Children of Psychiatrically Ill Parents: A prevention Perspective. *Hospital & Community Psychiatry*, **40**, 1257–1265.

89   Rubovits, P. (1996) Project CHILD: An intervention programme for psychotic mothers and their young children. In: M. Gopfert, J. Webster & M. V. Seeman, *Parental Psychiatric Disorder: Distressed Parents and Their Families.* Cambridge University Press.

90   Slade, M., McCrone, P. & Thornicroft, G. (1995) Uptake of welfare benefits by psychiatric patients. *Psychiatric Bulletin*, **19**, 411–413.

91   Merikangas, K. R. (1984) Divorce and assortative mating among depressed patients. *American Journal of Psychiatry*, **141**, 74–76.

92   Stoneman, Z., Brody, G. & Burke, M. (1989) Marital quality, depression & inconsistent parenting: Relationship with observed mother-child conflict. *American Journal of Orthopsychiatry*, **59** (1) 105–117.

93   Sims, A. (1992) Marital breakdown and health: More than a broken heart. *British Medical Journal*, **304**, 457–458.

94   Cox, A., Puckering, C., Pound, A. & Mills, M. (1987) The impact of maternal depression in young children. *Journal of Child Psychology Psychiatry*, **28**, 917–928.

95   Cleaver, H., Unell, I. & Aldgate, J. (forthcoming) *Parent's Problems – Children's Needs: Child Protection and Parental Mental Illness, Problem Alcohol and Drug Use and Domestic Violence.* Department of Health.

96   Egami, Y., Ford, D. *et al.* (1996) Psychiatric profile and sociodemographic characteristics of adults who

report physically abusing or neglecting children. *American Journal of Psychiatry*, **153** (7) 921–928.

97   Kaplan, H. & Sadock, B. (1988) *Synopsis of Psychiatry: Behavioral Sciences, Clinical Psychiatry,* p321. Baltimore: Williams & Wilkins.

98   Fadden, G. (1989) Pity the Spouse! Depression within marriage. *Stress Medicine*, **5**, 99–107.

99   David, H. P. & Morgall, J. M. (1990) Family planning for the mentally disordered and retarded. *Journal of Nervous and Mental Disease*, **178**, 385–391.

100   Apfel, R. J. & Handel, M. H. (1993) *Madness and Loss of Motherhood.* Washington: American Psychiatric Press.

101   Darton, K., Gorman, J. & Sayce, L. (1994) *Eve Fights Back: The Successes of MIND's Stress on Women Campaign.* London: MIND Publications.

102   Sayce, L. & Sherlock, J. (1994) Good practices in services for women with child-related needs. In: *Women and Mental Health: An information pack of mental health services for women in the United Kingdom.* London: Good Practices in Mental Health.

103   Grunbaum, L. & Gammeltoft, M. (1993) Young children of schizophrenic mothers: Difficulties of intervention. *American Journal of Orthopsychiatry*, **63** (1) 16–27.

104   Rudolph, B., Larson, G., Sweeney, S. *et al.* (1990) Hospitalised pregnant psychotic women: Characteristics and treatment issues. *Hospital & Community Psychiatry*, **41** (2) 159–163.

105   Kumar, R., Marks, M., Platz, C. & Yoshida, K. (1995) Clinical survey of a psychiatric mother and baby unit: Characteristics of 100 consecutive admissions. *Journal of Affective Disorders*, **33**, 11–22.

106   Hugman, R. & Phillips, N. (1993) *Like bees round the honeypot: Social work responses to parents with mental health needs.* **Practice 6** (No. 3) 193–205.

107   NSPCC Practice Development Unit (1997) *Long term problems, short term solutions: Parents in contact with mental health services.* Report for Department of Health & Brent ACPC.

108   Aldridge, J. & Becker, S. (1993) Punishing children for caring: The hidden cost of young carers. *Children & Society*, **7** (4) 376–387.

109   Bilsborrow, S. (1992) *You grow up fast: Young carers on Merseyside.* Carers National Association, RSS, Barnardos.

110   Jenkins, S. & Wingate, C. (1994) Who cares for young carers: Their invisibility is the first problem to be addressed. *British Medical Journal*, **308**, 733–734.

111   Department of Health, *Young Carers: Something to think about.* Report of 4 SSI workshops May – July 1995. Summary of SSI fieldwork project on families with disability or illness, October 1995 – January 1996. Available from: PO Box 410, Wetherby, LS23 7LN.

112   Edwards, A. & Smith, P. *Young carers & their parents with long term psychiatric disorders.* Paper presented at 12th Annual Conference of the Michael Seiff Foundation, September 1997.

113   Crosby, D. (1989) First person account: Growing up with a schizophrenic mother. *Schizophrenia Bulletin*, **15** (3) 507–509.

114   Brown, E. M. (1989) *My parents keeper: Adult children of the emotionally disturbed.* Oakland, California: New Harbinger Publications.

115   Marlowe, J. (1996) Helpers, helplessness and self-help: 'Shaping the silence': A personal account. In: M. Gopfert, J. Webster & M. V. Seeman, *Parental Psychiatric Disorder: Distressed Parents and Their Families.* Cambridge University Press.

116   Dunn, B. (1993) Growing up with a schizophrenic mother: A retrospective study. *American Journal of Orthopsychiatry*, **63** (2) 177–189.

117   Mckellar, S. & Coggans, N. (1997) Responding to family problems, alcohol and substance misuse: A survey of service provision in the Glasgow area. *Children & Society*, **11**, 53–59.

118   Diggins, M. (1996) *Partnership or Polarisation: How can Lewisham Social Services Department help facilitate joint agency & intra-agency work with families where the parents have mental health problems?* MSc dissertation, South Bank University.

119   Rooney, B. (1994) *Parental mental Illness: The social work view of its impact on children in the West Berkshire area,* MA dissertation, University of Reading.

120   Cowling, V. (1997) *Building Partnerships: Interagency collaboration to effectively meet the needs of families with*

dependent children where parents have a mental illness. The Southern Partnership Project Report, School of Social Work, University of Melbourne.

121   Dore, M. *et al.* (1995) Identifying substance abuse in maltreating families: A child welfare challenge. *Child Abuse and Neglect*, **19** (95) 531–543.

122   Scott, D. (1992) Early identification of maternal depression as a strategy in the prevention of child abuse. *Child Abuse and Neglect*, **16**, 345–358.

123   Zelkowitz, P. & Milet, T. (1995) Screening for post-partum depression in a community sample. *Canadian Journal of Psychiatry*, **40**, 80–86.

124   Department of Health (1988) *Protecting children: A guide for social workers undertaking a comprehensive assessment.* London: HMSO.

Chapter Two

*Impacts on children
and parents*

A conceptual framework

The mental health and well-being of children and adults within families in which an adult carer is mentally ill, are intimately linked in at least three ways:

- parental mental illness can adversely affect the development and in some cases the safety of children

- growing up with a mentally ill parent can have a negative influence on the quality of that person's adjustment in adulthood, including their transition to parenthood

- children, particularly those with emotional, behavioural or chronic physical difficulties, can precipitate or exacerbate mental ill-health in their parents/carers.

The evidence for influences and continuities involving mental health and adjustment between and within generations is strong. This chapter looks at what lies behind these links – the interactions between various factors and influences which produce negative outcomes in children and adults. There are a wide range of influences, including protective factors, which have been associated with successful adjustment in both parents and children, despite the adversities associated with parental mental illness.

The mechanisms must be considered within the broader developmental, family, cultural and social systems within which individuals live. For children, the earliest and most influential system is the family. Once they enter school, there is a progressive widening of social networks beyond the family. However, the family always remains important – as a source of support or unmet need.

Implications for parents and children

The fact that a parent experiences a mental illness does not automatically imply a negative impact on the parent-child relationship, nor does it suggest inevitable parental inability to parent and to adequately meet a child's needs. However, a conservative estimate is that a third of children living with a mentally ill parent will themselves develop significant psychological problems or disorders. A further third will develop less severe emotional/behavioural difficulties which may nevertheless be significant for their longer term development.[1-13]

The child of a mentally ill adult can be affected as a result of:

● Specific symptoms or characteristics of a disorder or disorders that the parent is experiencing; for example, symptoms which impinge directly upon and involve the child, such as delusions or self-harm.

● Any effect that mental illness has upon the parents, social and psychological functioning, and more particularly, their capacity to relate to and parent their child; for example:

  – self-preoccupation that reduces emotional availability

  – lack of energy affecting performance of household chores and appropriate provision for the child's needs (getting to and from school, structuring home activities – meals, bath and bedtime, monitoring homework, reading to child)

  – non-specific symptoms or effects of symptoms, such as poor concentration, which reduce a parent's capacity to ensure the (physical as well as emotional) safety of children.

● Associated alterations in family structure or functioning; for example:

  – separation from a parent due to hospital admission

  – alterations in family roles such as a well parent taking over more household/parenting tasks

  – parental relationship difficulties due to effect of mental illness and consequent separation or divorce.

● Associated risk and protective factors and resources; for example:

  – presence of an available supportive adult within the family

  – overcrowded or poor housing.

Diagram 1: The family model opposite illustrates the core components of the conceptual framework which includes relevant aspects of:

1 adult mental health

2 child mental health and development

3 parenting and the parent-child relationship

4 risk factors and stressors as well as protective factors including available resources.

All need to be considered for effective assessment and treatment when there is a parent with mental illness.

The interactions between each of these components are illustrated by the arrows. They highlight the relevance of a systems approach to assessment and intervention. Each component affects and is affected by every other component.

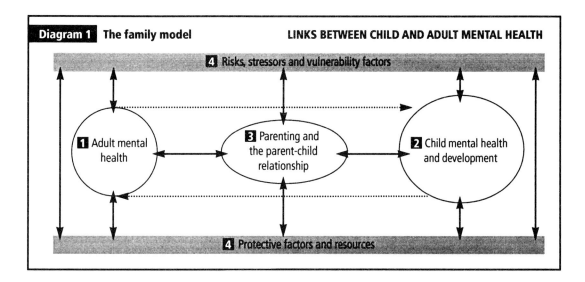

Diagram 1 The family model — **LINKS BETWEEN CHILD AND ADULT MENTAL HEALTH**

4 Risks, stressors and vulnerability factors

1 Adult mental health

3 Parenting and the parent-child relationship

2 Child mental health and development

4 Protective factors and resources

Such an approach requires consideration of:

● the tasks and responsibilities of parenthood and an individual's coping resources. This includes family of origin and childhood experiences as well as susceptibility to difficulties in the transition to parenthood

● unique aspects of the relationship between a parent and child

● the nature of the mental illness experienced by the adult

● the child's own needs according to their developmental stage and ability, as well as temperament, physical and mental/emotional health

● the family, social and environmental context in which these interactions take place, and the impact of this context on those interactions.

How these core components interact and influence each other determines the quality of an individual's adjustment within his or her family, as well as the adequacy of the whole family's adaptation to living with a mentally ill member.[14]

This model also attempts to convey a more dynamic understanding of how multiple factors within and between individuals and their environments interact over time.[15] The evolving nature of relationships between mentally ill parents and their children is an important consideration given the often sporadic, or one-off encounters that practitioners have with individuals or families, usually in acute crisis. These brief, sporadic contacts can hinder:

● the process of obtaining an overview of family experience over time

● the gathering of historical as well as current information

● an approach which emphasises strengths as well as difficulties.

This chapter will provide information on each of the individual components in **Diagram 1: The family model** and how they relate to each other. The aim is to facilitate an appreciation of the processes that underlie and influence how:

- parental mental illness affects children

- mental illness can affect parenting and the parent-child relationship

- parenthood can precipitate and influence mental illness

- children's mental health and developmental needs can have an impact on parental mental health.

Each component within the model is dealt with separately in the next four sections. However, it is vital that potential interactions of the various components and factors are always considered. For example, a parent who has experienced adversity in their own childhood will be vulnerable to mental ill-health as an adult and will also be more likely to have difficulty with the parental role. Their difficulties with parenting increase the likelihood that their child(ren)'s development will be adversely affected. If they then become mentally ill and the parent-child relationship and parenting deteriorate, the child may become emotionally and behaviourally disturbed. In turn, this will make the child even more difficult to parent and have a negative impact on the parent's own mental health. When they are ill, distressing memories of the parent's own childhood and relationship with their own parent may be recalled.

1 ADULT MENTAL HEALTH

The mental health of adults who are parents has already been highlighted as an important influence in the quality of parent-child relationships. This section focuses on aspects of mental health of relevance to practitioners in mainstream and statutory services, especially the more severe mental health problems including mental illness. This is particularly for those without direct training or experience in working with mentally ill adults. However, all professionals must consider how the parental role affects and is affected by mental illness, and how various factors can intensify these effects. Such factors include the influence of inequalities, co-morbidity, treatment compliance and the way in which the effects of stressors can be amplified by the parental role. For example, poor, cramped housing may contribute to mental ill-health – the presence of several children intensifies this impact because overcrowding makes it far harder to carry out parental responsibilities effectively.

    Given the breadth of the various subjects, the descriptions and information provided have been selected to support those undertaking the associated training and to promote better understanding of the interface between mental health and child welfare.

Definition: What is mental illness?

The World Health Organisation[16] has defined mental illness as:

> 'A term used by doctors and other health professionals to describe clinically recognisable patterns of psychological symptoms or behaviour causing acute or chronic ill-health, personal distress or distress to others.'

The context (including personal, family, cultural) in which symptoms arise, together with their severity and the degree of impairment and change occurring as a consequence of symptoms are all important to consider.

Prevalence[17]

- at least one in five adults suffers with mental health problems at any one time

- 40% of general practice consultations involve mental health problems

- suicide accounts for 5,000 deaths and more than 100,000 attempts annually

- around one in 600 people harm themselves sufficiently to require hospital admission

- 4·7% of adults show alcohol dependence

- 2·2% of adults living at home show drug dependence.

The causes (aetiology)

Mental illness occurs as a result of the interplay between:

- **predisposing** factors (such as genetic inheritance, adverse social circumstances)

- **precipitating** factors (such as life [loss] events, childbirth, cumulative daily stresses and pressures)

- **perpetuating** factors (ongoing, enduring difficulties, risks and/or absence of protective factors).

Thus biological, psychological and social perspectives are *all* essential to consider. This **bio-psycho-social approach** is best suited to understanding and addressing the needs of mentally ill parents and their dependent children within a family, developmental and social context. This conceptualisation includes biological, environmental (family and social) and psychological (how individuals think about and cope with their life within the system that they live) components. **The cause of mental illness within any individual is therefore multi-factorial.**

In addition to any symptoms or behaviours which are a cause of concern to the individual and/or to others, account must be taken of:

- genetic and hereditary factors

- quality of care and attachment relationships in childhood

- experience of childhood adversity including maltreatment (physical and emotional abuse and neglect and sexual abuse)

- educational achievements

- employment success and stresses

- quality of marital/domestic relationships

- general health

- personality

- habits (including alcohol and illicit drugs, misuse of prescribed drugs)

- life events

- experiences based on gender, race, culture

- housing and accommodation.

The strongest evidence for genetic transmission of mental illness has been found in schizophrenia and bipolar disorder (manic depression) (see pages 41 and 47), but evidence for a genetic contribution has been found for all of the major mental illnesses. A genetic predisposition does not inevitably lead to development of mental illness. **It is the combination of inherited predisposition and psycho-social experiences which will increase or reduce the likelihood of mental illness occurring.**[18] Access to treatment and psychosocial factors are of particular importance when considering mental illness related to parenting;[19,20] for example, the transmission of a predisposition to depression from parent to child will be by a combination of the genetic risk together with other factors, including the parenting pattern and style of the depressed parent.

Classification

In the UK the main classification system used is ICD-10 (*The International Classification of Diseases, version 10*).[16] This contains categories and criteria which psychiatrists and mental health professionals can use to assist in making a diagnosis once a person's mental state has been assessed and a comprehensive history obtained. Diagnostic categories reflect current knowledge and understanding about mental illness.

Classification brings together diagnoses which are related because they have similar symptoms, causes or outcomes. Making a diagnosis therefore assists in the process of assessing an individual's difficulties and planning treatment and care. However, a diagnosis is also a label which can lead to negative connotations or detract from seeing the ill person as an individual within a family and social context, and not a 'collection of symptoms'.

Comorbidity (dual/triple diagnoses)

Comorbidity occurs when more than one mental illness affects an individual at a given point in time. This increases the likelihood of a negative impact on parents, the parent-child relationship and their child's development and well-being.

Comorbidity is more common for certain mental illnesses, for example:

- depression in conjunction with personality disorder or alcohol abuse[21]

- personality disorder and schizophrenia[22]

- mothers with personality disorders are more likely to be dependent on alcohol or drugs[23]

- roughly one-third to a half of adults suffering from alcoholism exhibit depression at some point during the course of their illness; in addition, depression and alcoholism appear to occur together in the same families.

Treatment

In general treatment will involve one of the following approaches, individually or in combination:

1 Physical

- Medication; for example:
  - Antipsychotic drugs and injections (depot preparations)
  - Antidepressants
  - Mood stabilisers
  - Anti-anxiety agents
- Electroconvulsive therapy (ECT).

2 Psychological therapies; for example:

- Counselling
- Behaviour therapy
- Cognitive-behavioural therapy
- Psychodynamic therapy
- Group therapy
- Family therapy.

3 Social intervention; for example:

- Social skills training
- Occupational therapy
- Supported housing
- Practical assistance
- Welfare rights.

Compliance with treatment

Poor compliance with treatment is a crucial determinant of poor outcome.[17] Those who comply poorly with treatment are likely to be more severely ill at the point of re-admission to hospital, to have more frequent re-admissions, and are more likely to be admitted compulsorily and to have longer hospital admissions. **Poor compliance is therefore of major importance for all practitioners who support mentally ill parents and their children because it may prevent resolution of the episode or reduction in the severity of symptoms and consequent improvements in their capacity to meet their child's needs.**

Reasons for poor compliance involve problems with comprehension, comfort and collaboration:

- **Comprehension** – Problems include difficulties in realising the importance of taking medication due to inadequate understanding of the advantages and limitations of medication amongst affected individuals and family members.

- **Comfort** – Side-effects associated with use of medication are especially relevant. For example, patients with schizophrenia are highly likely to experience involuntary movements as a side-effect of their medication. Sedation, weight gain, sexual disturbances, blurred vision and galactorrhoea (breast milk production) in women are other side- effects that contribute to poor adherence. Some side-effects are experienced before any therapeutic effect, both with antipsychotic and antidepressant medication.

- **Collaboration** – Poor compliance can also occur as a result of a breakdown in the collaboration between patient and doctor/practitioner. It has been argued that schizophrenic patients, particularly young people and those from ethnic minorities, perceive psychiatric treatment as coercive and disempowering. Promising results have been obtained with programmes that combine giving information with efforts to encourage patients to collaborate with professionals in monitoring their treatment.

The cultural context

People from ethnic minorities comprise just over 3 million people (5·5% of the British population). Their geographical distribution is highly uneven and most live in London, the West Midlands and other urban areas.[17] Inequalities in the health and healthcare of ethnic and racial minority groups are evident and racism is the most disturbing of the explanations for these inequalities.[24]

Insufficient awareness and knowledge about other cultural beliefs and practices in relation to mental health can lead to errors in assessment, diagnosis and care planning together with inappropriate management and poor compliance.

Evidence from transcultural studies indicates that the major mental illnesses (schizophrenia and depressive illness) occur worldwide. However, culture will determine the content of the symptoms and the way in which they are expressed; for example, delusions amongst western societies often relate to technology (electricity being put into the brain, or being controlled by computer), whilst in Africa and India it is more common for delusions to have a religious basis (involving being taken over or harmed by gods or spirits).

Women and mental illness[25]

Over the past 30 years there have been significant changes in family structure and women's roles. Two changes affecting women and their mental health are the increase in lone parents and the growing numbers of women returning to the workforce who have children. These changes have important implications for those who provide services because meeting women's various needs requires different approaches. Women:

- are more likely than men to seek help for distressing symptoms and to be diagnosed with depression and anxiety[17]

- with severe mental illness are also more likely than men to live in families or to have a partner and/or children[26]

- with young children are at particular risk for developing depression. Brown & Harris identified that 25% of working-class women with young children in their study experienced depression following a significant life event.[27] **Factors which protected women against depression included a confiding relationship with a partner and paid work outside the home.**

The nature of the employment (quality, remuneration, and pattern [full- or part-time]) is an important determinant of mental health. For example, part-time work appears to have a protective effect whilst studies suggest that mothers in full-time employment who have responsibility for young children are particularly at risk. Lone mothers are especially vulnerable to mental illness,[28] perhaps because of the limited choices they face in relation to their and their children's circumstances.

Most studies identify impacts of *maternal* mental illness on children. Postnatal depression is described later in this chapter and implications of mental illness for women who have children is discussed in **Chapter 6**.

Inter-parental discord, domestic violence and parental mental illness

Associations between adult/parental relationship difficulties and mental illness are well documented.[29-32] There is ongoing debate about whether the illness (for example, depression) in a partner causes the relationship difficulty or whether the problematic relationship results in depression.[33,34] Family violence can take many forms and does not necessarily involve physical assault.[35]

Exposure to hostility and discord between parents is an important determinant of emotional and behavioural problems in children of all ages, especially if the discord is persistent over time and the child becomes embroiled in hostilities between the adults.[36]

Surprisingly few studies have systematically explored the combination of family violence involving both dependent children and their mentally ill parents.[37,38] Some have reported associations between the presence of specific mental illness and violence within families with dependent children.[21,39] However, more research is required to determine causal links and mechanisms. Studies of mothers in families where physical abuse of children has occurred have found associations with low income, youthful parenthood, less education, histories of abuse in their childhood, and alcohol or drug dependence.[40] Other studies have noted the combination of personality disorder and substance misuse in parents who have been both victims of violence (for example, by partner) and perpetrators (maltreatment of their children). Associations with chronic and recurrent depression have also been documented.[41]

Excessive alcohol consumption is an important accompaniment to violence in families and associated abuse and neglect of children together with children being 'looked after'.[19] Bland and Orne[21] found that alcoholism combined with anti-social personality and/or depression produced significantly high rates of violence within families. They also found that parents who had made previous suicide attempts were more likely to exhibit violent behaviour.

The following mental illnesses will be described:

- depression

- bipolar affective disorder (manic depression)

- postnatal mental illness

- psychotic depression

- anxiety disorders

- schizophrenia

- personality disorders.

Drug and alcohol misuse will not be covered separately, but dealt with in relevant sections, for example, treatment compliance and comorbidity with personality disorders.

Heide's story

'I became ill when Georgina was three and a half years old and Hannah was five. We had moved when Hannah was two and I was eight months pregnant and her father had left four months earlier. I coped reasonably well, although I did suffer from depression after Georgina was born just as I had when Hannah was born. This time, though, I had not sought help at all. The first time, I had refused treatment fearing that I would become addicted to the antidepressants.

I was living in a new area and did not think anyone could possibly be interested in how I was feeling. My parents had been certain that the marriage breakdown had been my fault and were not supportive.

I did not realise how depressed I was at the time and now looking back I feel quite shocked to think that I coped with a new baby and a toddler, having given birth by caesarean section for the second time, and believing that I could be living in a world where I thought I could hear and even see people who were not there. This eventually subsided over about five months, though I had felt unable to share the experience with anyone, sensing disbelief and feeling really afraid that I would be locked up and my children taken away.

Maybe I am fortunate or maybe it is because of my deep belief that it is wrong to cause distress to another person that I never had thoughts of harming my children. I was able to care for them at this time very well despite my inner suffering.

It was not until Georgina was three and a half years old that I became so clinically depressed that I needed to be hospitalised, voluntarily. Just before her third birthday, she underwent some tests following an infection for which she needed to be hospitalised. The effect of being present whilst Georgina was subject to the trauma of the tests was devastating to me. She clung to my arms and pleaded with me to take her home. Not only did I feel that I had betrayed her trust in me to keep her safe but it also finally broke down my own defences to my experience of abuse as a child.

My deterioration was swift. I felt extremely suicidal. My preoccupation became to prepare everything for my death, this included making sure that my accounts were in order and I also felt the need to sort out all of the drawers and cupboards so that everything was tidy.

I was prescribed antidepressants by my GP who also arranged an appointment with a psychiatrist when I mentioned that I felt suicidal. I began to forget things and became very muddled in my thinking. I was afraid to leave the house or to go into the garden. Everything and everyone became alien to me.

A day or two before I was admitted to hospital, my cousin arrived to find me counting out tablets, which I intended to take, and the children building a playhouse on the dining room table. I had begun to feed them when they said they were hungry because I could not keep track of time and I had already begun to feel remote from them and aware that they needed to be with someone who could care for them.

I even began to doubt whether I was in fact Hannah and Georgina's mother. I was unable to identify how I felt at the time but all feelings I would normally describe as maternal and of being able to show Hannah and Georgina how I loved them disappeared. I self-harmed. I became terrified that there was something genetically wrong with my brain, and that this could be inherited by my children. I believed that I had been a "dreadful child" and was therefore a dreadful mother and that my children would be better off if I was dead. They could then, as far as I reasoned at this time, be cared for by someone who was normal.'

Heide Lloyd

Depression [17]

Definition

Depression may range from normal unhappiness to psychosis. Within this spectrum, more severe and persistent lowering of mood which is disabling indicates clinical depression or a depressive disorder/illness. Many individuals present initially with physical symptoms (somatisation), and some may show multiple symptoms of depression in the apparent absence of low mood ('masked' depression).

Dysthymia refers to a persistent, less severe depressive state. This may be complicated by episodes of more severe depression, resulting in 'double' depression. Many patients do not fit neatly into categories of either anxiety or depression, and the concept of mixed anxiety and depression is now recognised. The presence of psychotic features such as delusions or halluncinations has major implications for treatment.

Classification (ICD-10)

The two main categories are unipolar and bipolar disorder. The unipolar variety consists of episodes of depression, single or multiple, of varying duration and severity. Bipolar consists of single or multiple episodes of depression and mania, of varying severity. Although not separately classified, maternal depression occurring before or soon after childbirth can have important effects on the developing child and parent-child relationship (see page 60).

Presenting features
In a typical episode of depression, the individual suffers from a number of symptoms:

● **Core symptoms:**
  – depressed mood
  – loss of interest and enjoyment
  – reduced energy, tiredness and diminished activity.

● **Supplementary symptoms:**
  – reduced concentration and attention
  – reduced self-esteem and self-confidence
  – ideas of guilt and unworthiness
  – bleak and pessimistic outlook for the future
  – ideas or acts of self-harm or suicide
  – disturbed sleep (initial insomnia, early waking or broken sleep)
  – loss of appetite and weight.

Severity is determined by the number, intensity and persistence of these symptoms:

In a mild episode, the sufferer experiences at least two core symptoms, plus at least two others from the supplementary list – all lasting at least two weeks. None are present to an intense degree. There is usually some difficulty continuing with ordinary work and social activities. A few mild but persistent symptoms suggest dysthymia.

More numerous or more severe symptoms suggest a depressive disorder. In a moderately severe episode, at least two core symptoms are likely to be present for at least two weeks. Several symptoms are likely to be present to a marked degree. Sufferers have considerable difficulty continuing with social, work or domestic activities.

In a severe episode, all three of the core symptoms are present together with at least four from the supplementary list, several of which are intense. Most people are unable to keep working or maintain social or domestic activities and the implications for any dependent children will be substantial. In extreme cases there may be psychotic symptoms such as delusions and hallucinations, typically involving ideas of guilt and self-criticism, poverty and disaster.

Prevalence
In recent community surveys, 2% of the population suffered from pure depression (evenly distributed between mild, moderate and severe), but another 8% suffered from a mixture of anxiety and depression. Even patients with symptoms not severe enough to qualify for a diagnosis of either anxiety or depression alone have impaired working and social lives and many unexplained physical symptoms, leading to greater use of medical services.

Depression in primary care:

- accounts for one in twenty visits to General Practitioner

- more than 100 depressed patients per doctor's list, but in half the depression is undetected

- 20% of those with acute depression develop chronic depression

- people may not mention their depression because of embarrassment and/or the wish to avoid annoying doctor, avoid stigma, avoid lack of sympathy, somatisation.

There are significant gender differences with depression occurring in 2·6%–4·5% of men in the general population compared to 5·9%–9% of women.[42] The difference has been attributed to genetic, hormonal and social factors, including the role of women in society, and responsibility for children and domestic chores.

There are important cultural aspects. For example, among people from the Far East and from lower socio-economic groups in Western cultures, depressive illness may present primarily as physical symptoms (somatisation). Individuals might complain of lethargy and joint pains rather than low mood. Failure to recognise the underlying depression may result in patients being subjected to unnecessary physical investigations, prolonging symptoms and reinforcing beliefs in their physical nature.

Aetiology

A combination of factors have been implicated, the combination varying from individual to individual.[43] Most depressions have triggering life events, especially in a first episode. Factors include:

- **genetic inheritance** (see **Table 2** below)

- **life (loss) events** (vulnerability factors such as early death of a mother or key carer;[44] discontinuity of care in childhood; [sexual] abuse;[45] job loss and unemployment)

- **quality of social support** (lack of confiding and warm relationships; burden of childcare; lack of employment outside the home or full-time employment as well as childcare responsibilities)

- changes in **brain chemistry and hormones.**

Table 2 Lifetime risk for depression (unipolar) based on relationship to affected individual[20]	
Relationship to the affected individual	**Lifetime risk of developing the disorder**
Offspring*	15–20%
Sibling	10–15%
Identical twin	40–50%
General population	2–3%

*Occurring at a younger age (12–13) compared to general population (16–17).

Treatment

Much depressive illness of all types is successfully treated in primary care settings.[17] The main reasons for referring depressed patients to a mental health team are that the condition is severe, failing to respond to treatment, complicated by other factors (such as personality disorder), or presents particular risks.

Basic treatment for mild, moderate and severe depression and the depressed phase of bipolar illness is generally similar and consists of medication, a 'talking therapy' or a combination of the two. Surveys have shown that most patients in primary care settings would prefer a talking therapy, but evidence of effectiveness is limited to particular forms of psychotherapy.

For mild to moderate depression, cognitive-behaviour therapy and antidepressants are equally effective. For more severe depression, antidepressant drugs are more effective. **Virtually all available antidepressants are equally effective if given at an adequate dose for a sufficient period but non-compliance with antidepressants may reach 50%.**

Newer drugs are now available which are more selective in their actions and hence have far fewer serious side-effects. Side-effects such as dry mouth, blurred vision and weight gain are thought to have a major effect on the frequency with which patients do not take antidepressants as prescribed. The capacity to tolerate the prescribed medication will have an important role in compliance.

The chronic nature of dysthymia may require long-term treatment, particularly when it is associated with episodes of more severe depression ('double depression') as recurrence of severe episodes is more likely if the dysthymia is not controlled. Cognitive-behaviour therapy and marital and family therapies benefit social functioning but have less effect on symptoms. The marked social and interpersonal debility associated with dysthymia and patients' need to acquire coping skills in managing symptoms and problems, suggest that an approach **combining antidepressants and focused psychotherapy is most likely to produce lasting benefit.**

Patients with psychotic depression are the most severely depressed, and they respond poorly to antidepressants alone. The combinations of antidepressant and antipsychotic drugs, and electroconvulsive therapy are effective.

Electroconvulsive therapy (ECT) is exclusively a hospital-based treatment, and most individuals remain as inpatients during the course of treatment. It is particularly effective in treating depression with psychotic features. There are no absolute contraindications to its use and it may be a life-saving treatment when depression is severe. There is also no evidence that it causes brain damage or permanent intellectual impairment.[46]

Poorer prognosis is associated with low self-esteem, social isolation and poor quality of relationships together with strongly held pessimistic ideas in the early stages of the illness. Dependent personality traits and comorbidity will also contribute to a poorer outcome in t he long term.

Implications for children and parents

Although symptoms may be less severe in dysthymia compared to acute depressive disorder or psychotic depression, it is the chronicity (enduring nature of symptoms) which can affect parenting and the well-being of children over time. This is especially so if symptoms are associated with parental irritability, inability to demonstrate warmth towards children and social isolation or other indices of socio-economic deprivation exist. Providing treatment and supporting and monitoring compliance is essential.

Comorbidity (dysthymia associated with substance misuse and/or personality disorder) will also make it much more difficult for a parent to meet a child's needs. From a public health (epidemiological) perspective, there are very many more parents suffering from dysthymia than, for example, psychotic depression. Children's physical safety may be of more obvious and immediate concern when psychotic symptoms are present in a parent, especially if the children have been actively incorporated into the parent's symptoms.

Where thoughts and intentions about suicide are explored, it is important to also inquire about homicidal ideas, especially where the individual has responsibility for young children.[47]

Bipolar affective disorder (manic-depressive illness/psychosis)

Definition
Bipolar disorder is a disturbance of mood in which episodes of mania alternate with periods of depression.

Presenting features
Mania typically presents with hyperactivity, an elevated or excessively irritable mood, sleep loss, rapid speech and a tendency to jump from topic to topic (flight of ideas). Psychotic symptoms, often indistinguishable from those seen in schizophrenia, occur. The latter may mimic forms of thought disorder, while grandiose beliefs (often delusional) may generate excess spending or a chaotic personal lifestyle. Psychotic symptoms may occur in both manic and/or depressive phases of the illness but are not invariably present. Hypomania is the term applied to a less severe form without psychotic features.

Prevalence
Lifetime prevalence has been found to be 1·3%.[22]

Aetiology
Genetic inheritance,[48] life events, personality factors and brain neurotransmitters and hormones are all implicated but the extent to which each plays a part will vary from individual to individual.

Table 3 overleaf shows that if an identical twin develops manic depression, there is a 75% chance that the other twin will also develop the condition. Adopted children of parents with a diagnosis of manic depression are at increased risk of developing the condition. The genetic inheritance could be seen as a 'vulnerability' factor which may exert its effects at certain times (for example following childbirth) or at times of stress or adversity. Hormonal changes following childbirth may result in puerperal psychosis, a condition with features of mania and/or depression. As with other disorders, life events may also precipitate episodes of mania or depression.

Table 3	Lifetime risk for manic depression (bipolar disorder) based on relationship to affected individual[20]	
Relationship to the affected individual		**Lifetime risk of developing the disorder**
Child with one affected parent		15–20%
Child with two affected parents		50–75%
Sibling/non-identical twin		15–25%
Identical twin		75%
General population		1%

Treatment

Acute episodes will require the use of antipsychotic or antidepressant medication, according to presenting features. Lithium, a mood stabiliser, has been shown to be effective in preventing relapse, but requires ongoing monitoring. Use of other treatment modalities should occur according to individual circumstances.

Suicide and deliberate self-harm [17]

There are about 5,000 suicides each year in England and Wales, of which 400–500 involve overdoses of antidepressants. Deliberate self-harm is 20–30 times commoner. Not all people who commit suicide have psychiatric illness, but, among those who do, depression is the commonest illness and 15% of depressed patients eventually kill themselves. Assessment of suicide risk is thus important and guides treatment.

Postnatal mental illness[49,50]

There are three main psychiatric conditions associated with childbirth:

● Maternity 'blues'

● Postnatal depression

● Postnatal (postpartum) psychosis.

Maternity blues involves less extreme, brief mood swings in the stage shortly after childbirth. Tearfulness and difficulty coping with the baby can occur. Symptoms are most prominent around the fifth day following the birth and from half to nearly three-quarters of women may report experiencing 'the blues' in the first week after childbirth.

Postnatal depression (PND) occurs in the first six weeks following childbirth. This presents in a similar way to depression at other times. There is now considerable evidence that non-psychotic postnatal depression (postnatal psychotic depression is rare) is associated with disturbances in mother-infant relationships, which in turn exerts adverse effects on child cognitive and emotional development.[51] The association is in part mediated by an impaired pattern of communication between mother and infant but other associated factors such as marital discord also play an important part.

The prevalence of non-psychotic major depressive disorders in mothers during the early weeks after childbirth is 10–15% with an estimated 50% of these cases going undetected.[52] Episodes usually last two to six months and some residual depressive symptoms are common up to a year after delivery.

Psychosocial factors including stressful life events, especially unemployment, the presence of marital conflict and the absence of personal support from spouse, family and friends have all consistently been found to raise the risk of PND. A psychiatric history is also commonly reported to be a risk factor for PND, especially a history of depressive disorder when combined with complications during delivery.

Detection, while generally poor, presents no difficulty and could be improved through consideration of:

● Maternity 'blues' in history taking

● the impact of neonatal (infant) factors such as temperament (irritability) and poor motor control

● use of brief self-report screening questionnaires administered by practitioners involved in postnatal services (for example, health visitors) to mothers.

Treatment

There is no systematic evidence to support the use of hormones (such as progesterone) but one study has shown a benefit of using oestrogen in severe and chronic cases. An antidepressant (Fluoxetine) has been shown to be helpful in elevating maternal mood but use of medication in mothers who are breastfeeding always requires expert advice.

Counselling has been shown to be of significant benefit in improving maternal mood and aspects of infant outcome, and counselling can be effectively delivered by trained health visitors. Treatment aimed at improving mother-infant relationships and preventive interventions have also been tested.

All practitioners, especially midwives, health visitors, social workers and community psychiatric nurses must ensure support networks are in place for vulnerable parents and infants.

Postnatal (postpartum) psychosis usually presents similarly to bipolar disorder (manic-depressive psychosis) or more rarely like schizophrenia. Poor sleep, overactivity and fluctuating mood are prominent. Mothers may appear perplexed and confused and may have suicidal and infanticidal thoughts. Hallucinations and delusions can also occur.

The condition affects one to two mothers in 1,000 and usually begins within the first two weeks of childbirth. During the first thirty days following delivery, mothers are twenty to thirty times more likely to be hospitalised for a psychotic disorder. Most at risk are women who have given birth to their first child within the previous month.[53] The incidence of postnatal psychosis in different cultures has remained constant over time.[54]

Postnatal psychosis requires similar treatment to other psychotic disorders, including major tranquillisers, mood stabilisers and antidepressants. Medication should be discussed with a GP or psychiatrist when a mother is breastfeeding.

Anxiety disorders

Definition

Anxiety is an unpleasant emotional state characterised by fearfulness and unwanted and distressing physical symptoms.[17] It is a normal and appropriate response to stress but becomes pathological when it is disproportionate to the severity of the stress, continues after the stressor has gone, or occurs in the absence of any external stressor. A recent British survey found that 16% of the population suffered from some form of pathological anxiety. Women are about twice as likely to develop anxiety.

General symptoms include:

- In the mind:
    - constant worry (tension)
    - poor sleep
    - feeling tired
    - unable to concentrate
    - feeling irritable, fearful, panicky.

- In the body:
    - irregular heartbeats
    - muscle tension and pains
    - sweating
    - faintness
    - indigestion
    - breathing heavily
    - diarrhoea
    - dizziness.

There are three common forms of anxiety:

1 generalised anxiety disorder

2 panic disorder

3 phobic anxiety (agoraphobia, social phobia, specific phobia).

Generalised anxiety disorder is characterised by anxiety that is persistent but not restricted to any particular circumstance. The predominant symptoms are irrational worries, motor tension, hypervigilance and physical (somatic) symptoms. For most sufferers, it tends to be mild, but in severe cases it may be very disabling. The subjective feeling of anxiety predominates.

Prevalence

It affects 2–5% of the general population, with a slight female preponderance, but accounts for almost 30% of 'psychiatric' consultations in general practice. Its onset is usually in early adulthood and its course may be chronic, with a worse prognosis in females.

Aetiology

Some genetic predisposition is present, childhood traumas such as separations may confer vulnerability, and it may be triggered and maintained by stressful life events.

Panic disorder is characterised by unpredictable attacks of severe anxiety with pronounced symptoms not related to any particular situation. Common features are shortness of breath, fear of dying or of going crazy, and an urgent desire to flee regardless of the consequences.

Prevalence

One year prevalence of panic disorder is 1–2%, with a lifetime prevalence of 1·5–3·5%. Onset is commonest in adolescents or in people in their mid-30s, while onset after 45 is rare. The course of the disorder is variable – sometimes chronic but waxing and waning in severity, or, rarely, it may be episodic.

Aetiology

There is evidence of genetic transmission, with first-degree relatives of patients at four to seven times greater risk than the general population.

Panic attacks are characterised by acute development of several of the following, reaching peak severity within ten minutes:

- escalating subjective tension
- chest pain or discomfort, palpitations ('pounding heart'), rapid heartbeat
- sweating, chills or hot flushes
- feeling of choking, smothering or shortness of breath
- nausea, 'butterflies' or abdominal distress
- dizziness, feeling light-headed or faint
- derealisation, depersonalisation
- tingling sensations in arms and legs
- fear of dying, loss of control or 'going crazy'.

Agoraphobia (with or without panic disorder) tends to start between the ages of 15 and 35 and is twice as common in women. Patients suffer acute anxiety attacks when they are in, or anticipate being in, places where escape might be difficult or help might not be available. They have an intense desire to be somewhere else, and their anxiety may be accompanied by the symptoms of panic disorder. Anxiety-inducing situations are avoided, and just thinking about going into such situations may produce anticipatory anxiety.

Social phobia is a persistent fear of performing in social situations, especially where strangers are present or where the person fears embarrassment. People fear that others will think them stupid, weak, or crazy, and exposure to the feared situation provokes an immediate anxiety attack. Patients recognise that their fear is excessive, but their anxiety and avoidance behaviour may markedly interfere with their daily routine, work or social life. Blushing is common, and patients may avoid eating or drinking in public.

There is some genetic predisposition, onset may follow a particular stressful or embarrassing experience or be insidious, and the disorder usually follows a chronic course. Symptoms often start in adolescence or even childhood and may be associated with poor social or academic performance. The incidence of social phobia is about 2%, but lifetime prevalence ranges from 3% – 13%. In some community studies, social phobia is more common in women than men, but the sexes are equally represented in clinical samples.

Specific phobic disorders are phobias restricted to highly specific situations such as spiders, heights, thunder and so on. These are very common throughout the general population and typically produce little interference with daily routine.

Treatment

● Medication:
  – benzodiazepines (usually short-term use)
  – antidepressants.

● Psychological treatment:
  – counselling and problem solving
  – anxiety management (relaxation, breathing exercises, distraction)
  – psychotherapy (cognitive-behaviour therapy, insight-oriented therapy).

Post-traumatic stress disorder
Anxiety and other symptoms may follow a severe trauma such as an assault or a serious accident. Although formal diagnosis requires an extremely severe stress to occur, similar features are often seen after milder stresses. There is considerable comorbidity with depression and suicide, anxiety states, and other psychosomatic syndromes.

Implications for parents and children
Anxious parents may view their children as having less social competence than their peers. Overwhelming feelings of anxiety can prevent parents from ensuring that children's needs are met. For example, a parent who is housebound because of anxiety may become excessively dependent on a child to accomplish chores outside the home which may interfere with educational needs or opportunities to spend time with friends. Some parents may fear being at home alone and keep a child from attending school. These feelings may be expressed in an overprotective parenting style or the child may be burdened with the parent's concerns.

Schizophrenia[17]

Sam, a 32-year-old father, attacked his eight-year-old son Alex with a spade. Sam had agreed to look after Alex and his sisters for a few hours but had become increasingly frustrated by what he described as Alex's 'defiant behaviour'. He had always felt that there was 'something different' about Alex compared to his sisters. Sam had recently begun to think that Alex had been 'sent' as part of a wider conspiracy to plot his downfall. He heard voices telling him to be careful because his son was 'out to get you' and he believed that television newsreaders were watching him as part of the conspiracy.

As Alex continued to refuse to tidy his toys, Sam heard voices muttering to him, directly: 'messing you about; laughing at you.' He also heard voices commenting: 'kid's got him; father's useless' over and over. Before Alex's sisters could help him, Sam 'snapped' and hit Alex with a spade.

Definition

At its simplest, **schizophrenia** can be described as a disconnection of thoughts, feelings and actions. The disturbance involves the aspects of daily functioning that give a person a sense of individuality and self-direction. The sufferer typically loses the ability to separate 'internal' feelings and thoughts from his/her perception of the external world.

Classification

Paranoid schizophrenia is the increasingly common form. In contrast, those presenting with only negative symptoms are described as having simple schizophrenia, while hebephrenia is a combination of negative and positive features associated with insidious onset in adolescence.

Clinical features

Diagnosis is usually based on the occurrence of one or more of the following symptoms which have been present for at least a month and cannot be explained by organic brain disease or substance misuse:

● **Positive symptoms and signs**

These are disturbances in the normal brain functions of thinking, perceiving, formation of ideas and sense of self. Those experiencing thought disorder may present with complaints of poor concentration or of their mind being blocked or emptied (thought block). Thinking is vague and the train of thought is difficult to follow.

Hallucinations are false perceptions in any of the senses: a patient experiences a seemingly real voice or smell, for example, although nothing actually occurred. The hallmark of schizophrenia is that patients experience voices talking about them as 'he' or 'she' (third person auditory hallucinations), but second person 'command' voices also occur, as do olfactory (smell), tactile (touch), and visual hallucinations.

Delusions are false beliefs held with absolute certainty, dominating the patient's mind, and untenable in terms of the socio-cultural background. Delusions often derive from attempts to make sense of other symptoms such as the experience of passivity (sensing that someone or something is controlling your body, emotions or thoughts). Typical experiences are of thoughts being taken or sucked out of the individual's head (a patient insisted that her mother was 'stealing her brain') or inserted into one's mind or of thoughts being known to others.

- **Negative symptoms**

  Apathy, poor motivation, limited speech, withdrawal and neglect of personal hygiene, appearance and physical health may be prominent. These involve loss of personal abilities such as initiative, interest in others, and the sense of enjoyment. The individual may withdraw from social contact.

Prevalence

Schizophrenia is a relatively common form of psychotic disorder (severe mental illness). The lifetime prevalence is nearly 1%, its annual incidence is 10–15 per 100,000 and the average general practitioner cares for 10–20 schizophrenic patients depending on the location and social surroundings of the practice. It is a syndrome with various presentations and a variable, often relapsing, long-term course. The diagnosis has good reliability across ages and cultures. Onset before the age of thirty is usual, with men tending to present about four years younger than women.

Aetiology

Table 4 Lifetime risk for schizophrenia based on relationship to affected individual[20]

Relationship to the affected individual	Lifetime risk of developing the disorder
Child with one affected parent	13% (10–16%)
Child with two affected parents	46%
Sibling	9%
Identical twin	48%
General population	1%

There is firm evidence for a genetic contribution: up to 50% of identical twins will share a diagnosis, compared with 9–15% for siblings and non-identical twins (see **Table 4**). The strength of genetic factors varies across families, but about 10% of a patient's first-degree relatives (parents, siblings, and children) will also be schizophrenic, as will 50% of the children of two schizophrenic parents. Thus a picture is emerging of a genetic brain disorder, enhanced or brought out by various forms of socio-environmental adversity.

Cultural implications

The prognosis is better in developing countries than in Western ones. This may relate to the quality and nature of support from families and interpretations made about the meaning of the affected individual's behaviour. Delusions and hallucinations draw on the symbols and images of the individual's cultural milieu. For example, in the West delusions often relate to technology and computers while in Africa and India they often have a religious basis.

Treatment

Schizophrenia requires a combination of drug treatment together with psychological and social interventions, determined by the stage of the illness.

Early use of **antipsychotic drugs** is central to resolving unpleasant symptoms and social impairment. Once stabilised, continuing treatment is available in the form of 'depot' injections which provide slow, stable release of medication over one to four weeks. They enhance compliance, a particular problem in those patients who lack insight. Relief of symptoms is achieved in at least 70% of patients with such treatment.

Side-effects are a particular problem, especially those affecting movement. Sedation or a sense of feeling flattened or depressed may also be distressing. Restlessness, either psychological or affecting the legs also occurs.

Psychological interventions can minimise distress and reduce frequency of relapse; they have centred on work with individual patients to improve social skills. Cognitive therapy to reduce the impact of delusional beliefs or hallucinations shows promise.

Family psycho-education approaches: relapse in schizophrenia seems closely associated with the level of the family's emotional expression as measured by formal assessments of critical comments or expressed hostility in family interviews. There is a close association between high arousal in the family and early relapse: this can be lowered by structured family education, reducing face-to-face contact via provision of alternative support (such as day centres) and formal family therapy.

Most psycho-educational programmes have focused on adults who have schizophrenia and their (adult) relatives who care for them. Whilst there has been some recognition of the 'ripple effects' of mental illness on all family members, none of the evaluated programmes has explicitly addressed burden/impact on dependent children.

Essential elements of existing programmes include:

- providing understandable information about mental illness (schizophrenia)

- working with patient/client and carers

- home-based

- flexible tailoring of any programme/approach to accommodate individual needs/ circumstances of families

- eliciting and facilitating positive coping strategies (emphasis on strengths and personal resources)

- providing information about access to additional resources (eg housing, finance, legal, voluntary agencies)

- contact opportunities beyond the acute crisis.

Such approaches could be made relevant to the needs of families with dependent children by:

- ensuring age-appropriate information about mental illness for children as well as adults

- involving children in discussions about coping with a family member who is mentally ill.

Social support is the cornerstone of community care. A keyworker can help with medication, disability benefits and housing needs. Hostels or group homes vary in structure and support, from the high-dependence units that provide 24-hour care to the semi-independence of a supported flat with someone visiting daily or less often. Day care, whether an active rehabilitation unit aimed at developing job skills or simply support with low key activities, can improve personal functioning (for example, hygiene, conversation skills, friendships and budgeting) as well as ensuring early detection of relapse. Targeted community support may reduce the need for respite care or compulsory admissions.

Prognosis

Prognosis depends on presentation, response to treatment and the quality of aftercare. Early and continued medication remains the key to good management.

A better outcome is associated with:

- acute onset over several weeks rather than many months

- social (family) support

- insight, intelligence and compliance with intervention

- positive rather than negative symptoms

- later age of onset (over 25 years)

- good response to low doses of medication.

Poorer outcome is associated with an insidious onset of illness over several years in a teenager from a disrupted family who shows possible brain damage or additional learning difficulties. Failure to comply with medication is often a key factor. These factors associated with poorer prognosis have important implications for an adult who also has responsibility for dependent children because they increase the likelihood that without assertive support they will struggle to meet the needs of their children and ensure their safety.

Up to 20% of sufferers will require long-term, highly dependent, structured care, sometimes under secure conditions.

About half of patients can live relatively independent lives, with varying levels of support, but require continuing medication.

The best 30% are independent, working full-time and raising families.

Implications for children and parents

The presence of positive or negative symptoms can impair a parent's ability to meet his/her child's needs. Negative symptoms particularly can result in lack of interest and neglect of children's needs – a two-year-old child without adequate food, an eight year old having to go to school unaccompanied and a fourteen year old 'on the streets'. Positive symptoms can affect children through observation of bizarre and frightening parental behaviour, such as a parent talking about symptoms inappropriate to the child's age, direct hostility towards the child or active incorporation of the child into parental delusions and hallucinations; for example, imbuing a child with special powers or qualities which may put a child in serious (physical) danger because of a parent's fixed beliefs that the child has malevolent qualities (a disciple of the devil) and must therefore be killed. Sometimes delusional thinking in a depressed or paranoid parent may involve the parent having to kill his/her child to prevent any further suffering because of the 'awfulness of life in this world', or because of a conspiracy to kidnap the child for torture or ritual abuse.

Personality disorders

Lizzie had a history of chronic depression complicated by problem drinking of alcohol. Her boyfriend of ten months resented her three children from a previous relationship. He would tolerate no noise and if any of the children questioned his authority or disobeyed him, he resorted to physical punishment using his belt or 'the stick' (a flexible bamboo cane). The older children had expressed their unhappiness and Lizzie had repeatedly asked her partner to be 'less strict'. Initially he had said discipline was important: 'It did me no harm when I got beaten'. More recently (after an argument at work and a subsequent drinking binge) he had told Lizzie to 'put up or shut up' after punching her repeatedly in front of the children.

Personality disorders are widespread and present a major challenge for all services.[17] They can be difficult to treat, complicate the management and adversely affect the outcome of other conditions, and exert a disproportionate effect on the workload of staff dealing with them.

Definition

There has been insufficient research (due in part to diagnostic difficulties and to problems in effectively engaging those with pervasive interpersonal relationship problems) and use of the term as well as responsibility for provision of services remains controversial.[55] The World Health Organisation defines these conditions as comprising *'deeply ingrained and enduring behaviour patterns, manifesting themselves as inflexible responses to a broad range of personal and social situations'*. They are associated with ways of thinking, perceiving and responding emotionally that differ substantially from those generally accepted within a person's socio-cultural environment. As a result, the person tends to exhibit a severely limited repertoire of responses across diverse social and personal contexts. These patterns are usually evident during late childhood or adolescence, but the requirement to establish their stability and persistence restricts the use of the term 'disorder' to adults.

Classification

There are dimensional as well as categorical systems. The former system involves the degree to which an individual displays a number of personality traits and behavioural problems. The WHO system[16] is based on the assumption that there are distinct types of personality disorder with distinctive features. For example, specific personality disorders include the paranoid, schizoid, dissocial (antisocial), emotionally unstable (includes impulsive and border-line types), histrionic, anxious and dependent types.

Presenting features

Individuals with personality disorder may come into contact with different services for various reasons including:

● acts of aggression

● alcohol and substance misuse

● anxiety and depression

● deliberate self-harm

● bingeing, vomiting, purging and other eating problems.

Some behaviours suggestive of personality disorder may be overt (such as extreme aggression), but others may be subtle (such as pronounced difficulty in assertiveness or avoidance behaviour). Temporary reactions to particular circumstances do not justify a diagnosis of personality disorder. Problems presenting for the first time in adulthood may point to a mental illness. A corroborating history from a relative or close friend is useful in distinguishing personality traits from mental illness. General practitioners, who may have known a patient since childhood, are in a good position to distinguish between transient and enduring patterns of behaviour.

The diagnosis of personality disorder of any type should not be made unless the individual concerned displays a pattern of:

● behaviour

● emotional response

● perception of self, others and the environment

which is:

● evident in early life

● persists into adulthood

● pervasive

● inflexible

● a deviation from patient's cultural norm

and leads to:

● distress to self, others, or society

● dysfunction in interpersonal, social, or working relationships

but is not attributable to:

● other psychiatric disorder (eg schizophrenia, depression, drug misuse)

● other physical disorder (eg acute intoxication, organic brain disease).

Prevalence

The prevalence of personality disorder ranges from 2–13% in the general population, with higher rates in institutional settings (hospitals, residential settings and prisons). Some diagnoses are made more commonly in men (such as antisocial personality disorder), while others are more common in women (such as histrionic and borderline personality disorders).

Aetiology

There are both biological and psychosocial theories of the aetiology of personality disorders. Biological and psychosocial theories are not mutually exclusive:

- there is mounting evidence to support a genetic component for some associated behaviours (such as alcoholism of early onset in men)

- neurochemical research has found serotonin metabolism in the brain to be related to abnormal impulsiveness and aggression

- psychological theories have focused on failure to progress through early developmental stages as a result of adverse conditions (for example, childhood maltreatment and experience of severe adversity and poor quality care), leading to problems in maintaining relationships in later life.

Treatment

The inclination to withdraw all treatment and support once a personality disorder is suspected should be resisted, especially if there are dependent children. Diagnostic uncertainty is an indication for referral to specialist mental health services and to child mental health services for assessment of parenting.

Inevitably, attempting to help a person who has difficulty in forming relationships may be hampered by that very difficulty. **The competing needs of parent and child create ample opportunity for confusion of roles and fragmented provision which may prevent needs being appropriately met and, in some circumstances, allow children to be exposed to acute (physical) dangers or longer-term emotional harm.**

Individuals with serious personality disorders have a propensity for casting professionals into extreme positions – idealising them as 'perfect' or denigrating them as 'useless'. Their complex needs may be in direct competition with the needs of their children. This creates fertile ground for professionals to be drawn into overzealous advocacy on behalf of 'their' patient/client (adult or child) which results in polarised views and associated actions which prevent effective collaboration between (adult and child) practitioners. The usual pattern is for adult practitioners to be seen as 'positive, helpful and understanding' whilst childcare practitioners are described as 'unhelpful, insensitive or stupid'.

When working with parents who have multiple problems and unmet needs, staff in all services must:

- ensure that while attending to the needs of the individual, they recognise the broader (family and social) context of their patient/client

- actively incorporate broader information into support strategies and interventions

- communicate early

- openly discuss how to assess and support competing (parent and child) needs in a balanced and objective manner.

Implications for parents and children

The presence of personality disorder in a parent requires professionals to consider experiences of all dependent children. In particular, professionals should note evidence of children:

- being exposed to parental hostility and violence

- living in chaotic, unpredictable environments with a family atmosphere of tension and low expression of warmth and intimacy to children

- experiencing emotional or physical neglect

- being exposed to effects of parental substance misuse

- living in homes where lack of safety is prominent.

Comorbidity

Amy, a mother whose two-year-old child, Helen, was in foster care, refused to agree to a residential assessment because of fears that having to live with other people would expose her and her child to germs. A mental state assessment by a psychiatrist confirmed the presence of psychotic symptoms.

Discussion with Amy's GP revealed a history of intermittent consumption of alcohol but no dependence and a pattern of 'difficulties in her dealings with professionals'. Details about her childhood were sparse but it was thought she had been rejected by her natural parents and had spent some time 'in care'.

Amy refused to accept medication and she was not thought to meet the legal criteria for compulsory admission to hospital.

She stated frequently how much she loved Helen. During contacts between Amy and Helen, Amy was observed to either interact positively with Helen or to ignore her and argue with Helen's social worker about why Helen was not living with her.

In view of the time Helen had already spent in temporary foster care (seven months), the local children's SSD were having to make more permanent plans for Helen's care. The social worker wondered how much, if any, contact there should be between Amy and Helen.

Comorbidity with personality disorder is common, with fewer than 10% having no additional diagnosis. Personality disorder commonly coexists with mental disorder, and a patient may have symptoms of both.

Alcohol and drug misuse[17]

Alcohol consumption is associated with:

- 80% of suicides

- 50% of murders

- 40% of road traffic accidents

- 80% of deaths from fire.

Alcohol consumption contributes to one-third of divorces and cases of child abuse and 20–30% of all hospital admissions.

The relationship between substance misuse and mental illness varies according to type, number and extent of substances used, personality and social factors. A substantial number of individuals who have been diagnosed with a mental illness are also dependent on drugs and/or alcohol. One extensive community-based survey found substance misuse or dependence in nearly half of those who also had a diagnosis of schizophrenia and a third of those with a mood disorder.[22]

Mental illness may be exacerbated by use of alcohol or drugs resulting in:

- poor compliance with treatment

- more severe (treatment resistant) psychiatric disorder including longer duration

- more frequent admission to hospital

- greater risk of self-harm and harm to others

- family discord, including domestic violence

- financial problems including unemployment, homelessness and criminal activities

- physical illness.

Each of the above factors, singly and (especially) in combination will lead parents to experience greater difficulties in effectively meeting the needs and safety of their children.

2 CHILD MENTAL HEALTH AND DEVELOPMENT

Any aspect of a child's development can be affected when living with a mentally ill parent, including cognition, language and communication, emotional and physical health, behavioural and social development. Existing emotional, behavioural or developmental problems or physical illness can be exacerbated and add to the burden of the mentally ill parent, or new difficulties may emerge. There is usually no simple, direct relationship between parental diagnosis and the nature of the child's difficulties; this is because outcomes depend on child characteristics, alterations in family functions and stressors and protective factors other than parenting.

Children vary in how they adapt to and cope with their parent's mental illness.[56–58]

Children who adapt well to a parent's mental illness will typically exhibit at least some of the following:

- older age at the time of the onset of their parent's illness due to less opportunity for exposure to difficulties and a greater range of potential coping resources

- more sociable and able to form positive relationships (easier temperament)

- greater intelligence

- a parent who has discrete episodes of mental illness with a good return of skills and abilities between episodes

- alternative support from adults with whom child has a positive, trusting relationship

- success outside of the home (for example at school, in sport).

Children who are more adversely affected may show some of the following:

- younger age at the time of the onset of their parent's illness

- difficulty forming positive relationships (less easy-going temperament)

- a parent who is chronically ill with poor pre-morbid functioning

- no external support for the child to turn to

- failure outside of the home

- family discord and disruption.

When considering the effects on children, professionals should consider:

A general guidelines for assessment

B developmental delays, disorders and physical illness

C more specific indicators of childhood developmental difficulty or psychiatric/psychological disturbance.

A *General guidelines for assessment*

When trying to decide whether a child is developing appropriately, professionals should consider:

- **Concerns**: is anyone concerned about this child's development – family, friends, professionals (GP, health visitor, school nurse)?

- **Observations**: a good description can greatly assist further discussion with an appropriate professional.

- **Comparisons**: how does the child's development compare with others (for example siblings, neighbours and children of the same age)? Comparisons must take into account issues of class, race, culture and language.

- **Impact:** is the nature of the child's development affecting the child or family? For example, are there frequent temper tantrums because the child cannot express her/himself? Is the child rejected and/or called stupid by their peers?

A list of what can generally be expected of children at each developmental stage is included in **Appendix iii**. It must be emphasised that this is not a comprehensive text. It provides (mental health) practitioners with a preliminary guide to supplement clinical assessment and should serve as a basis for further discussion with appropriate professionals in child health services.

B Developmental delays, disorders and physical illness

There are a number of conditions in children which will have an important influence on all aspects of child development and family life but which are not normally directly attributable to parental mental illness. They substantially increase the burden of parenting, and children who experience these conditions are more liable to develop emotional and behavioural disorders, but the children's needs are much less likely to be met when there is also parental mental illness. Lack of appropriate care may exacerbate the problems. Some examples include:

- **Developmental delays and disorders:** for example, speech and language disorders, learning disability, autism, Asperger's syndrome, dyslexia (a more specific educational-developmental disorder).[59]

- **Physical illness – acute and chronic** (not including the central nervous system): for example, asthma, eczema and cancer; chronic health problems are associated with mental health and adjustment problems.[60–62]

- **Physical illness involving the central nervous system:** for example, epilepsy – particularly temporal lobe epilepsy – which is strongly associated with psychiatric and psychological disorders in children.[63]

- **Physical disability/sensory impairments:** such as deafness, visual impairments, cerebral palsy.[59]

The presence of mental illness in a parent has been shown to affect children's:

- cognitive development
- language development
- attention and concentration span
- educational achievement
- social, emotional and behavioural development.

The effects will depend on the age and developmental stage of the child when the parent becomes mentally ill, together with the child's associated developmental needs. In general:

- older children will be better equipped to cope with their parent's mental illness

- children who remain well regardless of age at the time of their parent's illness will usually have other caring relationships, for example, other parent, extended family or substitute carer.[56,64]

Problems in children may not occur until later in the child's life or in adulthood.[65]

Table 5 summarises the various effects on children according to their age/developmental stage, using parental depression as an example. The comparisons are with children whose parents are not depressed.[11,12,66,67]

Table 5 Impact of parental depression on children according to age/developmental stage			
AGE (DEVELOPMENTAL STAGE) OF CHILD			
Infant	**Toddler**	**Primary school age**	**Adolescent**
· Disordered attachment relationships · Less responsive and spontaneous · More withdrawn and apathetic · 'Fussy' · Cognitive impairment (especially male infants)	· Less content, more distressed · Less persistent in completing tasks · More sensitive · More anxious or avoidant behaviour · More compassion (role reversal) · More behavioural problems (more demanding) · Developmental delays (eg language)	· Lower self-esteem · Greater rates of emotional and behavioural problems (eg depression, conduct disorder) · More somatic complaints (eg stomach-aches, headaches) · More anxious and less confident · Poorer concentration and attention span · Underachievement at school · Less competent peer relationships · More conflict in family relationships	· Lower self-confidence · More socially isolated · More care responsibilities (eg for parent or siblings, chores) · Conflict in relationships (family, peer) · Poorer academic performance · More behavioural and emotional disorders (depression, anxiety, conduct disorder, substance misuse) · Less supervision and greater rates of dangerous, illegal activities · Self-harm

C *More specific indicators of problems and developmental difficulties*

1 *Health and physical development*

- Is the child's physical development delayed or out of step with age-appropriate norms?

- Has the child had any accidents? What sort? How many?

- Has the child been admitted to hospital? Reason? Frequency?

- How often has the family attended their local doctor, nurse or health visitor? Reasons?

- Does the child have recurrent or persistent illness?

2 Education and cognitive development (including language)

- Is any aspect of a child's educational or cognitive development 'out of step'/delayed? For example:

- lack of imagination or co-operative play

- poorly developed or unintelligible speech for age; good speech but inability to relate with others; good practical problem solving, yet poor or absent language

- intelligent, yet not reading at the expected age/developmental level.

- How is the child's school attendance record and performance? Any adverse experiences (for example, bullying)? **A decline in school performance is an important indicator of difficulty.** Success in school is protective with regard to child mental health.

- Is the child struggling with schoolwork? Inability to learn (learning disabilities)? Is the child able academically but underperforming? Is there provision of sufficient support within school?

3 Emotional and behavioural development

- Has the child changed? For example, decline in schoolwork, unusually withdrawn or isolated, more clingy, easily upset, unusual behaviour?

- How does the child respond to daily routines and to changes in routines?

It is helpful to consider quantitative or qualitative differences in children's emotional and behavioural development. **Quantitative differences** refer to child behaviour which is like that of other children, but occurs more often, or in a more extreme way, such that it affects the child and their surrounding environment (for example, very severe or frequent temper tantrums in a young child, or persistent unhappiness affecting ability to concentrate on schoolwork). **Qualitative differences** refer to child behaviour that is different from their peers in general. For example, symptoms characteristic of severe developmental disorders such as lack of understanding of speech, or insistence on repeated routines or actions. In older children, examples are symptoms characteristic of adult disorders such as obsessive-compulsive disorder, manic depression or schizophrenia (such as repeated hand washing, delusions or thought disorder).

Only a few children will develop a major disorder such as psychosis. Such children may be genetically vulnerable to these disorders. Remember to check how the child is behaving and progressing outside the home, particularly at school.

4 Family and peer relationships

- Is there a persistent lack of friendships or recurrent conflict?

- Have there been instances of bullying and being bullied?

The quality of a child's relationships both influences and reflects their development. **This dimension is a good indicator of whether the child is suffering from a significant psychological or psychiatric disorder.**

Good relationships with family and/or peers can protect a child from emotional and behavioural problems.

5 *Self-care and competence*

● What is the child doing for themselves? Can they complete age-appropriate tasks? Are they responsible for all their own care?

A child's poor self-care (such as not washing) can adversely affect their general health as well as social relationships. Social competence can aid a child's development in other areas.

6 *Identity*

● Is the child self-confident? Do they express any concern about how they fit in socially?

● How are racial and cultural issues affecting the child?

A child who has conflict concerning their own identity may be vulnerable with regard to emotional and behavioural development, including development of self-esteem.

7 *Social presentation*

● Does the child adapt to different social settings?

● Does the child dress in a socially appropriate way?

● Has there been a change? Are they neglecting appearance or withdrawing from social contact?

❸ PARENTING AND THE PARENT-CHILD RELATIONSHIP

The needs of all children

To meet children's needs, parents should be able to:

● provide a safe physical and secure emotional environment

● model appropriate behaviour

● teach and give appropriate opportunities for their child's development

● show interest in and approval of their child, their activities and achievements.

The Department of Health *Looking After Children* material provides a framework consisting of seven dimensions to consider when assessing children's needs.[68] These needs should always be considered within the context of the child's environment:

1 *Health and physical development*

This includes parental consideration of children's:

- developmental checks and immunisations

- basic safety according to age-appropriate needs

- physical health, including onset of acute illness, prompt treatment and continuing compliance (for example, in cases of asthma or diabetes)

- healthy diet, exercise and age-appropriate activities.

2 *Education and cognitive development*

This includes parental consideration of children's:

- educational and cognitive development, both at home and at school

- needs for communication according to age

- needs for cognitive stimulation (for example, provision of appropriate toys and activities and joint activities such as reading stories)

- progress and achievements at school

- needs for activities out of school and away from home, according to age.

3 *Emotional and behavioural development*

This includes parental consideration of children's:

- quality of social interactions and attachments according to age-appropriate need

- understanding of their own feelings and those of others

- development of appropriate self-control and ability to manage their own behaviour to a healthy degree

- emotional security and support.

4 *Family and peer relationships*

This includes parental consideration of children's:

- negotiation of developmental stages within the family, including parental and sibling relationships

- achievement of success in relationships outside the home (school, friends, family network).

5 *Self-care and competence*

This includes parental consideration of children's:

- acquisition of age-appropriate levels of self-care and independence in feeding, toilet training, dressing, spending time away from home, using money, planning and self-organisation according to cultural expectations.

6 Identity

This includes parental consideration of children's:

- self-concept: the context of internal and social relationships

- achievement of self-confidence

- age-appropriate understanding of religious and cultural aspects of the family.

7 Social presentation

This includes parental consideration of children's:

- understanding of socially appropriate behaviour – both at home and in a wide range of social situations

- acquisition of culturally appropriate social skills.

A parent who provides adequately for most if not all of the child's dimensions of need, will probably be involved in a positive relationship with the child. However, **support (from partner, family, friends and neighbours) will be vital to sustain good parenting over time, especially through a period of mental illness**.

Parenting and parent-child relationships

A good-quality parent-child relationship requires appropriate degrees of:

Parental anticipation and facilitation
For example:

- anticipating the (non-verbal) infant's needs by learning to 'read' signals about hunger, discomfort, sleep or play

- anticipating behaviour problems in a toddler and facilitating ways of managing this effectively – for example, by the use of distraction

- preparing the child for changes (such as starting school, changing school, moving house, going to hospital).

Parental warmth and responsiveness
For example:

- demonstrating emotional investment in their child

- being aware of their child's emotions and providing sensitive responses at times of distress or excitement

- showing approval toward their child when appropriate

- listening to their child

- positive recognition rather than hostile or persistently negative behaviour or thoughts towards their child.

Child autonomy

For example:

- seeing their child as an individual in their own right

- being able to separate their own needs from those of their child; appropriately involved (not overprotective or neglecting)

- providing child with age-appropriate choices to develop competence that leads to independence.

Parent-child cooperation and control

For example:

- having reasonable control over children by effectively setting appropriate limits

- using strategies of mutual co-operation and influence between parent and child and via successful negotiation between parent and child.

Joint parent-child activity

For example:

- sharing and enjoying mutual activities

- conversations between parent and child not related to discipline.

Impact on children

Children's experiences of parental mental illness will be determined by:

1   the nature, severity and duration of the illness

2   involvement in and exposure to parental symptoms

3   alterations in parenting

4   alterations in family structure or functioning

5   the effects of parental treatment.

1   ***The nature, severity and duration of the illness*[69]**
    When considering the nature and severity of a parent's mental ill health in relation to the child's experiences, the following are important:

    - **Intrusiveness:** how the illness intrudes upon parental functioning and the parent-child relationship, and as a consequence prevents them from meeting their child's needs. For example, one parent may experience delusions, yet continue to parent adequately, whilst another parent with anxiety and agoraphobia may keep a school-age child at home to avoid being alone.

- **Modifiability of symptoms and behaviours**: some parents, despite being mentally ill, can modify their behaviour towards their child to reduce adverse effects. For example, once she was made aware of the effect of constantly criticising her child, a depressed mother was able to consciously reduce the frequency. This effort was helped by antidepressants which improved her low mood, tearfulness and irritability.

- **Pervasiveness**: symptoms and behaviours can impact on parental functioning across different settings and activities. For example, parents may be good at physically caring for their child or stimulating their child academically, yet be emotionally unresponsive.

- **Pattern of the illness**: a chronic, unremitting illness is likely to exert a greater negative effect compared to a single discrete episode. A moderately severe but chronic depression may have a greater adverse effect on children than recurrent, acute but circumscribed psychotic episodes.

- **Timing and duration**: timing refers to the relationship of the parent's mental illness to the age and stage of development of the child. In general, parents who have suffered enduring mental illness since their child was born will have greater difficulty in meeting their child's needs. A young child will have less opportunity to form stable attachment relationships and more exposure to symptoms and consequences of the illness. Duration refers to the length of exposure of the child to the parent's mental illness.

2 *Child involvement and exposure to parental symptoms*

A child can become involved with parental symptoms and dysfunctional behaviours in a number of ways. All can reflect a parent's inability to separate their own needs from those of their child. For example, a child could be incorporated actively into parental delusional thinking – particularly harmful if the child is viewed negatively – or witness disturbed behaviour.

3 *Alterations in parenting*

Children may not be exposed to or involved with specific symptoms, yet parenting can still be altered. The presence of mental illness can reduce and/or change a parent's respon-siveness towards their child. For example, a parent may become less emotionally involved, less interested, less decisive or more irritable with the child. This will affect the quality of the parent-child relationship, parenting capacity and the child's well-being.

When assessing the impact of parental mental illness on children, differentiate between:

- the nature of the child's experiences associated with their exposure to parental symptoms

- how the parents' actual parenting has changed due to the illness

- the quality of parenting skills when well.

4 Alterations in family structure or functioning

Children may take on more responsibilities and/or caring roles within the family when a parent is mentally ill. This includes practical tasks (chores, shopping) and emotional concerns (worrying about the ill parent). Hospitalisation of a parent may lead to changes in roles and/or living circumstances for the family. The impact on children following admission to hospital of a single, socially isolated parent will have quite different implications compared to hospitalisation of a mentally ill adult in a family where good quality alternative carers are available.

5 The effects of parental treatment

All types of treatment for mental illness can affect parents and children, directly or indirectly.

● **Medication:** for example, antipsychotic medication (major tranquillisers and depot injections) can result in reduced energy, drowsiness or feeling physically unwell. The parent may be less alert to when the child is ill or in danger, or they may be less emotionally responsive. It is therefore important to assess whether the difficulties a parent is having in meeting their child's needs are due to effects of the actual illness or effects of the medication.

● **Talking therapies:** counselling or forms of 'talking therapy' may result in the emergence of difficult and painful past experiences, which could make a parent more distracted, irritable, depressed or angry.

Poor compliance

Refusing to take medication or taking it inconsistently can prevent resolution of the episode or reduction in the severity of symptoms which affect parenting and children. Side-effects are an important cause of poor compliance. For example, some parents worry that medication will impair their parenting. In addition, parenting or other responsibilities may prevent a parent from keeping appointments. The core dilemma is weighing up the reasons for and consequences of poor compliance including effects of ongoing symptoms and impact on children (see also page 33).

Impact on parenting

Parenthood is stressful for all parents. The presence of mental illness imposes additional burdens which can alter the efficiency and effectiveness of parenting and the capacity to meet children's needs.

The presence of a mental illness can affect how parents:

● **Provide physical care:** lack of energy, poor concentration, altered belief systems and fear of going out can adversely affect tasks such as responding to a child's physical illness, shopping, cooking and other household chores.

● **Manage children's behaviour:** this requires energy, decisiveness, concentration and emotional control. All can be impaired by excessive emotional lability, poor concentration, distorted thinking and despair.

- **Respond emotionally in order to support and contain children:** mental illness may be associated with self-preoccupation and need for emotional support that can impair the capacity to accept and tolerate feelings of others. The parent may turn to the children for emotional support.

- **Develop self-confidence in parenting:** symptoms can lead to or be associated with a sense of failure as a parent, which generates further anxiety, guilt and low self-esteem, all of which can further impair parenting and exacerbate symptoms.

General patterns in problematic parent-child relationships

There are certain observable qualities/styles in parent-child interaction that can occur with parental mental illness. These may be styles that pre-date the parent's illness, or reflect changes subsequent to the onset of mental illness. Most of these patterns are not unique to parents who are mentally ill and these features are themselves not specific to any particular mental illness; for example, less emotional responsiveness, increased irritability or lack of decisiveness.

These patterns can be conceptualised along **quantitative** (how much) and **qualitative** (how appropriate) dimensions.

The **quantitative** dimension emphasises that normally occurring parental behaviour may be inappropriate; for example, if there is excessive interaction (too severe or frequent) or insufficient involvement (neglect – physical or emotional). Excessive interaction may be positive (over-involvement and overprotection) or negative (critical, hostile and lack of empathy in interactions or too frequent discipline).

The **qualitative** dimension draws attention to interaction which is inappropriate regardless of its frequency (for example, involvement of children in parental delusions).

Difficulties are more likely when the parent-child relationship is characterised by more extreme or inappropriate patterns of interaction. It is when these patterns occur that children's needs, including the need for protection, are least likely to be met. These will also be the situations which generate most uncertainty for practitioners when deciding about intervention and balancing children's needs for safety with the needs and rights of their mentally ill parents. Outcomes for individual children and families must always be considered within their broader family, social and cultural context.

Examples of general relationship difficulties include parental:

- **Intrusiveness and/or overprotection:** a parent may be unable to maintain developmentally appropriate boundaries with their child. For example, they may transmit their own anxieties so that there is an inappropriate emotional dependence on the child or the child may be drawn into their symptoms (eg extreme suspiciousness associated with delusions). The overprotective parent stops the child joining in appropriate age-related activities with peers, or prevents the child going out due to 'fear' of what could happen.

- **Under-involvement and neglect:** this can result in insufficient emotional and physical care and support for a child. For example, lack of supervision can expose children to antisocial influences. A failure of emotional support may predispose to depression. Physical neglect, such that the child appears unkempt and uncared for, can lead to teasing, bullying and social ostracism.

- **Inconsistency:** this can impair provision of day-to-day stability, predictability and structure. The presence of mental illness can prevent a parent from creating or maintaining daily structure and organisation within the home. Associated unpredictable changes in mood and/or behaviour can further contribute to uncertainty and confusion for children.

- **Hostility and irritability:** consistent criticism associated with a lack of expressed warmth is likely to have a significant effect on a child's self-esteem and emotional development. Children exposed to persistent hostile, blaming and rejecting behaviours have the poorest outcomes; for example, phrases like:

'You're making me ill.'

'If you don't listen to her (parent) she'll end up back in hospital again.'

'I hate being a mother – you are so demanding.'

'If you go on like that, I'll put you in a home.'

'Just leave me alone.'

- **Problems with discipline and control:** difficulties in achieving appropriate levels of control are not unique to parents with mental illness. Lack of support (social isolation), lack of energy, irritability and self-preoccupation with thoughts or symptoms are some of the factors which may impair a mentally ill parent's ability to negotiate and use consistent forms of discipline and control. Unpredictable responsiveness can lead to children having to be very persistent to gain a parent's attention. This can precipitate an irritable or negative response (a pattern of escalating, coercive parent-child interaction).

'Child approaches mother: "I want a drink." Parent ignores.

"Mum, David said a rude word." Parent ignores.

"I'm thirsty." Child leaves mother's side.

"Can we go to the park?"

Mother: "I'm busy – I've told you I'm busy."

Child leaves room and fight with sibling occurs.

Mother: "You little sods – I've told you not to fight. Go and get some sweets and be quiet. Just leave me alone." '

- **Difficulties in relating to their child:** these may reflect the parent's own adverse upbringing and/or current illness (for example due to self-preoccupation). The parent may struggle to separate her/his own needs from the child's, or lack knowledge or experience in communicating with the child at a developmentally appropriate level. There may be developmentally inappropriate expectations or a lack of personal emotional resources to meet the child's needs.

Specific mental illnesses and parenting behaviours[70–78]

Although there is no clear one-to-one relationship between particular parental mental health problems and specific parenting behaviours, some problems/patterns are more common with certain parental mental illnesses. **Table 6** overleaf illustrates the possible effects on parenting for a number of mental illnesses including substance misuse and personality disorder.

Table 6	Examples of some mental illnesses and their effects on parenting behaviours	
Parental mental illness	**Parental symptoms**	**Effect on parenting/ parent-child relationship**
Depression: Dysthymia	Lack of energy, lethargy and low mood	· Physical and/or emotional neglect (insufficient involvement) · Irritability, criticism (negative involvement) · Lack of communication and emotional support for child · Inconsistent parenting (over- and under- involvement
Depressive disorder	Guilt, despair, hopelessness, self-blame, suicidal thoughts, tearfulness, helplessness	· Mother seeks comfort from child (role reversal) · Inconsistent parenting (over- and under-involvement)
Psychotic depression	Delusions of guilt, despair and nihilism, hallucinations, suicidal and/or homicidal thoughts or plans	· Severe neglect · Involvement in delusions
Schizophrenia	**'Positive' symptoms** (delusions and hallucinations)	· Inconsistency · Over-involvement (positive or hostile) · Involvement in delusions
	'Negative' symptoms (apathy and withdrawal)	· Neglect (unresponsive to child's needs – physical and/or emotional)
Dissocial/Borderline personality disorder	Unstable relationships, impulsiveness, recklessness, hostility and violence, associated alcohol and substance misuse, symptoms associated with other mental illness, lack of empathy, self-harm	· Over-involvement (intrusive interactions, positive or negative) eg harsh discipline and criticism, lack of empathy, modelling of antisocial behaviour · Exposure to discord/violence · Inconsistency · Inappropriate expectations for self-care by child · Comfort seeking from child · Neglect (emotional and/or physical) and intolerance of child's needs for care
Substance misuse	**Acute intoxication:** (inappropriate behaviour, impulsiveness, unpredictability, physical violence, verbal aggression, self-harm)	· Over-involvement – positive/negative (hostility, criticism, discord, violence) · Comfort seeking from child · Inconsistency
	Post-intoxication: (eg 'hangover', 'passed out')	· Neglect (developmentally inappropriate expectations; inadequate supervision) · Irritability · Inconsistency
	'Pre'-intoxication: (effects of substance-misusing culture or lifestyle) such as drug-acquiring activities	· Neglect (developmentally inappropriate expectations) · Inconsistency · Exposure to inappropriate lifestyle

Common patterns of difficulty in parent-child interaction occur across all disorders but the effects must always be considered in relation to the needs of the individual child according to age, and the particular constellation of stressors and resources available to individual family members.

Parents with a diagnosis of dissocial (antisocial) personality disorder are more likely than parents with any other disorder to exhibit hostile and irritable behaviour towards their children. Given the long-standing difficulties in making and sustaining relationships, such parents can find it particularly difficult to relate to a child in an age-appropriate way. This may be due to difficulty in distinguishing their own needs from those of their child or lack of an understanding about differences in children's needs compared to adults.[23] Impulsivity may lead to ill-considered physical discipline (smacking/assault) rather than verbal negotiation.

Associations of personality disorder with mental illness, substance dependence and discordant relationships (comorbidity) means that some of these parents are least able to meet children's needs and present the greatest risk to their safety and future development. The presence of mental illness in the partner of an adult with a personality disorder may impede efforts to meet children's needs and ensure their safety.

Child maltreatment and parental mental illness

The majority of mentally ill parents do not abuse or maltreat their children. Furthermore, individual risk factors and stressors tend to be insufficient as sole causes of serious inability to meet children's needs. It is the combination of personality factors, coping skills, social supports and factors within the child as well as the presence of mental illness in a parent, that cumulatively determines whether maltreatment occurs.[79]

There is a small but significant number of families in which the presence of a mental illness in conjunction with other risks and stressors serves to outweigh parental coping capacities and social supports; this prevents parents from meeting their children's needs and ensuring their safety. At its most extreme, fatal abuse and neglect can occur.[80]

Depression, substance dependence and personality disorders occurring together in various combinations and at various points in time are the most frequently reported psychiatric conditions affecting parents who abuse their children.

4 PROTECTIVE FACTORS, STRESSORS AND RESOURCES[81–84]

There are many factors that influence (both positively and negatively) the overall impact on children and adults when a parent is mentally ill. Vulnerability and protective factors can be either **intrinsic** to individuals (for example, genetic composition, personality or temperament, intelligence)[85,86] or **external** to the individual (for example, socio-economic circumstances, social class, cultural context, education and employment).[9,87–91] The surrounding environment and an individual's biological make-up will continually interact and influence each other in aiding or hindering their ability to cope with and adapt to living with parental mental illness.[92,93] These factors will also influence the pattern of the illness, including severity and duration.

Individual risk or stress factors, on their own, do not necessarily have a serious effect on an adult's mental health, their parenting capacity, the parent-child relationship, or a child's mental health. It is when environmental (external) and/or personal (intrinsic) factors occur in combination that an impact on child and/or parental mental health is much more likely. For example, **when three or more stress factors occur together without the presence of associated complementary resources or protective factors, the likelihood is substantially increased that an adult's mental health, parenting skills, the parent-child relationship and the child's mental health/development will be affected.** Protective factors such as mutually supportive interpersonal relationships, or the presence of children with 'easy' temperaments, may offset risk/stressful factors.

Strengthening protective factors

It may not be possible to readily change some adversities which families experience (such as poor housing, poverty, or even the parent's mental illness). However, promoting and supporting protective factors (such as social support and compensatory experiences) can help mitigate negative effects and adversities when a parent is mentally ill. This is particularly true when considering effects on children. In practice, it is not always possible to alleviate stressors, but it is usually possible to promote or build up protective factors.

These factors must always be considered as part of the holistic approach to supporting children and adults (see **Diagram 1**, page 29); for example, chronic poor quality housing may directly affect a parent's mental health which in turn can exacerbate underlying relationship difficulties with a partner. The escalating parental discord can have a particularly damaging effect on the children's emotional well-being and their mental health. The presence of emotional and/or behavioural difficulties in children will place additional burdens on the parental relationship and exacerbate adult mental health problems.

Tables 7 and **8** summarise factors which can exacerbate or buffer the experiences and circumstances of children and adults. These factors relate to:

● the intrinsic make-up of the individual (personal attributes)

● the immediate circumstances (family) or broader social environment within which the individual lives

● life events experienced by the individual.

Table 7	Risks/stressors and protectors/resources relevant to parents[27, 30, 94–99]	
Risk/stressor	**Factor**	**Protector**
Intrinsic		
Adverse experiences (eg trauma, abuse/neglect, multiple changes in carers, 'looked after', developmental problems, physical illness, self-harm, poor educational attainment); poor quality early attachments and relationships	**Childhood experiences**	Good experiences and relationships
Belonging to minority group – being 'different', experience of oppression, discrimination, racism	**Ethnicity**	Belonging to majority group
Persistent, personal relationship difficulties	**Personality**	Good social skills, capacity for harmonious relationships
General or specific learning disabilities	**Cognitive abilities**	Above average cognitive abilities and educational skills
Comorbid substance misuse, alcoholism, personality disorder	**Other mental disorder**	No comorbidity
Disability, chronic illness	**Physical health**	Healthy, no disability present
Immediate Circumstances		
Absent, discordant	**Partner relationships**	Present, harmonious, mutually supportive
Discordant, disturbed, critical, lack of warmth and empathy	**Parent-child relationship**	Harmonious, praise, expressions of warmth and empathy
Present	**Domestic violence**	Absent
Absent, discordant	**Social relationships (family and friends)**	Present, supportive
Multiple moves within and between countries (for example, refugees)	**Geographic mobility**	Stability and security
Unemployed, multiple job changes	**Employment**	Stable, rewarding
Low	**Socio-economic resources**	Financially secure
Poor conditions, crowded	**Housing**	Good conditions, spacious
Racism, threats, alienation and exclusion	**Community**	Support networks, mother and toddler groups, after-school clubs
Life Events		
Losses and other negative events/experiences	**Life events and experiences**	Positive experiences

Table 8	Risks/stressors and protectors/resources relevant to children[11,100–110]		
	Risk/stressor	**Factor**	**Protector**
Intrinsic			
	Younger	**Age**	Older
	Male	**Gender**	Female
	General or specific learning disabilities, developmental disorder, lack of educational skills	**Development** (language and cognitive abilities)	Good cognitive and language abilities and educational skills
	Chronic physical illness/disability	**Physical health**	Healthy
	Predisposition to mental disorder, or increased risk	**Genetics**	No adverse predisposition
	Difficult	**Temperament**	Easy
	Belonging to minority – being 'different', experience of oppression, discrimination, racism	**Ethnicity**	Belonging to majority group
Immediate Circumstances			
	Discordant/distant	**Parent-child relationship**	Warm/mutual
	Lax/hostile/no control Neglect, abuse	**Parenting**	Positive, eg co-operation and good control, age-appropriate interactions
	Distant/discordant/violent	**Inter-parental relationship**	Mutually supportive/ co-operative
	Comorbidity, both parents ill, single parent ill	**Parental mental health**	Partner well
	Absent/discordant/oppressive	**Sibling and peer relationships**	Warm/supportive
	Material hardship	**Socio-economic resources**	Financially secure
	Crowded, unhygienic	**Housing**	Good, spacious
	Poor ethos, low support, bullying, punitive	**School**	Good ethos, supportive
	Absent supports, anti-social influences	**Community**	Support, provision of child activities
Life Events			
	Loss and other negative life events and experiences	**Life events and experiences**	Positive life events, acknowledgement of achievements

Implications for practice

Diagram 1 (see page 29) illustrates the key components which should be addressed when working with a mentally ill adult who is also a parent. In assessing the needs of adults with mental illness and child-care responsibilities, these various components and the processes/interactions between them must be taken into account when assessing and planning support and intervention.

Each individual must be seen as a 'whole' person within their family and cultural context. Examples of *processes* include:

- the mechanisms whereby adverse childhood experiences generate susceptibility to adult mental illness and/or difficulties in the transition to parenthood

- whether the mentally ill parent complies with recommended medication; this may be influenced by potential side-effects and how these affect the relationship with their child

- housing problems (such as high rise flats with no lift, or damp, cramped conditions) which create stress for a parent, affecting both their mental health and the relationship with their child.

General principles of assessment

For individual children and families there will be a dynamic interaction between the various factors in their living circumstances. By implication, a crisis indicates that difficulties are outweighing supports and coping mechanisms at that point in time.

If outcomes are to be improved, assessment must include examination of the context in which mental illness occurs, including supports and assets, not just vulnerabilities and problems. **Practitioners must consider how the provision of support will assist the family, not only at the point of initial contact, but in the future.**

Each family will have a lifetime of individual and collective experience which contributes to the overall level and quality of adjustment at any point in time. Assessment must include this **historical perspective** (illustrated in **Diagram 2**, see page 75) which will assist decisions about the nature and amount of support required to meet needs effectively both in the short and long term.

Parental inability to meet a child's needs may be a consequence of any one or combination of the following:

- the impact of the illness on the adult (being a parent *and* having a mental illness)

- parental personality factors (pre-existing and/or exacerbated by the illness – irritable, hostile, unable to cope, self-preoccupied)

- a combination of mental illness, personality factors and substance misuse (comorbidity)

- environmental stressors outweighing support and protective factors

- a parent's own childhood experiences of adversity and care.

The various domains to assess are summarised in **Diagram 2** (opposite) which highlights:

● the **historical perspective** (including family of origin experiences of mentally ill adults/carers)

● **current family, social and cultural context**

● **linking assessment to outcomes** (for adult mental illness, family relationships, child mental health and development, parenting and the parent-child relationship).

Guidelines for assessment

Observe interactions between parents and their children. With children old enough to talk, try to engage in conversation in order to begin to establish a relationship.

Include partners in any assessment of a mentally ill parent's circumstances. A partner is important as a potential source of:

● alternative care and support

● additional burden because they may also show evidence of mental illness

● direct harm for children if the partner has maltreated children and mental illness prevents a parent from adequately protecting children

● indirect harm for children – for example, if domestic violence is witnessed; a woman who is unable to adequately protect herself will struggle to ensure her children are adequately protected.

Treating symptoms in isolation is not sufficient. Difficulties in the parent-child relationship have been shown to persist well beyond the period of mental illness.[111] Addressing the social context of parents and children is essential. In particular, **practitioners should not assume that resolution of the episode of illness will also mean an automatic return of good quality and appropriate parenting.** In situations where there are serious concerns about parental inability to meet a child's needs when unwell, professionals will need to **reassess the adequacy of parenting and the parent-child relationship once psychiatric symptoms have resolved.**

Further dilemmas can also arise in terms of the time required for a parent to recover and the continuing uncertainty this generates for children, carers and professionals. Ways need to be found to **support children while parents are being rehabilitated.** There is a danger that services which are purely crisis-oriented will not give adequately sustained support for the child, or will fail to address whether parenting is satisfactory despite resolution of the illness.

Where concerns about **personality disorder** arise, pay particular attention to:

● the presenting problems

● childhood history and experiences, especially of severe illness, abuse or behavioural disturbance

● violent outbursts or episodes, and their precipitating factors

● risk-taking behaviour (self-harm, harm to others including children)

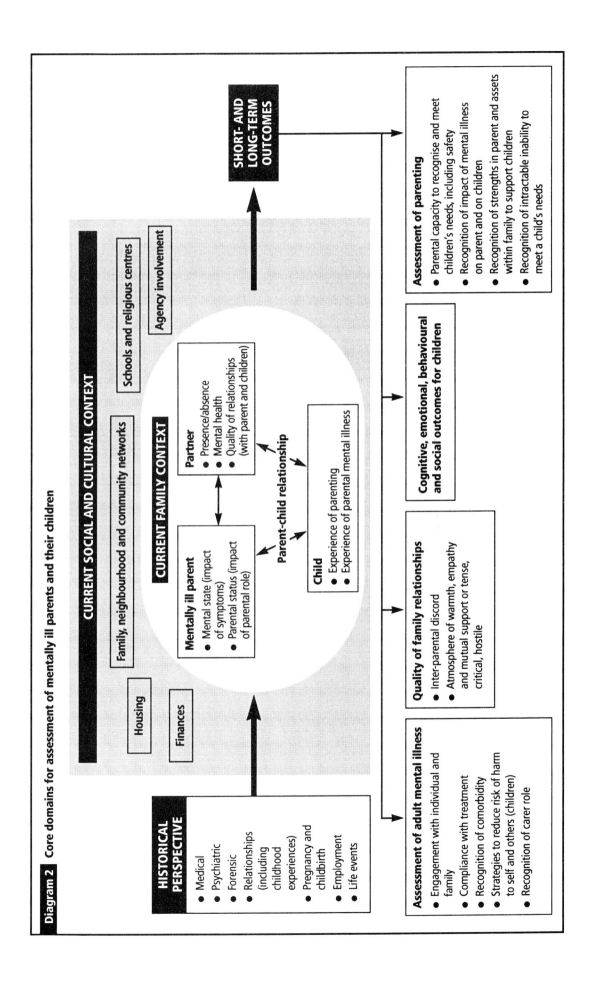

Diagram 2 Core domains for assessment of mentally ill parents and their children

CURRENT SOCIAL AND CULTURAL CONTEXT

Family, neighbourhood and community networks

Schools and religious centres

Agency involvement

Housing

Finances

HISTORICAL PERSPECTIVE

- Medical
- Psychiatric
- Forensic
- Relationships (including childhood experiences)
- Pregnancy and childbirth
- Employment
- Life events

CURRENT FAMILY CONTEXT

Partner
- Presence/absence
- Mental health
- Quality of relationships (with parent and children)

Mentally ill parent
- Mental state (impact of symptoms)
- Parental status (impact of parental role)

Parent–child relationship

Child
- Experience of parenting
- Experience of parental mental illness

SHORT- AND LONG-TERM OUTCOMES

Assessment of adult mental illness
- Engagement with individual and family
- Compliance with treatment
- Recognition of comorbidity
- Strategies to reduce risk of harm to self and others (children)
- Recognition of carer role

Quality of family relationships
- Inter-parental discord
- Atmosphere of warmth, empathy and mutual support or tense, critical, hostile

Cognitive, emotional, behavioural and social outcomes for children

Assessment of parenting
- Parental capacity to recognise and meet children's needs, including safety
- Recognition of impact of mental illness on parent and on children
- Recognition of strengths in parent and assets within family to support children
- Recognition of intractable inability to meet a child's needs

- relationships, type and stability (parental discord and violence)

- mental health of partner (children living with two parents who have personality problems and/or mental illness)

- comorbid physical or mental disorders including substance misuse

- implications for dependent children of practitioner's inability to engage with a parent.

Following admission of a parent subsequent to an **overdose or self-harm**, seek information about:

- the presence and whereabouts of dependent children

- any agencies involved with parents and/or children

- the support required for a parent to meet the needs of the children, including their safety; for parents with responsibility for young children, **questioning about homicidal as well as suicidal thoughts is necessary.**

References

1   Laucht, M., Esser, G. & Schmidt, M. H. (1994) Parental mental disorder and early child development. *European Journal of Child & Adolescent Psychiatry*, **3** (3) 125–137.

2   Radke-Yarrow, M., Nottelmann, E., Martinez, P. *et al.* (1992) Young children of affectively ill parents: A longitudinal study of psychosocial development. *Journal of the American Academy of Child & Adolescent Psychiatry*, **31**, 68–77.

3   Sharp, D., Hay, D., Pawlby, S. *et al.* (1995) The impact of postnatal depression on boys' intellectual development. *Journal of Child Psychology & Psychiatry*, **36** (8) 1315–1336.

4   Canino, G., Bird, H., Rubio-stipec, M. *et al.* (1990). Children of parents with psychiatric disorder in the community. *Journal of American Academy of Child and Adolescent Psychiatry*, **29**, 398–406.

5   Rutter, M. & Quinton, D. (1984) Parental psychiatric disorder: Effects on children. *Psychological Medicine*, **14**, 853–880.

6   Weissman, M. M., Gammon, D. G. (1987) Children of depressed parents: Increased psychopathology and early onset of major depression. *Archives of General Psychiatry*, **44**, 847–853.

7   Barnett, M. F., Guzman, A. M. & Parker, G. B. (1991) Maternal anxiety: A 5 year review of an intervention study. *Journal of Child Psychology & Psychiatry*, **32** (3) 423–438.

8   Weissman, Leckman, Merikangas, Gammon & Prusoff (1984) Depression and anxiety disorders in parents and children. *Archives of General Psychiatry*, **41**, 845–851.

9   Feldman, R. A., Stiffman, A. R. & Jung, K. G. (1987) *Children at risk: In the web of parental mental illness.* New Brunswick and London: Rugters University Press.

10   Schachar, R. & Wachsmuth, R. (1990) Hyperactivity and parental psychopathology. *Journal of Child Psychology & Psychiatry*, **31** (3) 381–392.

11   Lee, C. & Gotlib, I. (1989) Clinical status and emotional adjustment of children of depressed mothers. *American Journal of Psychiatry*, **146**, 478–483.

12   Beardslee, W., Schultz, L. & Selman, R. (1987) Level of social-cognitive impairment, adaptive functioning, and DSM-III diagnoses in adolescent offspring of parents with affective disorder: implications of the development of the capacity for mutuality. *Developmental Psychology*, **23**, 807–815.

13   Larsson, G. & Larsson, A. (1982) Health of children whose parents seek psychiatric care. *Acta Psychiatrica Scandinavica*, **66**, 154–162.

14   Keitner, G. & Miller, I. (1990) Family functioning and major depression: An Overview. *American Journal of Psychiatry*, **147** (9) 1128–1137.

15   Rutter, M. (1989) Pathways from childhood to adult life. *Journal of Child Psychology and Psychiatry*, **30**, 23–51.

16   World Health Organisation (1992) *The ICD-10 Classification of Mental and behavioural Disorders: Clinical Descriptions and Diagnostic Guidelines.* Geneva: WHO.

17   Davies, T. & Craig, T. K. J. (Eds.) (1988) *ABC of Mental Health.* London: BMJ Books.

18   Parnas, M. D., Teasdale, T. W. & Schulsinger, H. (1985) Institutional rearing and diagnostic outcome in children of schizophrenic mothers. A prospective high risk study. *Archives of General Psychiatry*, **42**, 762–769.

19   Sheppard, M. (1997) Double Jeopardy: The link between child abuse and maternal depression in child and family social work. *Child and family social work*, **2**, 91–107.

20   Judge, K. (1988) Genetic issues in treatment. In: H. Lefley & M. Wasow (Eds.) (1994) *Helping Families Cope with Mental Illness*, Ch. 9, pp184. Harwood Academic Publishers.

21   Bland, R. & Orne, H. (1986) Family violence and psychiatric disorder. *Canadian Journal of Psychiatry*, **31**, 129–137.

22   Regier, D., Farmer, M., Rae, D., *et al.* (1990) Comorbidity of mental disorders with alcohol and other drug abuse. *Journal of American Medical Association*, **264**, 2511–2518.

23   Constantino, J. N. (1993) Parents, mental illness and the primary health care of infants and young children. *Zero to Three*, **13** (5) 1–10.

24   Bhopal, R. (1998) Spectre of racism in health and health care: Lessons from history and the United States. *British Medical Journal*, **316**, 1970–1973.

25   Jenkins, R. & Clare A. (1985) Women and mental illness. *British Medical Journal*, **291**, 1521–1522.

26   Test, M., Burke, S. & Wallisch, L. (1990) Gender differences of young adults with schizophrenic disorders in community care. *Schizophrenia Bulletin*, **16**, 331–344.

27   Brown, G. W. & Harris, T. (1978) *Social origins of depression.* London: Tavistock Publications.

28   Meltzer, H., Gill, B., Petticrew, N. & Hinds, K. (1995) The prevalence of psychiatric morbidity among adults aged 16–64 living in private households in Great Britain. *OPCS Surveys: Report 1.* London: OPCS.

29   Birtchnell, J. & Kennard, J. (1983) Does marital maladjustment lead to mental health? *Social Psychiatry*, **18**, 79–88.

30   Birtchnell, J. (1983) Marriage and mental illness. *British Journal Psychiatry*, **142**, 193–198.

31   Noh, S. & Avison, W. (1988) Spouses of discharged psychiatric patients: Factors associated with their experience of burden. *Journal of Marriage & the Family*, **50**, 377–389.

32   Mors, O., Sorensen, L. & Therkildsen, M. (1992) Distress in the relatives of psychiatric patients admitted for the first time. *Acta Psychiatrica Scandinavica*, **85**, 337–344.

33   Ulrich-Jakubowski, D., Russell, D. & O'Hara, M. (1988) Marital adjustment difficulties: Cause or consequence of depressive symptomatology? *Journal of Social & Clinical Psychology*, **7**, 312–318.

34   Merikangas, K., Prusoff, B., Kupfer, D. & Frank, E. (1985) Marital adjustment in major depression. *Journal of Affective Disorders*, **9**, 5–11.

35   Emery, R. (1989) Family violence. *American Psychologist*, Feb, 321–328.

36   Emery, R. (1982) Interparental conflict and the children of discord and divorce. *Psychological Bulletin*, **92** (2) 310–330.

37   Bentovim, A. (1990) Family Violence: Clinical aspects. In: R. Bluglass & P. Bowden, *Principles and Practice of Forensic Psychiatry.* Churchill Livingstone.

38   Wolfner, G. & Gelles, R. (1993) A profile of violence towards children: A national study. *Child Abuse and Neglect*, **17**, 197–212.

39   Pawl, J. H. (1997) Intervention to strengthen relationships between infants and drug abusing or recovering parents. *Zero to Three*, Aug/Sept.

40   Oliver, J. E. (1985) Successive Generations of Child Maltreatment: Social and medical disorders in the parents. *British Journal of Psychiatry*, **147**, 484–490.

41   Falkov, A. (1997) Parental psychiatric disorder and child maltreatment Part 11: extent and nature of association. *Highlight No. 149.* London: National Children's Bureau.

42   Wing, J. K. & Bebbington, P. (1985) Epidemiology of depression. In: E. E. Beckjma & W. R. Leber (Eds.) *Treatment, assessment and research,* pp 765–794. New York: Dow Jones-Irwin.

43   O'Connell, R. & Mayo, J. (1988) The role of social factors in affective disorders: A review. *Hospital & Community Psychiatry*, **39**, 842–851.

44   Harris, T., Brown, G. & Bifulco, A. (1987) Loss of parent in childhood and adult psychiatric disorder: the role of social class position and premarital pregnancy. *Psychological Medicine*, **17**, 163–183.

45   Bifulco, A., Brown, G. & Adler, Z. (1991) Early sexual abuse and clinical depression in adult life. *British Journal of Psychiatry*, **159**, 115–122.

46   The ECT handbook. London: Royal College of Psychiatrists, 1995 *(Council report CR39).*

47   West, D. J. (1965) *Murder followed by suicide.* London: Heinemann.

48   Kirov, G. & Owen, M. (1998) The genetics of bipolar affective disorder. *Progress in Neurology & Psychiatry*, **2**, 30–32.

49   Murray, L. & Cooper, P. (Eds.) (1997) *Postpartum Depression and Child Development.* Guilford Press.

50   Brockington, I. (1996) *Motherhood and mental health.* Oxford University Press.

51   Cooper, P. J. & Murray, L. (1998) Postnatal depression. *British Medical Journal*, **316**, 1884–1886.

52   Ramsey, R. (1993) Postnatal depression. *The Lancet*, **341**, 1358.

53   Kendell, R., Chalmers, J. & Platz, C. (1987) Epidemiology of puerperal psychosis. *British Journal of Psychiatry*, **150**, 662–673.

54   Kumar, R. (1994) Postnatal mental illness: A transcultural perspective. *Social Psychiatry and Psychiatric Epidemiology*, **29**, 250–264.

55   Cawthra, R. & Gibb, R. (1998) Severe personality disorder – whose responsibility? *British Journal of Psychiatry*, **173**, 8–9.

56   Shachnow, J. (1987) Preventive intervention with children of hospitalised psychiatric patients. *American Journal of Orthopsychiatry*, **57** (1) 66–77.

57   Anthony, E. J. (1976) How children cope in families with a psychotic parent. In: E. Rexford., L. Sander & T. Shapiro (Eds.). *Infant psychiatry: a new synthesis,* pp239–247. New Haven Conn: Yale Universities Press.

58   Rutter, M. (Ed.) (1988) *Studies of psychosocial risk: The power of longitudinal data.* Cambridge University Press.

59   Rutter, M., Taylor, E. & Hersov, L. (Eds.) (1994) *Child and adolescent psychiatry: Modern approaches.* Oxford: Blackwell Scientific Publications.

60   Breslau, N. (1985) Psychiatric disorder in children with disabilities. *Journal of the American Academy of Child & Adolescent Psychiatry,* **24**, 87.

61   Pless, I. B. (1984) Clinical assessment. Physical and psychological functioning. *Ped Clin North A.* **32**, pg 33.

62   Slater-White, B. (1978) Impact of chronic illness on child and family. An over-view based on five surveys. *International Journal of Rehabilitation Research,* **1**, 7.

63   Goodman, R. (1994) *Brain disorders.* In: M.Rutter, L. Hersov & Taylor, E. (Eds.) *Child psychiatry: Modern approaches.* 3rd Edition, pp19–22 Oxford: Blackwell Scientific Publications.

64   Kaufman, C., Grunebaum, H., Cohler, B. & Gamer, E. (1979) Superkids: Competent children of psychotic mothers. *American Journal of Psychiatry*, **136** (11) 1398–1402.

65   Goodman, S. H. & Isaacs, L. D. (1984) Primary prevention with children of severely disturbed mothers. *Journal of preventive psychiatry*, **2** (3&4) 387–402.

66   Radke-Yarrow, M., Cummings, E. M., Kuczynski, L. & Chapman, M. (1985) Patterns of attachment in two and three year olds in normal families and families with parental depression. *Child Development,* **56**, 884–93.

67   Morrison, H. (Ed.) (1983) *Children of Depressed Parents: Risk, identification and intervention.* New York: Grune & Stratton.

68   Parker, R., Ward, H., Jackson, S., Aldgate, J. & Wedge, P. – DH LAC (1991) *Looking After Children: Assessing outcomes in childcare.* London: HMSO

69   Keller, M., Beardslee, W., Dorer, D. *et al.* (1986) Impact of severity, and chronicity of parental affective illness on adaptive functioning and psychopathology in children. *Archives of General Psychiatry*, **43**, 930–937.

70   Rutter, M. (1990) Commentary: Some focus and process considerations regarding effects of parental depression on children. *Developmental Psychology*, **26** (1) 60–67.

71   Goodman, S. & Brumley, H. E. (1990) Schizophrenic and depressed mothers: Relational deficits in parenting. *Developmental Psychology*, **26**, 31–39.

72   Webster, J. (1990) Parenting for children of schizophrenic mothers. *Adoption and Fostering*, **14** (2) 37–42.

73   Bettes, B. A. (1988) Maternal depression and motherese: Temporal and intonational features. *Child Development*, **59**, 1089–1096.

74   Sheppard, M. (1993) Maternal depression and child care: The significance for social work and social work research. *Adoption and fostering*, **17** (2) 10–15.

75   Barnett & Parker (1986) Possible determinants, correlates and concensens of high levels of anxiety in primiparous mothers. *Psychological Medicine*, **16**, 177–185.

76   Weissman, M. & Paykel, E. (1974) *The depressed woman*. University of Chicago Press.

77   Keitner, G. (Ed.) (1990) *Depression and Families: Impact and Treatment*. Progress in Psychiatry Series, American Psychiatric Press.

78   Links, P. (Ed.) (1990) *Family Environment and Borderline Personality Disorder*. Progress in Psychiatry Series, American Psychiatric Press.

79   Cleaver, H., Unell, I. & Aldgate, J. (forthcoming) *Parent's problems – Children's needs: Child protection and parental mental illness, problem alcohol and drug use and domestic violence*.

80   Falkov, A. (1996) Study of working together. Part 8 reports: Fatal Child abuse and parental psychiatric disorder. *DoH – ACPC Series – Report no. 1*.

81   Luthar, S. & Zigler, E. (1991) Vulnerability and competence: A review of research on resilience in childhood. *American Journal of Orthopsychiatry*, **61** (1) 6–22.

82   Rutter, M. (1987) Psychosocial resilience and protective mechanisms. *American Journal of Orthopsychiatry*, **57** (3) 316–331.

83   Garmezy, N. (1987) Stress, competence, and development: Continuities in the study of schizophrenic adults, children vulnerable to psychopathology, and the search for stress-resistant children. *American Journal of Orthopsychiatry*, **57** (2) 159–174.

84   Werner, E. High-risk children in young adulthood: A longitudinal study from birth to 32 years. *American Journal of Orthopsychiatry*, **59** (1) 72–81.

85   Wertlieb, D., Weigel, C., Springer, T. & Feldstein, M. (1987) Temperament as a moderator of children's stressful experiences. *American Journal of Orthopsychiatry*, **57** (2) 234–245.

86   Beardslee, W. (1989) The role of self-understanding in resilient individuals: The development of a perspective. *American Journal of Orthopsychiatry*, **59** (2) 266–278.

87   Rutter, M. (1966) Children of sick parents: An environmental and psychiatric study. *Institute of Psychiatry Monographs*, no. (**17**). Oxford University Press.

88   Sameroff, Barocas, A. J., Barocas, R. & Safer, R. (1984) Rochester Longitudinal study progress report. In: N. Watt, E. J, Anthony, L. C. Wynne & J. Rolf. (Eds.) *Children at risk for schizophrenia: A longitudinal perspective*. Cambridge University Press, New York.

89   Jensen, P., Bloedau, L. Degroot, J. *et al.* (1989). Children at risk: 1. Risk factors and child symptomatology. *Journal of the American Academy of Child & Adolescent Psychiatry*, **29** (1) 51–59.

90   Jenkins, J. & Smith, M. (1990) Factors protecting children living in disharmonious homes: maternal reports. *Journal of the American Academy of Child & Adolescent Psychiatry*, **29** (1) 60–69.

91   Breier, A. & Strauss, J. (1984) The role of social relationships in the recovery from psychotic disorders. *American Journal of Psychiatry*, **141** (8) 949–955.

92   Tienari, P., Sorri, A., Lahiti, I. *et al.* (1985) Interaction of genetic and psychosocial factors in schizophrenia. *Acta Psychiatrica Scandinavica*, **71**, Supplement 319, 19–30.

93   Pellegrini, D., Kosisky, S., Nackman, D. *et al.* (1986) Personal and social resources in children of patients with bipolar affective disorder and children of normal control subjects. *American Journal of Psychiatry*, **143** (7) 856–861.

94   Fadden, G., Bebbington, P. & Kuipers, L. (1987) The burden of care: the impact of functional psychiatric

illness on the patients family. *British Journal of Psychiatry*, **150**, 285–292.

95   Sheppard, G., Kellam, M. D., Ensminger, M. A. & Turner, R., J. (1977) Family structure and the mental health of children. 1977. *Archive of General Psychiatry*, **34**, 1012–1022.

96   Hammen, C., Adrian, C., Gordon, D., Burge, D., Jaenicke, C. & Hiroto, D. (1987) Children of depressed mothers: Maternal strain and symptom predictors of dysfunction. *Journal of Abnormal Psychology*, **93** (3) 190–198.

97   Landerman, R., George, L. K. & Blazer, D. G. (1991) Adult Vulnerability for psychiatric disorders: Interactive effects of negative childhood experiences and recent stress. *The Journal of Nervous and Mental Disease*, **179** (11) 656–662.

98   Bryer, J., Nelson, B., Miller, J. & Krol, P. (1987) Childhood sexual and physical as factors in adult psychiatric illness. *American Journal of Psychiatry*, **144** (11) 1426–1430.

99   Bifulco, A. & Moran, P. (1998) *Wednesday's Child: Research into women's experience of neglect and abuse in childhood and adult depression.* London: Routledge.

100   Pilowsky, D. (1995) Psychopathology among children placed in family foster care. *Psychiatric Services*, **46** (9) 906–910.

101   Bebbington, A. & Miles, J. (1989) The background of children who enter local authority care, *British Journal of Social Work*, **19** (5) 349–369.

102   Gross, D. (1989) At risk: Children of the mentally ill. *Journal of Psychosocial Nursing and Mental Health Services*, **27** (8) 14–19.

103   Patterson, G. R. (1986) Performance models for anti-social boys. *American Psychologist*, 432–444.

104   Goodyear, I. M., Cooper, P. J., Vize, C. M. & Ashby, L. (1993) Depression in 11–16 year old girls: The role of past parental psychopathology and exposure to recent life events. *Journal of Child Psychology and Psychiatry*, **43**, 1103–1115.

105   Cohler, B. J. (1987) Adversity, Resilience and the study of lives. In: E. J. Anthony & B. J. Cohler (Eds.) *The invulnerable child,* pp363–424.

106   Graham, P. J. (1986) Behavioural and intellectual development in childhood epidemiology. *British Medical Bulletin,* **42** (2) 155–162.

107   Weissman, M. M., Gammon, G. D., John, K. R., Leckman, J. F. & Kidd, K. K. (1984) Psychopathology in children (ages 6–18) of depressed and normal parents. *Journal of the American Academy of Child and Adolescent Psychiatry*, **23**, 78–84.

108   Silverman, M. (1989) Children of psychiatrically ill parents: A prevention perspective. *Hospital and Community Psychiatry*, **40** (12) 1257–1265.

109   Hill, M., Laybourn, Brown, J. (1996) Children whose parents misuse alcohol: a study of service and needs. *Child and Family Social Work*, **1**, 159–167.

110   O'Hagan, R. (1995) *Emotional and psychological abuse of children.* Milton Keynes: Open University Press.

111   Stein, A., Gath, D., Bucher, J., Bond, A., Day, A. & Cooper, P. (1991) The relationship between parental depression and mother-child interactions. *British Journal of Psychiatry*, **158** (1) 46–52.

Chapter Three

Legal and policy frameworks

All practitioners working with mentally ill parents and children require an understanding of childcare and mental health legislation and relevant policies and procedures to ensure good practice. This includes being able to relate and communicate effectively with colleagues across age, service, geographic, cultural and training-related barriers. The challenge for all parties is to develop greater shared understanding of legislation, policy and practice in different services and to translate this into more integrated and collaborative joint working.

Although the basic legislation in mental health has remained the same since 1983, there have been significant changes in recent years which have affected professional practice in the field, particularly since the implementation of the *NHS and Community Care Act, 1990*[1] and some of the specific recommendations arising from the inquiry into the homicide by Christopher Clunis.[2]

These changes have included additions to the legislative framework and a range of new guidance for professionals concerning the way in which services for people with mental illnesses should be delivered. It is important to note that both health authorities and social services departments have been directed to target resources on people with *severe* mental illnesses, and that this may have important implications for many parents with mental illness in terms of access to services.

In many respects, adult mental health legislation, policy and guidance reflect a continuing preoccupation with tensions which are very similar to those found in childcare policy and legislation; in particular, the need to respect the rights of individuals whilst ensuring the safety of others.

Key documents in adult mental health, childcare and protection are listed in **Appendix i.**

Learning Resources
Centre

Adult mental health legislation and policy

The Mental Health Act, 1983 and the Code of Practice

Most treatment of mental disorder is undertaken voluntarily in the community, in outpatient departments or during a hospital admission. Compulsory admission of a person must be for one or more legal reasons set out in the *Mental Health Act, 1983* (MHA). This is the key legislation which provides the framework for compulsory admission to hospital, including a range of provisions for the care and treatment of in-patients and also legal requirements for aftercare services.

A key resource for all mental health professionals is the *Mental Health Act Manual,*[3] which contains not only the Act itself but also details of related legislation and Government guidance and circulars. This manual also contains the *Code of Practice*, which provides guidance to statutory authorities and staff on how to follow their duties under the Act.

Admission for assessment or treatment of a person with a mental disorder may be necessary for the person's health, the person's safety, the protection of others, or all of these.

Broad principles

People being assessed for possible admission under the MHA should:

● receive respect for and consideration of their individual qualities and diverse backgrounds – social, cultural, ethnic and religious

● have their needs taken fully into account though it is recognised that, within available resources, it may not always be practicable to meet them

● be delivered any necessary treatment or care in the least controlled and segregated facilities practicable

● be treated or cared for in such a way that promotes to the greatest practicable degree, their self-determination and personal responsibility consistent with their needs and wishes

● be discharged from any order under the Act to which they are subject immediately after it is no longer necessary.
(DOH, 1993)

Key professionals

The two main professional groups given powers under the MHA are **social workers** and **doctors**. Social workers have to be qualified for two years and then undertake specific training provided by a local authority and be awarded a special warrant before they can practice as an **Approved Social Worker** (ASW) under the Act. They also have to undertake regular 'refresher' training to update their knowledge of the Act and good practice issues.

Many psychiatrists and some GPs are also approved under the MHA, and are known as Section 12 doctors (the section of the Act that applies). Not all psychiatrists are approved and the approval has to be renewed at regular intervals. This approval recognises particular skills and experience in the diagnosis and treatment of mental disorders.

ASWs have a wide range of responsibilities and duties under the Act. The main duty of the ASW involves acting as applicant for compulsory admissions to hospital. Normally, when a person is detained under the MHA, an ASW makes an application to the managers of the hospital where the person is to be admitted, addressing the application to the managers and naming on the form the hospital concerned. The responsibilities of an ASW are set out in **Section 13** of the Act and can be summarised as:

1   *It shall be the duty of an ASW to make an application…where s/he is satisfied that such an application ought to be made.*

2   *Before making an application…an ASW shall interview the patient in a suitable manner and satisfy her/himself that detention in a hospital is in* all the circumstances *of the case the most appropriate way of providing the care and medical treatment of which the patient stands in need.*

3   *An application…may be made outside the area of the local social services authority by which s/he is appointed.*

4   *It shall be the duty of a local social services authority, if so required by the nearest relative of a patient residing in their area, to direct an ASW as soon as practicable to take the patient's case into consideration under (1) above with a view to making an application; and the ASW shall inform the nearest relative in writing if s/he decides not to make an application.*

The duty to make an application for compulsory admission to hospital is placed *on the ASW* and not his/her employer; this means that ASWs have personal liability for the decisions they make about applications for admission:

> '*He should exercise his own judgement, based upon social and medical evidence, and not act at the behest of his employers, medical practitioners or other persons who might be involved with the patient's welfare.*' (Jones, 1996, p71)

The *Code of Practice* provides more detailed information about the individual responsibilities of ASWs, in which it is re-emphasised that the ASW has overall responsibility for co-ordinating the assessment and implementing any decision to admit someone to hospital. The ASW must attempt to identify the person's nearest relative, and specific responsibilities in relation to nearest relatives are laid out in the Act. Furthermore, the ASW should ascertain the views of other people, including friends and relatives of the patient as well as the views of other professionals, and should take these into account in reaching a decision.

The legal role of the doctor under the MHA is to provide a medical recommendation to support an application if satisfied that the grounds for admission (as specified in the relevant section of the Act; see below) are met. Substantial detailed information is given in Section 12 of the Act and in the *Code of Practice* regarding the way in which this role should be carried out.

Key definitions

Section 1 of the MHA defines the legal categories of mental disorder which include mental illness, psychopathic disorder and mental impairment. The mental disorder must be so severe as to warrant assessment or treatment in hospital rather than in the community. The definitions of psychopathic disorder and mental impairment include a disorder of behaviour.

> *'Mental disorder' means mental illness, arrested or incomplete development of mind, psychopathic disorder and any other disorder or disability of mind.*

> *'Severe mental impairment' means a state of arrested or incomplete development of mind which includes severe impairment of intelligence and social functioning and is associated with abnormally aggressive or seriously irresponsible conduct on the part of the person concerned.*

> *'Mental impairment' means a state of arrested or incomplete development of mind (not amounting to severe mental impairment) which includes significant impairment of intelligence and social functioning and is associated with abnormally aggressive or seriously irresponsible conduct on the part of the person concerned.*

> *'Psychopathic disorder' means a persistent disorder or disability of mind (whether or not including significant impairment of intelligence) which results in abnormally aggressive or seriously irresponsible conduct on the part of the person concerned.*

There has been much debate about these terms, their meaning and how they should be applied in assessments under the MHA. Some key points are:

- 'Mental illness' is the category used in 97% of formal admissions to hospital. However, it is not defined in either the MHA or in the *Code of Practice*. Its 'operational definition and usage is a matter for clinical judgement in each case' (Memorandum quoted in Jones 1996). *The Mental Health Act Manual* also quotes the judicial view that 'mental illness' has no medical or legal significance in its own right, and that decisions about whether or not a person may be described as being mentally ill depends on what 'the ordinary sensible person'[3] might say of someone's behaviour, otherwise described as 'the-man-must-be-mad' test.

- 'Abnormally aggressive conduct' is defined in the *Code of Practice* as behaviours which are *'outside the usual range of aggressive behaviour, and which cause actual damage and/or real distress occurring recently or persistently or with excessive severity.'* (DOH, 1993, p113)

- 'Irresponsible conduct' is defined in the *Code of Practice* as *'behaviour which shows a lack of responsibility, a disregard of the consequences of action taken, and where the results cause actual damage or real distress, either recently or persistently or with excessive severity'* (DOH, 1993, p113). It has also been noted that behaviour which involves failure to protect oneself from abuse by others is being defined under this term.[3]

- 'Psychopathic disorder' is another term which has been the subject of intense debate for many years. A fairly helpful definition has been provided by a DOH and Home Office Working Group as follows:

'..the term "psychopathic disorder" does not represent a single clinical disorder but is a legal category describing a number of severe personality disorders, which contribute to the person committing anti-social acts, usually of a recurrent or episodic type. One important feature may be an inability to relate to others, and to take account of their feelings and safety. It has often proved difficult to influence this behaviour by means of social, penal and medical interventions.'[3]

The notion of 'treatability' is an important one in relation to personality disorders under the MHA, in that someone can only be compulsorily admitted for treatment if that treatment 'is likely to alleviate or prevent a deterioration of his condition'. (There is more about treatability in Section 3 on page 87.)

Grounds for admission

A patient may be compulsorily admitted under the MHA where this is necessary:

- in the interests of his/her own health; or
- in the interests of his/her own safety; or
- for the protection of other people.

The *Code of Practice* provides detailed guidance on what should be considered before reaching a decision about compulsory admission in addition to the statutory criteria above, including the patient's own wishes and perception of their needs; the impact of a compulsory admission on their life after discharge, and the possible burden on those close to the patient should s/he not be admitted to hospital.

- **Health:** this includes mental as well as physical health, and an admission can be considered under the Act with a view to preventing the deterioration of someone's physical and/or mental health

- **Safety:** an admission should be considered on this ground if the person is being exposed to the risk of being harmed unless they are detained

- **Protection of others:** this phrase has been interpreted as referring not only to risks from the patient to the general public, but also to specific individuals; furthermore:

    'Although the matter is not free from doubt, it is likely that this phrase covers both protection from physical harm and protection from serious emotional harm.'[3]

The main sections of the MHA used in relation to compulsory admission to hospital are found in Part 2 of the Act. Sections 2, 3 and 4 are of particular importance.

Section 2: Compulsory admission for assessment

Grounds:

- he is suffering from mental disorder of a nature or degree which warrants the detention of the patient in a hospital for assessment (or for assessment followed by medical treatment) for at least a limited period; and

- he ought to be so detained in the interests of his own health or safety or with a view to the protection of other persons.

Application: by ASW or nearest relative of patient, founded on two medical recommendations.

Duration: up to 28 days.

Discharge: can be made at any time by the patient's Responsible Medical Officer (RMO), the hospital managers, or through an appeal to the Mental Health Review Tribunal which must be made by the patient within the first 14 days of the admission. Subject to certain conditions, the nearest relative can also order discharge.

Although **a nearest relative** can make an application for admission under this section of the Act, the *Code of Practice* clearly states that the ASW 'is usually the right applicant', given their professional training, knowledge of local resources and of the legislation. Furthermore, an application by a nearest relative may well detrimentally affect the applicant's relationship with the person being assessed, and so is usually to be avoided.

The two medical recommendations can be provided either jointly or separately, and the *Code of Practice* stresses that the second recommendation should be made by a doctor 'with previous acquaintance of the patient' (p11) if practicable.

A **Section 2** cannot be extended beyond the 28-day duration but may be followed by a **Section 3** within the 28-day period, providing that the grounds under that section of the Act are met.

Mental Health Review Tribunals (MHRTs) were set up under the Act to safeguard the rights of people compulsorily admitted to hospital. The MHRT offers an independent review of individual cases from both medical and non-medical perspectives, and has to consider the justification for continued detention in hospital at the time of the hearing. Having reviewed the person's condition, the Tribunal can direct the person's discharge if it sees fit, or if the grounds for compulsory detention are no longer met.

Section 3: Compulsory admission for treatment

Grounds:

- he is suffering from mental illness, severe mental impairment, psychopathic disorder or mental impairment and his mental disorder is of a nature or degree which makes it appropriate for them to receive medical treatment in hospital; and

- in the case of psychopathic disorder or mental impairment, such treatment is likely to alleviate or prevent a deterioration of his condition; and

- it is necessary for the health or safety of the patient or for the protection of other persons that they should receive such treatment and it cannot be provided unless he is detained under this section.

Application: by ASW or nearest relative of patient, founded on two medical recommendations.

Duration: up to six months, renewable for a further six months, then annually.

Discharge: by the patient's RMO; by hospital managers or through the MHRT within the first six months; subject to certain conditions, by the nearest relative.

The decision regarding whether Section 2 or Section 3 is the most appropriate order to be made is discussed in *The Code of Practice*. It states that Section 2 is more appropriate in cases where someone has not been admitted to hospital on any basis before. Section 2 is also more appropriate where the diagnosis of someone's illness is unclear and the prognosis uncertain and there is therefore a need for further assessment in hospital. Where a patient is well-known, but the nature of their condition appears to have changed, Section 2 is also the more appropriate order.

An admission under Section 3 is considered more appropriate, according to the *Code of Practice*, when the person is known to mental health services, where they have recently been assessed by the team and their condition appears to be the same.

One particular issue which has received close attention in relation to Section 3 of the Act is the '**treatability test**'.[3] Subsection (b) takes account of the substantial evidence which strongly suggests that people suffering from **mental impairment**, but more especially **psychopathic disorder**, suffer conditions which are not readily responsive to currently available treatment. In these cases, the idea of a compulsory admission to hospital for 'treatment' becomes relatively meaningless. The fact that this subsection applies only to these two categories is significant in that it allows for the detention of someone with either a mental illness or severe mental impairment even though their condition may not respond to treatment. This is specifically to allow for admissions which may be of benefit at times of crisis for such people.

Section 4: Compulsory admission in an emergency

Grounds: where there is an urgent need for admission for assessment and compliance with the procedure under Section 2 would cause undesirable delay.

Application: by an ASW or nearest relative of the patient, founded on one medical recommendation.

Duration: up to 72 hours.

Discharge: only by the RMO and hospital managers. No appeal to MHRT.

The *Code of Practice* emphasises that Section 4 is only for use in cases of genuine emergency, and explicitly warns against its use 'for convenience', for example when a second doctor is simply unavailable. 'Emergency situations' are those arising from the existence of significant risk of harm to the patient, to others or to property, or from the need to physically restrain the person. Section 4 has been criticised because of the frequency with which it appears to be used, especially given the wide regional variations in its use. This section has therefore been subject to close monitoring by the Mental Health Act Commission.

Holding powers for doctors and nurses

Under **Section 5 (2)** of the MHA, a doctor can apply for someone who is already an in-patient in hospital to be formally detained by applying in writing to the hospital managers. This holding power lasts for up to 72 hours, allowing enough time for detention to be arranged under Section 2 or 3.

Under **Section 5 (4)**, nurses can apply in writing to the hospital managers for someone to be detained for up to six hours, or until a doctor applies for a Section 5 (2) if earlier.

Guardianship

The purpose of Guardianship is to provide a statutory basis for community care, although it has been a little-used provision to date. The grounds for the use of Guardianship are that the person must be suffering from one of the four categories of mental disorder and two medical recommendations are required. The order must be made in the interests of the welfare of that person or to protect others. It is renewable after six months if the grounds are still met, and there is also a right of appeal to the MHRT. Under Guardianship, the local authority is given powers to:

● require the person to live in a specified place

● attend places for treatment or rehabilitation

● require access to specific professional staff (Section 8).

People subject to criminal proceedings

Part III of the MHA relates to people who are subject to criminal proceedings. Only some of these sections will be summarised here. Under **Section 37**, courts have the power to make a **hospital order** where someone is convicted of an offence for which they would normally receive a prison sentence. Two medical recommendations are required to confirm that the person is suffering from one of the four forms of mental disorder, and the 'treatability test' applies as for Section 3.

Sections 47, 48 and 49 allow for the transfer of mentally disordered offenders from prison to hospital.

Section 117: Aftercare

Section 117 of the MHA places a specific duty on health and local authorities in relation to people who have been admitted to hospital under Sections 3, 37, 45(a), 47 or 48 of the Act to provide aftercare on discharge. The aim of this provision was to ensure that people had the necessary support after their stay in hospital to be able to adjust to life in the community, and that any necessary care and treatment would continue.

Section 136: Police powers

Under this section, the police can remove from a public place to a place of safety, someone who appears to be suffering from a mental disorder and to be in immediate need of care or control.

Grounds: if the police constable thinks it necessary in the interests of that person or other people.

Application: a police constable.

Duration: up to 72 hours.

The *Code of Practice* stresses that good practice in relation to the use of Section 136 depends upon local agreement between the social services department, the health authority and trusts and the police in establishing a clear policy to guide those responsible for its implementation. According to the *Code of Practice*, the principal aim of this Section should be *'to secure the competent and speedy assessment by a doctor and an ASW of the person detained under the power'* (p33).

NHS and Community Care Act, 1990

With this Act came the introduction of **care management**. The term 'care management' defines both the structures which needed to be put into place in terms of separating those staff responsible for **assessment and care planning** from those responsible for **service provision** (the 'purchaser/provider split'). It also defines the process by which these activities should be undertaken.

The process of care management was divided into seven stages in the guidance:

1 publishing information

2 determining the level of assessment

3 assessing need

4 care planning

5 implementing the care plan

6 monitoring

7 reviewing.

The Care Programme Approach

The Care Programme Approach (CPA) was introduced in April 1991, with lead responsibility for its implementation given to health authorities. It applies *only* to people with a mental illness, and was intended to introduce a more systematic approach to the care of such people. The responsibility under CPA is to arrange an individual package of care for all patients prior to their discharge from hospital and for those using specialist psychiatric services.

Key elements:

● assessment of need

● care planning

● allocation of a keyworker

● regular reviews of progress.

Key steps:[4]

● enter patient's details on CPA information system

● initial assessment of need – further assessment for those with complex needs, with larger team – consider supervision register

● identify keyworker

● formulate and record care plan

● ensure patient and carer understand and, if possible, agree care plan

● circulate care plan to all who *need to know*

- ensure that elements of care plan necessary for discharge are carried out *before* in-patients are discharged

- keyworker to monitor delivery of care plan

- review care plan at agreed intervals, or sooner if necessary.

The assessment process should include a full assessment of risk to both the patient and to others. A 'tiered care programme' has been developed in response to the varied needs of clients who require CPA; a full multidisciplinary CPA will most often be required for people with a severe and enduring mental illness, whilst people with less complex needs will often require a less intensive form of CPA.

As with care management, although the key principles have been laid out by government, the guidance has made it clear that 'it has no intention of prescribing precisely what should be done at a local level.'[4] The guidance emphasises that CPA is an approach to the care of people with a mental illness, based on a systematic assessment of their needs. There is therefore substantial local variation in how CPA has been implemented. As a result, there are also very different experiences in terms of how care management and the CPA have been integrated as systems which should, in theory, work together to meet the needs of clients with a mental illness.

Integrating care management and the CPA

Care management and the CPA are clearly based on the same guiding principles:[4, p56]

- assessment of need

- care planning

- implementation, monitoring and review of care plans.

The keyworker and care manager functions are essentially the same in terms of each being concerned with co-ordinating care.

> *'One way of looking at the CPA is as a specialist variant of care management for people with mental health problems, and the two systems should be capable of being fully integrated with one another.'*[4]

According to this guidance, this capability for integration should apply *whatever* model of care management is in operation. It stresses that the *minimum* requirements for local arrangements to succeed are that:

- all agencies involved should agree **a single care plan**

- each client should have **a single keyworker**

- all those involved in delivering the care plan should know who the named keyworker is.

Keyworkers should carry out the care management function of co-ordinating, managing and revising the care plan, and should therefore have the support of all agencies involved in its implementation. It is stressed that it is the keyworker who holds the responsibility for the *co-ordination* of services, whilst responsibility for their *delivery* still remains with the appropriate individual agency. The guidance acknowledges that keyworkers are also likely to provide services to clients in their own right (such as counselling), in which case their role as provider should not be confused with their role as co-ordinator of the overall care plan for clients:

> 'The provider role should not be allowed to dominate the co-ordinating and managing roles, nor vice versa.' [4, p59]

Our Healthier Nation

The Green Paper *Our Healthier Nation*[5] builds on the success achieved under *Health of the Nation* and has maintained mental health as a priority. It suggests a national target *'to reduce the death rate from suicide and undetermined injury by at least a further sixth (17%) by 2010 from a baseline at 1996.'* It also sets out a national contract on mental health covering some of the measures that might be taken to meet the national target. This national contract addresses some of the complex social, economic and environmental causes of ill health and aims to 'tackle the much harder task of improving the health of the unskilled and socially excluded.'

New legislation and guidance

There has been increasing concern about the care being received in the community by people who are mentally ill, particularly since the inquiry into homicide by Christopher Clunis in 1992[2] and subsequent inquiries into other serious incidents. These concerns have led directly to a number of new initiatives in mental health by the government, an outline of which was contained in a ten-point plan issued in 1993. This plan included new guidance on the discharge of mentally-disordered offenders into the community, the setting up of supervision registers for people considered to be high-risk, and the introduction of a new power under the MHA of supervised discharge.

Supervision registers

Supervision registers were introduced in 1994 in order to help prioritise those patients under the CPA who could be identified as being most at risk, either to themselves or others. There are clear parallels between supervision registers and the child protection register used in children's services.

The initial assessment undertaken at the CPA meeting should include consideration of adding the person's name to the supervision register, which has the status of an NHS record. In order for their name to be added, the person should be suffering a severe mental illness and should also pose:

- significant risk of suicide

- significant risk of serious violence to others

- significant risk of severe self-neglect.

The decision to include someone's name on the supervision register rests with the consultant psychiatrist and multidisciplinary team involved in the care of the client/patient. All those subject to supervised discharge should be included on the supervision register.

The Mental Health (Patients in the Community) Act, 1995

This legislation was implemented in 1996 and is intended to provide powers for the supervised discharge of some patients who have been subject to compulsory detention under Section 3 of the MHA. It specifically addresses the problem of 'revolving door patients', who are readmitted to hospital due to the failure of care arrangements made for them on discharge, and who may still be regarded as presenting a risk either to themselves or others.

Grounds for an application for supervision specified in this Act are substantial risks of serious harm:

- to the health of the patient; or

- to the safety of the patient; or

- to the safety of other persons; or

- arising from the patient being seriously exploited.

'Substantial risk of serious harm to others' can include psychological harm to a potential carer.

The two further conditions which must also be met for an application to be made are that the person should be suffering from one of the four categories of mental disorder specified in the MHA, and that the Order is likely to help ensure that the person will receive Section 117 after-care services which will help reduce the risks they face.

Under this Act, an individual will be required to co-operate with a care plan developed under the CPA, and their supervisor (who will normally be the CPA keyworker) will have the power to require that:

- the patient reside in a specified place

- the patient attend a specified place for medical treatment or rehabilitation

- the supervisor (or person authorised by them) be allowed access to the patient at the place they are currently residing

- the supervisor (or person authorised by them) may take and convey the patient to any place where they are required to reside or attend for medical treatment or rehabilitation.

Application: can only be made by the patient's RMO whilst the person is still an in-patient under Section 3 or 37 of the MHA.

Duration: six months, extendable for a further six months, and then annually, with a right of appeal to the Mental Health Review Tribunal.

The requirement to attend for medical treatment does not imply any powers to impose medication on someone without their consent, although the review of a case where someone fails to meet the above requirements can include consideration of a further period of detention under the Act.

Carers (Recognition and Services) Act, 1995

All those caring for someone who is eligible for services under the *NHS and Community Care Act* are entitled to an assessment of their own needs and these should be taken into account in the assessment of the person for whom they care. Services can be provided to young carers under *The Children Act, 1989* and should take into consideration both the needs of the young person and the adult for whom they are caring.

Childcare support and protection systems

The Children Act, 1989

The Children Act, 1989 (CA) provides the key legislative base for childcare work.
The Act is arranged in twelve parts:

- **Part I** states that the welfare of the child is always the paramount consideration of the Courts and introduces the concept of parental responsibility.

- **Part II** deals with orders concerning children in family proceedings. This is the section generally referred to as 'private law'. Central to this part of the Act are the Section 8 Orders (see page 98 below).

- **Part III** describes a range of duties and powers for the provision of local authority support for children and families in need (Section 17 provisions).

- **Part IV** deals with care and supervision orders and provides 'threshold criteria' which must be satisfied before a court can make an order. Central to the child protection provisions in Parts IV and V is the concept of 'significant harm' when a child may be at serious risk of maltreatment.

- **Part V** deals with the protection of children and provides for a child assessment order and emergency protection order and establishes the duty to make enquiries where there are concerns about a child's welfare.

- The rest of the Act (**Parts VI–XII**) deals with a range of provisions concerning children who are living away from home, residential care, fostering, daycare and childminding, Secretary of State's supervisory functions and responsibilities, and other matters.

Principles

Central to the CA is a set of principles which determine how children should be treated under the law and by local authorities:

1 Children's welfare must be safeguarded and promoted

The Act recognises that some parents may need support in meeting their children's needs and that in certain situations children may need protection from maltreatment. There is a range of provisions in the Act dealing with child protection matters. The Act states that the local authority has a duty to safeguard and promote the welfare of children in their area.

2 Wherever possible, children should be brought up by their own families

As far as is consistent with their welfare and safety, children should be brought up and cared for by their own families. When families experience difficulties, such as when a parent is mentally ill, services for children in need should be provided to support the family. When children cannot live with their parents, parents retain parental responsibility for the child which only ends if the child is adopted. Contact with parents is a child's right and should be encouraged as long as it is in a child's interests.

3 If children cannot live with their families, there should be high-quality substitute care

It is vital that any alternative childcare provision, if children cannot live with their families, meets children's needs and achieves good short- and long-term outcomes for the children.

4 The concept of parental responsibility

Parents have rights as well as responsibilities regarding their children. Parental responsibility is defined as *'all the rights, duties, powers, responsibilities and authority which by law a parent of a child has in relation to the child and his property'*.[6]

- **Both parents** have parental responsibility where they were **married** to each other at or after the child's birth.

- In the case of **unmarried parents**, when the child is born the mother has parental responsibility; the father does not, unless he acquires it. This can be done by applying to a court or he can make a parental responsibility agreement with the mother on the requisite form.

- **More than one person may have parental responsibility** for the same child at the same time, and the person who has parental responsibility will not lose it because some other person subsequently acquires parental responsibility.

- Parental responsibility is something which parents **have**, and, short of adoption (or freeing for adoption) or death, do not lose until the child is 18.

- Local authorities acquire parental responsibility when a child is looked after whilst the subject of a Court Order, and they **share** parental responsibility with the parents.

- A **guardian** who is appointed by the court or by a parent also acquires parental responsibility.

Implications for practice

When working with parents who are mentally ill, it is important to know who has parental responsibility for their children. Parents may be divorced, separated or in new relationships. If a mother is admitted to hospital, it will be important to ascertain who else has parental responsibility and to decide, with the mother, whether it is appropriate for such a person to share the parenting role, including where and with whom children should live whilst the mother is in hospital.

Where a local authority acquires parental responsibility by virtue of a Court Order (such as a Care Order or Emergency Protection Order), the local authority may only exercise parental responsibility to the extent of safeguarding and promoting the welfare of the child for the duration of the Order.

5 Partnership and co-operation

One of the aims of the CA is to try to keep children and families together, as it has been demonstrated that working in partnership results in better outcomes for children. Another core theme is to encourage greater collaboration between those with responsibilities for children and statutory and voluntary agencies. This includes practitioners working with mentally ill adults.

Implications for practice

There have been many efforts to define what 'partnership' means. The Department of Health publication *The Challenge of Partnership*[7] describes a number of different types of partnership from information sharing to full partnership. Good practice means that, as far as possible, parents, the child concerned (if 'of sufficient age and understanding') and other professionals such as mental health workers, if appropriate, are involved in the decision-making processes in an open and honest way. Efforts must be made to offer services that are ethnically and culturally appropriate. As far as this is consistent with promoting the welfare and protection of their child, parents' wishes should be respected and their views taken into account when arrangements are being made. Once completed, these plans are generally recorded in a parental agreement. Parents then receive a copy of this agreement.

6 Children's wishes and feelings should be ascertained and taken account of

7 The court should be responsive to the needs of children

When the court makes any decision about a child, it has to comply with three important principles:

i **The child's welfare is paramount**

When a court is making any decision involving a child, the welfare of the child comes before any other consideration. In day-to-day practice, this also means that where adults and children have competing interests – such as in the cases of adults who are mentally ill – the welfare of the child takes precedence over the welfare of the adult.

ii **The no delay principle**

Strenuous attempts must be made to minimise delays in the court process, during which time children, family members and alternative carers face uncertainty and experience high levels of distress and anxiety. Studies have shown that children are harmed by this 'drift' and delay.

iii **The presumption of no order (no order principle)**

When making an order, the judge must have sufficient and clear evidence to demonstrate that a particular order is required and that making such an order would be in the best interests of the child.

Welfare checklist

The **Welfare checklist** must be considered by the court when making any decision about a child. This checklist provides a list of good practice in all matters relating to children which must be taken into account when the Court is making a decision about the child, including:

- the wishes and feelings of the child; these must be ascertained by a social worker working with the child, but these wishes need to be balanced with the needs of the child and the views of others and therefore do not necessarily determine the decisions made; however, they must be taken account of when making judgements about what will be in the child's best interests

- the child's physical, emotional and educational needs

- the likely effect on the child of any change in circumstances

- the child's age, sex, background and any characteristics which the court considers relevant

- any harm the child has suffered or is at risk of suffering

- the parents'/carers' ability to meet the child's needs

- the range of powers the court has in the proceedings.

Section 17: Services for children and families in need

Part III of the CA specifies the duties of local authorities to provide services for children and their families. Under Section 17, it is the duty of every local authority to safeguard and promote the welfare of children in need living in their area. As far as is consistent with this, local authorities have to promote the upbringing of children by their families, if necessary by providing (Section 17) services appropriate to their needs.

A child is 'in need' if he or she is unlikely to achieve or maintain, or to have the opportunity of achieving or maintaining, a reasonable standard of health or development without the provision of services by a local authority under Part III, or the child's health or development is likely to be significantly impaired, or further impaired, without the provision of such services, or the child is disabled.

The local authority has a duty to provide such services as they consider appropriate with respect to children in need within their area. Services may include: day care for children under five; accommodation; family centres; services from voluntary organisations; advice, guidance and counselling; occupational, social, cultural and recreational activities; home helps; facilities to make use of services (such as transport); assistance to have a holiday; help to enable children return to live with their families or to contact their families. Services should take account of the cultural, religious and linguistic background of the child and family, including any disability. In order to fulfil their responsibilities, social services may ask for help from other local authority agencies including education and housing departments and the health service.

Summary of Child Care Orders

Although it has no strict legal basis, lawyers and courts tend to make a distinction between what is known as private and public law. **Public law** deals with those areas where local authorities intervene to protect children or to promote their welfare. **Private law** deals with matters between individuals such as disputes between parents who are divorced about where their children will live. Section 8 Orders are the most important of the private law aspects of the CA.

Private law – Section 8 Orders

Section 8 Orders include:

- **Residence Order** – an order to settle the arrangements as to the person with whom a child is to live

- **Contact Order** – an order requiring the person with whom the child lives to allow contact with the person named on the order

- **Specific Issue Order** – an order giving directions for determining a specific issue (such as consent for medical treatment, education, religion)

- **Prohibited Steps Order** – an order prohibiting a parent taking a step specified in the order without the consent of the court (such as taking a child out of the country).

In addition, the court has the right in any family law proceedings where a question arises concerning the welfare of a child, to ask the local authority to investigate the child's circumstances (Section 37) where it appears to the court that it may be appropriate for a care or supervision order to be made. Under Section 16 (1), in exceptional cases, and with the agreement of all parties, the court may also direct that a probation officer or social worker be made 'available to advise, assist and (where appropriate) befriend' any person named in the Order.

Public law orders – Section 47: The duty to make enquiries

Section 47 (1) gives the local authority a duty to investigate where they:

'*(a) are informed that a child who lives, or is found in their area*

  (i) is the subject of an emergency protection order; or

  (ii) is in police protection; or

'*(b) have reasonable cause to suspect that a child who lives, or is found, in their area is suffering, or is likely to suffer, significant harm,*

the authority shall make, or cause to be made, such enquiries as they consider necessary to enable them to decide whether they should take any action to safeguard or promote the child's welfare.'

Child protection orders

There are two short-term orders specifically related to child protection. The first is the **Emergency Protection Order** and the second is the **Child Assessment Order**. In addition, the police have powers (Section 46) to take children into 'police protection' where a police officer has reasonable cause to believe that a child will otherwise suffer significant harm.

An **Emergency Protection Order** (EPO):

- requires a person to produce the child; or

- authorises the removal of a child to safeguard his/her welfare; or

- prevents the removal of a child from a hospital or other place.

An application can be made by **any person** where there is reason to believe **that the child is likely to suffer significant harm** or where social workers are making enquires regarding child protection and access is denied. The application can be made without notice to the parents and the CA requires the court to be '*satisfied there is reasonable cause to believe that a child is suffering or likely to suffer significant harm*'. The child's welfare is the paramount consideration and the Welfare Checklist does *not* apply. The EPO lasts for a maximum of eight days. An application can be made for an extension of a further seven days if serious concerns for the child's safety persist. The child must be returned home as soon as it is safe to do so. The court may issue a warrant authorising a police officer (using force if necessary) to assist any person attempting to exercise powers under the EPO. Application is normally made to a single magistrate or to a sitting Magistrates Court. Where a child, parent or other person with parental responsibility was not informed about, and/or was not present at the hearing, they may apply for a discharge of the EPO after 72 hours. There is no right of appeal against the making (or refusal to make) an EPO.

A **Child Assessment Order** (CAO) can be made where:

- there are reasonable grounds to suspect that the child is suffering or is likely to suffer significant harm; and

- an assessment is required to determine this question; and

- it is unlikely that any such assessment will be made without such an order.

The CAO requires the person named in the Order to produce the child and to comply with the directions to have the child assessed. (Note that a child of 'sufficient understanding' can refuse medical/psychiatric examination.) The CAO is hardly ever used. In an emergency where there are serious concerns about a child's safety, it is likely that an EPO will be necessary.

Implications for practice

EPOs are often used to keep children in hospital when there are serious concerns about their safety rather than removing them from their home. Mental health workers will find children and family services social workers reluctant to consider an EPO which involves taking children from their parents, unless there is a serious risk involved, because of the psychological consequences of traumatic separation. However, given the unpredictable nature of mental illness, some emergencies cannot be avoided. The emotional trauma for children, however, is less if a relative or other known person is able to care for them at these times. Good practice is about acting in a planned way, but there will be occasions when an EPO is necessary.

Care and Supervision Orders

These orders include:

- **Care Order** (Section 31) – an order receiving a child into local authority care

- **Interim Care Order** (Section 38) – an order receiving a child into local authority care pending a final hearing

- **Supervision Order** (Section 35) – an order requiring a local authority or probation officer to advise, assist and befriend a child.

A Care Order:

- lasts until the child's 18th birthday unless it is brought to an end earlier

- can be ended by a successful application to the court to discharge the Order by the child, the local authority or any person with parental responsibility for the child; making a Supervision Order or a Residence Order

- is also terminated when an **Adoption Order** or a **Freeing Order** is made.

Similar conditions apply for an Interim Care Order but here the court does not have to be satisfied that the threshold criteria (see below) have been met, but only that there are 'reasonable grounds' to believe that they have. Initially, an Interim Care Order can only be made for eight weeks but can be renewed at four-weekly intervals (without limit) subject to the general principle of avoiding delay. Supervision Orders may require a child to comply with the specific directions of the supervisor. The Order lasts for one year with a possible extension of up to three years.

Implications for practice

Before making any decision about a child whom the local authority proposes to look after, the childcare social worker must consult with the child, the parents, and any other person with parental responsibility and any other person who may be relevant to the situation. The local authority is obliged to take these views into consideration.

When talking with parents, childcare practitioners must consider the implications of known or possible mental health problems in a parent. This will mean talking with colleagues in the local mental health service or with the general practitioner. This is an opportunity to ensure that unmet parental needs can be addressed and that appropriate support can be provided for parent and child if the care order is granted.

The local authority must also give 'due consideration to the child's religion, racial origin and cultural and linguistic background' when deciding where to place the child. Attempts should always be made to place the child with someone who has a significant connection with the child, such as a family member. As far as possible, siblings should be placed together; unless there are specific dangers involved in doing so, they should be placed near their original home.

If it is in the child's interests, the local authority must allow the child reasonable contact with parents and any other person with whom the child has been living before they came into care, or with whom they have a relationship, such as friends and relatives. The local authority can apply, in exceptional cases, for an Order to refuse contact (Section 34 [4]) Social workers are required to hold regular reviews of the child's circumstances and, as far as possible, parents and children should be involved in these reviews.

Significant harm and the threshold criteria for care and supervision orders

Threshold criteria apply to Care Orders, Interim Care Orders and Supervision Orders.

Both in the short term and in the longer term, when children cannot safely live with their parents, decisions will have to be made for these children to enable them to grow and develop in a safe environment. Under Part III of the CA, children can be offered accommodation (Section 20). This is a voluntary arrangement between the local authority and parent(s). Parents can return their child home at any time. This provision is useful for parents who have periodic mental health problems and who have limited social support.

The **use of statutory powers** may be necessary where parents do not recognise that their children would be better living elsewhere or where they may need supervision to ensure that their parenting is not placing the child at risk of significant harm. Before a Care or Supervision Order is made, the court must be satisfied that certain conditions have been met.

These are:

(a)   that the child concerned is suffering or is likely to suffer significant harm; and

(b)   that the harm, or likelihood of harm, is attributable to –

   (i)   the care given to the child, or likely to be given to him if the order were not made, not being what it would be reasonable to expect a parent to give him; or

   (ii)   the child being beyond parental control.

There are a series of conditions to be satisfied in making the assessment:

1   Is the child suffering or likely to suffer harm?

The child must be shown to be suffering or likely to suffer **a substantial deficit in the standard of health or development which it is reasonable to expect him/her to achieve.**

'Harm' includes both:

(a)   ill-treatment (which includes sexual abuse and non-physical ill-treatment such as emotional abuse), and

(b)   the impairment of health or development. 'Health' means physical or mental health and 'development' means physical, intellectual, emotional, social or behavioural development.

Thus, the child does *not* have to have a visible injury to suffer ill-treatment. Emotional and psychological harm are included. For example, a child who was being taunted by a deluded parent that he/she was the devil incarnate and the child was being extremely distressed by this, could be deemed to be suffering ill-treatment. In order for the criteria to be met, the court will require clear evidence – for example health records, medical and psychiatric reports.

2   Is the harm significant?

Minor shortcomings in health or development should not give rise to compulsory intervention. When assessing whether the impairment of health or development is significant, the courts must compare the health or development of the child in question with that which could be expected of a similar child, that is a child with similar attributes and needs. The CA makes it clear that for harm to be 'significant' there must be the likelihood of long-term damage to the child.

To prove a child is 'likely' to suffer significant harm is more difficult. Where a parent is mentally ill, this would probably be based on the previous behaviour of the parent, for example, the parent had previously attacked the child when in a psychotic state, or a depressed mother had said that she wanted to kill both herself and her child. In other situations it may be that the child's long-term development and health have already been significantly harmed as demonstrated by medical and other evidence, or are likely to be harmed by continuing to live in the same circumstances. This could occur, for example, in situations where a chronically depressed parent is frequently critical of a child, has developmentally inappropriate expectations of the child and shows little warmth or empathy towards the child.

3 Is the harm suffered, or the likelihood of harm to be suffered, attributable to the absence of a reasonable standard of parental care?

An absence of a reasonable standard of care need not imply that the parents are at fault. This is important in relation to the needs of parents with severe mental health problems. For example, the child may be beyond parental control and thus overwhelm parental attempts to provide reasonable care for the child. Living in poor accommodation may be damaging a child's health, but for court purposes, the harm has to be attributable to the parental care. If a parent is suffering from severe illness and does not make adequate provision for the child and refuses reasonable/appropriate offers of help, then the harm could be deemed to be attributable to the care given by that parent. For professionals working with mentally ill parents, their knowledge and expertise of the parent's illness and its likely course will be an important contribution to the assessment.

4 In reaching its decision has the court ensured that:

● the child's welfare has remained paramount

● the requirements of the welfare checklist have been adhered to

● the child would be better off by an order being made than no order being made?

Implications for practice

Before a court will make a Care or a Supervision Order, there are numerous evidential tests to be overcome. Mental health workers who believe that a Care Order would be the best option for their client's children may be frustrated by their children and families' colleagues who appear reluctant to agree. In reality, it may not be that they disagree, but they are aware that there may not be sufficient evidence to meet the threshold criteria. Awareness by adult mental health workers of the likely responses or thresholds applied by local children and families social workers on the basis of previous referrals should not discourage new referrals and discussion.

Refocusing children's services

In 1995, the Department of Health launched a major new initiative, based on the findings summarised in *Child Protection – Messages from Research.*[8] This report posed challenges for practitioners and policy makers by asking whether professionals had achieved the correct balance between child protection, family support and child welfare. It suggested a 'refocusing' of services, to ensure that support was provided for children and family members when difficulties and concerns arose, whilst at the same time safeguarding the child's welfare. This means that **practitioners should simultaneously focus on both mental health and child care issues in families.**

The five key findings found to be associated with good outcomes for children were:

● sensitive and informed professional/client relationships

● an appropriate balance of power between key professionals

- a wide perspective on child abuse: greater emphasis on meeting needs and supporting families

- effective supervision and training of social workers

- a determination to enhance the quality of children's lives.

Implications for practice

The refocusing of children's services will have an impact on mental health staff working with mentally ill parents. Although the need to protect children remains the priority, those working with children and families are being asked to think about how support to families can be offered in situations where instigating child protection procedures is inappropriate, for example where the child protection process ends following a Section 47 enquiry or child protection conference.

Supporting vulnerable families requires child and family practitioners to work closely with their adult mental health colleagues within and between social services and all other agencies. Children will only be able to remain safely with their families if workers from the different services share information and are involved in joint planning and service provision. In the long term, family support work where the children are safe is likely to lead to the best outcomes for most children, especially where the needs of their mentally ill parents are also considered and support provided to enable them to look after their children on a long-term basis.

Working together

Working Together Under The Children Act, 1989: A guide to arrangements for inter-agency co-operation for the protection of children from abuse sets out the government's guidance on how to respond to and manage child protection concerns.[6] This document, currently being revised, takes into account the requirements of the CA and lessons learned from practice. In particular, it is concerned with **inter-professional and inter-agency co-operation** and should be complied with unless local circumstances indicate exceptional reasons which in child abuse cases justify a variation. With regard to the importance of inter-agency collaboration in supporting families and protecting children, *Working Together* provides information on **the role of the Area Child Protection Committee** (ACPC).

ACPCs develop, monitor and review local child protection policies to promote effective co-operation between agencies. The ACPC has the responsibility for developing the local procedural handbook which should be available to all staff. ACPC members are drawn from social services; health services, including medical, psychiatric and nursing staff, GPs and their managers; the education service, including teacher representatives; the police; the probation service; the voluntary sector; and, where appropriate, the armed services. A member of the social services department usually chairs this committee.

Working Together details the roles of the professionals involved. Each professional – whether GP, nurse, midwife, hospital worker, mental health worker or educator – has a paramount responsibility to safeguard the child's welfare although each has a different role to play. Although the police, for example, are concerned about the welfare of the child, their prime role is to investigate crime and to protect the community. *Working Together* notes that:

> *'Ethical and statutory codes concerned with confidentiality and data protection are not intended to prevent the exchange of information between different professional staff who have a responsibility for ensuring the protection of children.'*

Social services have lead responsibility for enquiries in cases where there is reasonable cause to suspect that a child is suffering or likely to suffer significant harm. This process will involve gathering information from key professionals, the child and family, and liaising with different agencies. At all stages, thought needs to be given to the provision of co-ordinated services to children and their families.

Stages of a child protection enquiry

Following **referral**, an assessment of the child's needs is required, including the need for protection. In doing so, a working partnership with the family should be established if possible. In some circumstances, immediate statutory action such as the taking of an Emergency Protection Order and use of police powers of protection may be required to ensure the physical safety of children.

After **initial checks** have been carried out, a strategy meeting must be convened if a Section 47 enquiry is being considered. This meeting must consider whether an Section 47 enquiry is required and, if so, to discuss and plan how to undertake enquiries. In addition, services may need to be provided whilst an Section 47 enquiry is ongoing. A decision may be taken not to proceed with the Section 47 enquiry but to offer services under Section 17.

Following an Section 47 enquiry, if there is evidence of significant harm, a **child protection conference** will be convened. The purpose of this is to decide if the child's name should be added to the **Child Protection Register** (CPR) and, if so, to appoint a keyworker to take responsibility for the case and to co-ordinate a comprehensive assessment, child protection plan and delivery of services to the child and family. If a child is not registered on the CPR, the family should receive appropriate services under Section 17 as required, and in accordance with the child's and family's needs.

If a child's name is placed on the CPR, a **comprehensive assessment** will be undertaken. In situations where parental mental illness is a factor, **assessments about the ability of the parent(s) to meet the child's needs and the harm the child has suffered or may suffer will be enhanced by the active involvement of both mental health and childcare workers.** The mental health worker will have greater knowledge of the course, prognosis and impact of mental illness on the parent, while childcare workers will have more knowledge of the impact of parental mental illness on the child.

Following the assessment, an analysis of the information and communication with relevant professionals and family members, including children, a plan will be formulated as part of the written **child protection plan**. This will be based on findings from the assessment, including discussions with parents/carers and children. It will also describe the contributions to be made by staff from other agencies, including mental health services, participating in the plan to support all family members and to ensure children's safe and optimal development. The plan will be reviewed at a minimum of every six months while the child's name remains on the CPR.

Finally, for a small number of children, it may be necessary to instigate **childcare proceedings**. The Court will appoint a *Guardian ad Litem* to give independent social work advice, to investigate a child's circumstances, and to provide a report for the court, based on the Welfare checklist. The duty of a Guardian ad Litem (GAL) is to represent the interests of the child in court proceedings. Each GAL will appoint a solicitor to represent the client. All agencies should be aware that GALs have a right of access to local authority records in particular circumstances. GALs are appointed from special local panels.

From a child protection perspective, most referrals do not proceed beyond the initial enquiry stage. There is either insufficient evidence of the child suffering significant harm, or the welfare of the child can be promoted by providing services that support parents/carers more effectively in their parenting tasks. *Messages from Research*[8,p28] provides a breakdown of figures for each of the stages in the process.

Conclusion

The Children Act, 1989 was intended to lay the framework that would lead to better practice when working with children and families. Those working with the mentally ill deal with some of the most complex and difficult situations. Whether the outcomes for children and families are good will not depend so much on the legislation but on the skills of practitioners to translate legislation and guidance into good practice.

Confidentiality and information sharing

Confidentiality and Child Protection

All those working with children and families, and those working with people who are mentally ill are continually faced with different and at times difficult ethical dilemmas. The particular dilemma for those working with mentally ill parents is that they have two clients. Confidentiality and trust are central to the worker's relationships with the client. **Where joint working and communication occur at an early stage in the referral process, good practice will ensure that relevant information is shared routinely, rather than at the point of crisis.** Where more complex issues arise, the competing needs of parent and child will require practitioners to address difficult dilemmas. The safety – physical as well as emotional – of children must be the paramount consideration. Sharing information is essential to safeguard the welfare of children.

Some guidance on this includes:

● Department of Health (1996): *The Protection and Use of Patient Information:*

> '*Patients have an expectation that information about them will be treated as confidential... Patients would be unlikely to trust staff with detailed information about themselves and their clinical condition if they thought this might be passed onto others without proper controls...' (p2)*

'In general...any personal information given or received in confidence for one purpose may not be used for a different purpose or passed to anyone else without the consent of the provider of the information. This duty of confidence is long-established... but with proper safeguards need not be construed so rigidly that, when applied to the NHS or related services, there is a risk of its operating to a patient's disadvantage or that of the public generally. Indeed, as a number of inquiry reports have shown, the prompt flow of accurate information in sensitive areas such as mental health and child care can often be for the benefit and safety of all concerned.' (p5)

'In child protection cases, the overriding principle is to secure the best interests of the child. Thus, if a health professional (or other members of staff) has knowledge of abuse or neglect, it may be necessary to share this with others on a strictly controlled basis so that a decision relating the child's welfare can be taken in the light of all relevant information.' (pp12–13)

Department of Health (1991): *Working Together Under The Children Act, 1989:*

'Ethical and statutory codes concerned with confidentiality and data protection are not intended to prevent the exchange of information between different professional staff who have a responsibility for ensuring the protection of children.' (p21)

'In child protection work, the degree of confidentiality will be governed by the need to protect the child. Social workers and others working with a child and family must make clear to those providing information that confidentiality may not be maintained if the withholding of the information will prejudice the welfare of a child.' (p13)

Department of Health (1995): *Building Bridges – A guide to the arrangements for inter-agency working for the care and protection of severely mentally ill people:*

'In the course of their work with adults, it is possible that disclosures of child abuse will be made to mental health professionals. They will therefore need to be aware of their responsibilities under The Children Act, 1989 *and familiar with local Area Child Protection Committee (ACPC) procedures. Mental health services may be involved in assessing and treating adult abusers, and it is therefore vital that appropriate liaison takes place with health, social services and other relevant agencies.*

'Mental health professionals who work in the community, particularly in people's homes, should ensure that the welfare of the child in those settings is paramount at all times. Assessment of an adult who is a parent or carer should include consideration of whether the adult's mental illness poses any risk to the child.' (pp41-42)

The Caldicott Committee (1997): *Report on the Review of Patient-identifiable Information*

This most recent document tightens up the definition of what information can and cannot be shared in child protection cases and when. There is a useful flowchart giving examples.

The Report concludes that it is justified to share information to inform the decision-making process in proceedings and to share information in child protection cases where the mother has mental health problems. In the second instance, eight specific purposes for sharing information are identified. This suggests that, for some purposes – for example, arranging support for a mother and child – a more limited range of information should be shared.

These four documents indicate that where a child's welfare is at stake, information with or without the consent of the parent, but preferably with, should be shared with the appropriate bodies. However, what is shared, and with whom is best decided on a 'need to know' basis.

Information sharing

Sharing and exchanging information is crucial to the provision of services to children and their carers, including those experiencing mental health problems.

A thorough assessment of needs has implications for numerous services and agencies, if individuals' diverse and at times multiple needs are to be addressed. A generic approach to assessment, with extensive sharing and pooling of information, is better than an exclusively specialist focus where broader needs, or the needs of relevant others, may be missed. Global, rather than tunnel vision is required. For example, a single referral may indicate childcare needs, mental health needs, a carer's needs, possibly substance misuse, and many other elements.

Childcare assessments are better done 'in the round', looking at the child in the context of their whole family's circumstances. This involves a shift in emphasis. Rather than investigating whether children are at risk of abuse by their mentally ill parents, practitioners should firstly consider **whether a parent's mental ill-health affects their parenting skills and what supports are required to improve the quality of the parent-child relationship.** The burden of parenting when there are co-existing mental health problems must be recognised, as well as the contribution made by the child's health and behaviour. This approach should narrow down to a child protection focus at the point or for the period in which children's needs, including the need for safety, are not being met. **This holistic approach would enable professionals from different agencies to bridge each other's domains more successfully.**

References

1   *The NHS and Community Care Act, 1990.* London: HMSO.

2   Ritchie, J. H. (1994) *The report into the care and treatment of Christopher Clunis.* London: HMSO.

3   Jones, R. (1996) *Mental Health Act Manual* 5th Edition. London: Sweet & Maxwell.

4   Department of Health (1995) *Building Bridges: A guide to the arrangements for inter-agency working for the care and protection of severely mentally ill people.* London: HMSO.

5   Department of Health (1998) *Our Healthier Nation.* London: HMSO.

6   Department of Health (1991) *Working Together Under The Children Act, 1989. A guide to the arrangements for inter-agency co-operation for the protection of children from abuse.* London: HMSO.

7   Department of Health (1995) *The Challenge of Partnership in Child Protection: A guide for practitioners.* London: HMSO.

8   Department of Health (1995) *Child Protection – Messages from Research.* London: HMSO.

Chapter Four

Systems and organisational frameworks

The organisational context for service provision to children and families affected by parental mental illness is complex. There is no single, coherent or integrated service response to their needs. Central and local government, as well as private and voluntary organisations are all involved in managing, planning and contributing to the provision of services and, as described in **Chapter Three**, mental health and children's services each have separate legal frameworks with associated guidance and regulations on policy and practice. Most health and social care professionals will have experienced at least one, and more likely several, structural changes in their organisation during their working careers. For professionals *and* service users, these changes pose numerous challenges. Although there has been some attempt to promote greater integration within services and between agencies, there is still much to be done to ensure coherence in policy and practice.

The organisational context

Various barriers to effective joint working exist. Specialisation in training and practice, fragmented adult and children's services and purchaser/provider splits have all hampered attempts to develop services which can effectively address the needs of all family members.[1-3] Some of the difficulties relate to organisational issues, others relate to gaps in professional awareness about the relevance of working together to meet the diverse needs of all family members.

Organisational factors include:

- separate legal frameworks for children and adults

- increasing involvement (not necessarily effectively co-ordinated or mutually informed) of contracted-out services for both adults and children

- separation of service delivery structures for adults and children and consequent specialisation of knowledge and management structures.

Professional awareness and gaps in service provision include:

● lack of support for the families of mentally ill adults, including their children

● lack of AMH support for parents whose children are the designated client group

● insufficient support for early and effective intervention involving all family members

● inadequate development of services for children in need

● increasing pressure on all mental health services

● lack of culturally and ethnically sensitive services

● absence of formal structures to ensure routine consideration of both children's needs and parental mental health needs (see **Chapter One**).

The quality of structures and organisational systems makes a significant difference to service delivery. One study[4] relating to child deaths involving mentally ill parents suggested that the core conclusions in each of the 32 cases studied were strikingly similar:

> *'Service provision is fragmented and there is poor inter-agency communication. In general, professionals working with children lack expertise in adult mental health and there is insufficient emphasis on child welfare and child protection amongst adult psychiatric services.'*

Similarly, in adult mental health services, enquiries into homicide by mentally ill adults have also drawn attention to common concerns about poor communication and the sharing of relevant information.[5,6]

During the past several years, there have been substantial changes in service configurations and delivery, including purchaser/provider splits within health and social services and the division of social work services into specialist mental health and children and family services.

Inter-agency planning arrangements

The needs of children and families affected by mental illness cross existing organisational frameworks and boundaries. They also cross the strategic and planning frameworks both in health and social services. There are now two major statutory service-planning frameworks:

● Children's Service Plans

● Community Care Plans.

These are intended to produce greater local inter-agency integration. However, they do not readily address requirements for service provision at the interface between adult mental health and children's services. All practitioners and managers will need to work actively to address this if the needs of mentally ill parents and their children are to be routinely and systematically met.

Inter-agency operational arrangements

By their very nature, services for families affected by mental illness have to operate in an inter-agency context. **A shared understanding of relevant issues across services and agencies is essential.**

Professionals have differences in background, culture and understanding which affect practice and their ability to co-operate with each other. Each service may well have coherent systems for assessing need and planning intervention, but across agencies and divisions, priorities and definitions of outcome will differ. This requires all staff, at all levels within and between services and agencies, to acquire **a better understanding of different perspectives and approaches to assessment and treatment.**

If communication between staff and agencies is poor, risks to both children and their parents inevitably increase. The competing needs of children and their parents can highlight important differences between practitioners even within the same agency. Mental health staff may advocate for the very parent who is threatening the well-being of a child whom childcare staff are attempting to protect. The tensions, rather than being resolved, may be reproduced amongst professionals. There is no doubt that **co-operation between individual practitioners and collaboration of services across agency boundaries is particularly important for families affected by mental illness.**

Identifying a sense of common purpose across the children's services and adult mental health interface must replace over-zealous advocacy for either parent or child. Such a shift can only come from considering the needs of *both* child *and* parent. **An objective appraisal of the issues is essential to ensure safety and a balanced consideration of needs and interests.** Shared understanding can provide the basis for good decision making in assessment and intervention.

Exchange of information

Given the organisational complexity in which practitioners work and the multiple, at times competing needs of mentally ill parents and their children, information sharing can become a focus for professional/service polarisation. Such splits are always unhelpful and serve to distract from addressing the needs of children and parents. It is therefore important that:

● **Communication and collaboration between various practitioners working with a family occurs as early as possible following a referral.** Such an approach promotes greater understanding between individuals and ensures that discussing the needs of a family becomes routine rather than exceptional. When discussion occurs only in crisis, anxiety distorts communication.

● **Confidentiality is not used as a cover for the absence of good practice**, or a platform for over-zealous advocacy on behalf of a client/patient. For example, knowing which adults in contact with a mental health service have dependent children is vital to ensure that the needs of both parent and children can be addressed.

● If difficulties arise, clarity should be sought about **whose interest** is or is not being served by sharing information, as well as the **potential consequences** of sharing or not sharing information.

Needs-led services

Epidemiologically-based needs assessments for both adult and child mental health have been conducted in recent years as a basis for planning services. These assessments have clarified the manner in which **individuals have different needs and different levels of need for services**. Mental health needs assessments for adults[7] and children[8] both point out the necessity for relevant agencies to undertake local population assessments of need for services because of **the great variation between communities in both needs and existing provision**. Services should aim to meet the full range of health and social care needs so that availability and effectiveness are not impaired by an individual, family or community's:

- age
- gender
- cultural background and context
- physical disability
- family resources
- social context
- race and ethnicity.

Framework of services

Key components of mental health services include:

1 **Primary care services**

- primary health care, voluntary agencies and education service.

2 **Specialist mental health and social care services**

- personal social services, occupation and leisure activities
- out-patient and day-patient care
- supported accommodation including 24-hour nursed beds
- local in-patient care including low-security units
- medium and high security units, including long-stay facilities.

1 *Primary care services*

- Within adult mental health services, most physical and mental health care is provided by GPs or other members of the primary care team.
- The same is also true in child mental health services, with health visitors playing a key role when dealing with younger children (under the age of five).

- For school-age children, teachers are of vital importance when considering mental health needs. Valuable contributions can also be made by school nurses.

- Across the child and adolescent range, community and hospital paediatricians are involved with many children who have mental health problems.[9]

- Other services such as housing, social services and voluntary agencies all play a part in, for example, pre-school and after-school provision.

2 Specialist mental health and social care services

- These services are intended to respond to higher levels of need than those which can be met by primary care. They are contributed to by a wide range of agencies.

- Specialist mental health services include community mental health teams (CMHTs). These teams provide a wide range of support, and they treat individuals at home as well as through day and residential care and hospital services.

- Local authorities should provide significant community resources, and social workers involved in adult mental health will collaborate with these services when they are assessing and treating individuals.

- In-patient services should be available for any child or adolescent who is in need of such a service. However, they cannot be expected to be present in all localities.

- In most localities, the main health provision for children and adolescents in need of specialist services is community and hospital out-patient based. An important role is played by special educational services and social services including field, residential, and fostering and adoption services.

Patterns of integration between health, local authority and social work services vary. Within both adult and child services, the importance of working closely with a wide range of other agencies has been repeatedly emphasised. These agencies include those responsible for:

- housing
- social security benefits
- education
- employment
- training
- leisure
- criminal justice
- voluntary support.

Service providers and purchasers should recognise that needs vary not only *between* individuals, but also *within the same individual over time*. It is vital that all practitioners also recognise and work with the needs of other family members where there is a mentally ill parent. They must therefore acknowledge both:

- the consequences of being mentally ill when an adult has a parental role

- the implications for others (especially children and young people) living in a household where a parent/carer is mentally ill.

Community care services

Local authorities are required to assess people who may require community care services, and can decide on the basis of that assessment what, if any, services they should arrange to meet those needs.

When they carry out the assessment they must inform the housing and health authorities if they think there are also health and housing needs, and must invite those authorities to become involved in the assessment. The services that are likely to be available from those authorities should be taken into account.

Local authorities are also required, under *The Carers (Recognition and Services) Act, 1995*, to assess carers who provide, or intend to provide care on a regular basis. In addition, it is also the duty of the health and local authority to provide after-care for certain categories of adults discharged from hospital, including mentally-disordered offenders (MHA, Section 117).

Child mental health service delivery

When considering mental health and social services responses to children's mental health needs the *Handbook on Child and Adolescent Mental Health; Together We Stand*, and the *Epidemiologically-Based Needs Assessment for Child and Adolescent Mental Health* (see **Appendix i**) all advocate that resources should be deployed in accordance with levels of need for those services. The levels of need are those that can be expected to be met by:

- primary care services

- solo specialist child mental health professionals

- multidisciplinary out-patient services

- multidisciplinary in-patient services.

The tiers or levels of need and responses to need are *not* a prescription for service organisation, but are a *description* for the targetted deployment of resources.

However, despite the fact that all documents concerned with child mental health services advocate links with adult mental health services, **there are currently no established models of joint provision to meet the needs of families where *both* adults and their children require services.** Within current practice and service organisation, adults in families who are in contact with child services, and children in families who are in contact with adult services, have inadequate access to appropriate service provision in order to meet their needs.

The settings in which these services are delivered are broadly similar to those for adults but a smaller proportion of children and adolescents are hospitalised. Specialist services are also delivered to families and children in GP surgeries and health centres, in schools and day nurseries.

The way forward

Corporate approaches and consensus-building at the local level – seeing people in their full family and social context, rather than each separate agency seeing a small part of the whole – are far from easy, but they have to be developed if services are to be connected, co-ordinated and achieve successful outcomes for children and their mentally ill parents.

Structural and organisational arrangements for services to children and families affected by mental illness must be sufficiently flexible to facilitate liaison between practitioners and to accomplish statutory as well as supportive work.

Current service provision could be improved by attending to seven key principles for the development of inter-agency and inter-professional co-operation:

1   **Develop coherent, co-ordinated and integrated service *structures*** so that opportunities are created for effective communication and consultation between services.

2   **Develop *procedures* to ensure that the needs of children and parents are jointly considered.** Health visitors, teachers, community psychiatric nurses, GPs, social workers, and nursery workers all need to know how to get advice and to provide co-ordinated support. Open consultation and joint service and agency protocols can assist in this process.

3   **Promote inter- and intra-agency *communication* about needs at an individual, family and community level.**

4   **Put *long-term support* strategies and a variety of different services in place** wherever needed to enable parents to care appropriately for their children. Involve a wide range of agencies and professionals and ensure this support is carefully co-ordinated.

5   **Make available a flexible and accessible range of *community-based resources*** – family aides, home care, home visiting schemes (for example, Homestart), family resource centres, groups for children and parents and respite care.

6   ***Support the family as a whole*** – provide information and skills to promote successful coping strategies. Facilitate individual members' personal growth and development; for children this means helping them to make sense of their experiences and promoting age-appropriate support and opportunities. Practitioners must recognise strengths and competence in individuals and incorporate these assets into planning and support.

7   **Develop *inter-agency training*** and provide opportunities for all staff to acquire the necessary knowledge, skills and values for supporting mentally ill parents and their children.

References

1   White, S. (1996) Regulating mental health and motherhood in contemporary welfare services: anxious attachment or attachment anxiety? *Critical Social Policy*, **16** (1) 67–94.

2   Blanch, A. K., Nicholson, J. & Purcell, J. (1994) Parents with severe mental illness and their children: The need for human services integration. *The Journal of Mental Health Administration*, **21** (4) 388–396.

3   Hugman, R. & Phillips, N. (1993) 'Like bees round the honeypot': Social work responses to parents with mental health needs. *Practice 6* (3) 193–205.

4   Falkov, A. (1996) Dept of Health Study of Working Together 'Part 8' Reports: *Fatal child abuse and parental psychiatric disorder.* Department of Health, Social Care Group, ACPC Series, Report No. 1. London: HMSO.

5   The Woodley Team Report (1995) *Report of the Independent Review Panel to East London & the City Health Authority & Newham Council, following a homicide in July 1994 by a person suffering with a severe mental illness.* London: East London & City HA.

6   Boyd, W. (1996) *Report of the Confidential Inquiry into Homicides and Suicides by Mentally Ill People.* Royal College of Psychiatrists.

7   Wing, J. K., Brewin, C. & Thornicroft, G. (1993) Defining mental health needs. In: G. Thornicroft, C. Brewin, J. Wing (Eds.) *Measuring Mental Health Needs.* London: HMSO.

8   Wallace, S. A., Crown, J. M., Berger, M. & Cox, A. D. (1997) Child and adolescent mental health. In: A. Stevens, & J. Raftery (Eds.) *Health care needs assessment: The epidemiologically based needs assessment reviews.* Abingdon, Oxon: Radcliffe Medical Press.

9   Kurtz, Z., Thornes, R. & Wolkind, S. (1994) *Services for the Mental Health of Children and Young People in England – A National Review.* London: Maudsley Hospital and South Thames (West) Regional Health Authority.

Chapter Five

*Service user
perspectives*

'When I did not know how to begin writing this I asked Hannah and Georgina for some ideas.
Georgina helpfully told me to begin by writing, "One day when I was ill..." and Hannah advised
me that I could begin by saying something like, "When I was ill it was like..." The reason why
it is not easy to start writing about my experience of suffering from mental ill-health – and in
particular the effect of that upon my children, myself in relation to them and our relationship
together – is because of the consuming emotional turmoil it stirs up, as I know it must for
anyone who has experienced mental ill-health and later tries to explain to some degree what
it is like.'
Heide Lloyd

This chapter considers young carers with responsibility for looking after a parent with
mental health problems and also describes a joint project by the London Borough of
Brent (LBB) and the National Society for the Prevention of Cruelty to Children (NSPCC) in
which mentally ill parents and their children were consulted about services. This is an
example of good practice where users were actively involved in local service planning
and development.

Young carers

What is a 'young carer'?

Children most likely to take on a burdensome role looking after a parent/carer include those
from single-parent families or those from families where a non-caring partner does not take
an active role in caring for the parent (for example, if engaged in full-time work). In situations
of social isolation and poor support, it is not just parents/adults who need looking after but
siblings and the general running of the household.[1] The additional impact on a child caring
for a mentally ill parent has been neglected both by researchers and practitioners.[2] Young
carers can be defined in terms of the care they provide and the effect this has on their lives.
The Carers National Association gives the following definition:

'Anyone under the age of 18 whose life is in some way restricted because of the need to take responsibility for the care of a person who is ill, has a disability, is experiencing mental distress or is affected by substance use.'[1]

The Department of Health provides the following definition:

'A child or young person (under age 18) who is carrying out significant caring tasks and assuming a level of responsibility for another person, which would usually be taken by an adult.'[3]

Note that:

- The definition does not refer to young people under the age of 18 caring for their own children.

- The term does not refer to those children who accept an age-appropriate role in taking an increasing responsibility for household tasks in homes with a disabled, sick or mentally ill parent.

- There is an important cultural component to acceptable norms of care provided by children.

Experiences of young carers ('little heroes and lost childhoods')

A description by an 11 year old:

'When I was younger, mum had a problem. She had difficulty with us four kids – sorting us out for school – she wasn't getting a lot of help and she was shouting a lot. Her words were all jumbled up – didn't come out properly. She was having too many cups of tea… always asking me for cups of tea so I was late for school. I told the teachers an excuse that mum overslept and I had to make breakfast for the younger ones – mum didn't want them to know she was sick because she thought they were watching her and coming round.'[4]

This child went on to state that she thought it very unlikely anyone was watching because *'if there were watchers I'd have seen them – but I didn't tell mum this because she would have said,"How do you know it's unlikely?"'*

A young carer grown-up ('survivor'):

'People tend to protect children and young people. For me, this translated into ignoring my need to be informed and involved. My life was affected anyway and if I had had guidance it might have made the experience more positive. I needed good, age-specific information about my mother's condition and its consequences. And I needed someone to talk to who would listen in confidence and help me to express and explore the complex feelings and situations I was dealing with.'[5]

The impact of caring[1, 5, 6, 7]

Grown-up (adult) young carers are more able to articulate their needs (what would have made a positive difference to them as children). Those who are currently looking after mentally ill parents are burdened with dilemmas around loyalty to parents, shame and secrecy. Sometimes they simply do not know that what they are doing is 'developmentally inappropriate'.

Some children derive important benefits from their role as carer. It may be an important source of competence and confidence-building.

It is the *consequences* of caring which may lead to difficulties, including:

- impaired educational opportunities, poor concentration, teasing and bullying

- isolation from peers and extended family

- lack of time for usual childhood activities

- conflict between the caring role and the child's own needs leading to feelings of guilt and resentment

- feeling that there is no-one there for them, that professionals are working with the adult

- lack of recognition, praise or respect for their contribution

- feeling stigmatised

- feeling that no-one understands their experience

- lost opportunities and limited horizons.

The Loughborough research project[1] found that educational problems and the intimacy of their caring role were the two factors that young carers felt separated them from the 'normal' child population.

How many young carers are there?

Estimates depend on the breadth of definition used; these have ranged from 10,000 to 212,000. The Office of National Statistics Survey estimated a total of 32,000 young carers in the UK, with perhaps one-third (10,000) having a mentally ill parent.[8,9] This is the currently accepted figure, but acknowledged as being a crude estimate. Whilst this represents a substantial number in itself, it is likely that individual areas/caseloads will have small numbers which can itself be a barrier to developing services which address the needs of young carers in general and those looking after a parent with mental health problems specifically.

Identifying young carers

A substantial obstacle to addressing the needs and concerns of young carers has been a lack of awareness of their existence.[2, 9, 10] The failure to identify young carers[9,11] has led to a 'chicken and egg' situation whereby lack of existing services results in failure to identify, and failure to identify precludes service development.

The situation for those young people caring for adults with mental illness is further compounded by the stigma associated with mental illness and the absence of readily observable evidence of the 'illness'. In addition, many young carers do not want to become known to services because of:

- guilt (asking for help seen as failing in their task) and/or loyalty towards their parent and family

- fear of family break-up and separation

- being labelled as 'having a problem'.

These fears can induce self-imposed isolation and longer-term difficulties in asking for help. (See **Chapter One: Grown-up 'survivors'**, page 17.)

In addition to the problems already described, young carers living in families from minority ethnic groups have to:

- live with racism; harassment; refugee status and fear of deportation[12]

- contend with inequality of access to support from and contact with services.[13]

Finding this 'hidden' group constitutes an inter-agency challenge requiring improved co-ordination and accessibility of services so that realistic opportunities are created for young carers to come forward and talk. Listening to their concerns is a key priority to improve access and support.

What young carers say

When asked about **barriers to receiving help**, they:

- are reluctant to seek help and make known the extent of care provided (they may not see it as abnormal or inappropriate)

- fear professional intervention: for example, viewing social workers with suspicion for fear of care proceedings as a response to asking for support

- fear punitive responses to school non-attendance or educational under-performance rather than sensitive exploration of underlying causes.

When asked about **immediate needs**, they say they would like:

- to be able to talk about difficulties and to have someone listen to them sensitively and with respect, and to believe them when they describe the circumstances in which they live

- opportunities for normal activities/outings

- to keep school and friends separate from caring responsibilities

- to achieve their full potential

- support at school if required
- to be able to participate in age-appropriate activities
- to be able to share the care responsibilities
- their parent to receive treatment and to get better and to be appropriately involved in the process.

When asked about **concerns regarding a mentally ill parent**, they:

- worry about the person they care for
- may need to protect the person they care for from teasing/taunting/bullying.

When asked about **long-term needs**, they:

- have concerns about becoming mentally ill
- worry and feel guilty about becoming independent, leaving home and wonder who will care for their parent.

(See **Chapter One**, pages 17 and 18.)

Thoughts and feelings described by children whose parents have a mental illness include:

- anxiety
- guilt
- fear and uncertainty
- embarrassment
- concerns over their own mental health
- confusion
- anger
- isolation
- worry
- depression
- frustration.

Young carers want:

- information about the illness and prognosis
- recognition of their role in the family
- practical and domestic help
- a contact person in the event of a crisis regarding their parent
- someone to talk with – not necessarily formal counselling.

Service implications

> '*A sensitive worker can aid a child's development as a child and empower their caring role as part of that.*'[5]

To identify young carers, workers need to be prepared to listen and then to provide *appropriate* support. Appropriate use of Community Care Plans and Children's Services Plans can strengthen inter-professional working, and help to formulate policies and practice relevant to the needs of these young people and their parents.

A key issue is getting the correct balance between usefully supporting young carers as opposed to removing their 'role' by providing input without direct discussion and understanding of the nature of the young person's role within the family (the pendulum swing from neglect to intrusive, insensitive provision). Furthermore, young people want 'long-term, adaptable, supportive, empowering and low-key provision'[5, p105] not just crisis involvement.

Children's experiences will depend upon the nature and extent of caring, the child's constitutional strengths and vulnerabilities, family context and socio-economic circumstances. It is therefore important to consider the person within a developmental, family and environmental context.

Good practice points

Practical aspects

Listen to what children and young people have to say about their experiences with their parents. Ask about what they do – is there a carer role? They may participate in the full range of care tasks, including:

- personal (physical) care
- paperwork
- keeping company
- giving medicines
- practical care (chores)
- taking out their ill parent
- checking up on how an ill parent is managing
- looking after siblings
- 'role reversal' (bringing themselves up, 'child parenting the parent')
- being responsible for an ill parent's emotional well-being.

Is the young carer missing out on age-appropriate activities? How is the young carer doing at school?

Emotional aspects

- Is the young person burdened by the responsibility? Where caring involves an 'invisible' but burdensome emotional component, the young carer may need help to realise the impact of the caring role. Forming a relationship will take time but will enable a better understanding of the needs of the young carer.

- Acknowledge the young carer's loyalty to family and thus the real dilemma about seeking help, and address fears about splitting the family, openly and honestly.

Sources of support

- Does the young carer have a supportive peer group, or engage in activities away from the home?

- Does the young carer have someone in whom they can confide? If not, it is important to consider ways to provide such an opportunity – schools, voluntary services (for example, young carers project) and primary care access may be sufficient. Where there are concerns about a young person's mental health, mainstream or specialist referral may be appropriate. Such efforts will be helpful in reducing distress in the short term as well as having preventive potential for the young carer in the future.

- Access to support can be provided at various points within services and agencies – the key will always be to ensure a co-ordinated response.

- Make information about support widely available – schools, youth clubs, GP surgeries and health clinics.

Barriers to support and protection

- Parents may struggle with the implications of having to be parented. Some may resist others' efforts to support their children. They may feel guilty about not being able to care adequately for their children or they may resent the intrusion which serves to highlight their difficulties. Recognise the varied individual responses to the caring role and the range of cultural norms and expectations of different children and young people.

- The term 'young carer' is a label. There are times when it may be perceived as stigmatising and unhelpful.

Preventive aspects

- Provide opportunities for a young carer to have age-appropriate leisure time – either via direct participation in local schemes or clubs or by having time to spend with friends away from home whilst a service provides support for the parent.

- Ensure that practitioners know their duties and powers regarding key legislation.

Key learning point

Recognise the delicate balance between **provision of adequate support** for children and young people who look after a parent who is mentally ill, whilst not removing **the competence-enhancing responsibilities** the young person has taken on.

Relevant legislation

The duties and powers of authorities to help young carers and their families are established in three key pieces of legislation and are further developed in the *Policy Guidance and Practice Guide* to the 1995 *Carers Act*.[14] The provisions of the Act cover children and young people who provide or intend to provide 'a substantial amount of care on a regular basis'.

Section 17 of *The Children Act, 1989* covers young carers who may be eligible for services (described in greater detail in **Chapter Three**). Young people whose health and development are likely to be impaired without the provision of local authority services are deemed to be 'children in need' under Section 17 (10).

The *NHS and Community Care Act* places a duty on local authorities to carry out an assessment where it appears to the local authority that an individual may have a need for community care services. Guidance has stressed that a carer should be consulted when an assessment is carried out under this Act.

Involving users in service development

This section describes a joint collaboration between the NSPCC and the London Borough of Brent from January 1997 to February 1998. The aim of the project was to consult mentally ill parents and their children about their experiences related to mental illness and the quality of support they received from local mental health and childcare services. They were also invited to participate in discussions to develop services which would meet their needs more effectively. The project demonstrated that users, commissioners and providers of mental health and child welfare services were able to work together to debate and plan the development of greater integration between services.

The project occurred in three phases. Initially, a group of local parents and children were interviewed about their experiences of mental illness and views about services. This was followed by two workshops in which users participated. The final phase consisted of partner agencies working together to develop policy and practice in response to interview information and feedback from the workshops.

Interviews with mothers about their experiences revealed a number of themes including:

● suicidal thoughts and actions:

> '*I wouldn't answer the phone and I kept the curtains drawn. I just wanted to sleep. I dreaded tomorrow. I used to wish I wouldn't wake up and the baby wouldn't wake up either.*'

- social disadvantage and material deprivation (including poor housing, poverty, lack of employment and racism); housing problems were identified by some as being the precipitating factor in mental-health crises

- social isolation, marital discord and violence

- ethnic minority status

- poor access to support and services for parents which contributed to a cycle of further deterioration and at times ended with compulsory admission to hospital

- gender imbalances (all the service users were mothers).

Children and young people's experiences revealed wide-ranging unmet needs. Many of the children were young carers who provided both physical and emotional support for parents and siblings.

> *'My mum was depressed, I was unable to be with my friends... I looked after her all the time, I did the cleaning, the tidying, the washing up and the shopping. If I was out, I worried about her and I would come rushing back.'*

Young carers also experienced distress and anxiety, stigma and shame, loss, guilt and bullying. Many missed out on opportunities to form positive peer relationships and to do well at school.

> *'People cuss us for having a mad mother all the time.'*

> *'She is always wanting cigarettes. Once she was eating a biscuit and she kept the crumbs. She told me to give them to our neighbour and to make sure to get a cigarette in return.'*

> *'When I was being bad at school, I thought I made my mum ill.'*

> *'I thought we were winding her up. I asked her and she said it wasn't us, but I thought it was.'*

> *Father: 'The children began to cry when they saw her. She looked like a zombie, not their mother.'*

Nearly half the children had also been separated from both parents at some point, mostly as a result of being looked after in foster care or in residential homes. It was not surprising to discover some of the children becoming users of mental health services in mid and late adolescence.

> *'I did terrible things to N. when she was little, I know now it's best they are not with me, I have to take care of myself.'*

> *'Father: 'She [the mother] took an overdose and went and lay in E.'s bed. E. [aged seven] was frightened when she couldn't wake her up.'*

Parents' views about services included a wish for:

● co-ordinated and consistent services

● help before and after a crisis

● information, explanation about the illness and treatment, including counselling

● safety when in hospital.

Involving users

One of the aims of this project was to engage users in the process of planning and developing local services. Three approaches were taken:

1 organising workshops

2 establishing a steering group

3 using broader planning forums.

1 Workshops

The benefits of combining the input of service users and professionals into workshops included:

● family members making moving presentations with considerable impact on the audience

● findings being more readily accepted coming 'first-hand'

● family involvement facilitating constructive debate by focusing professionals' attention directly on their difficulties and needs

● some users feeling 'heard'.

Factors that contributed to the success of the workshops are thought to have included:

● ongoing engagement between families and professionals

● preparation for users who had agreed to present

● offering choices about modes of presenting; for example, speaking 'live', pre-recording, video, being interviewed in front of the audience, having someone else read out a written presentation

● establishing clear ground rules

● identifying professionals to support families on the day

● paying users an attendance fee plus expenses

● providing a separate family room and a crèche

● having the NSPCC as independent 'broker'.

2   Steering group

Whilst users are 'experts' on issues of service delivery, they are likely to have considerably less information about the identity and role of various professionals and inter-agency management issues. In order to prevent service user attendance becoming a token gesture, a number of strategies were adopted. These included:

● explanations of professional roles and responsibilities

● written briefings from professionals circulated in advance

● pre-meetings of the Chair with users to go over the briefings and to give users the chance to raise agenda items.

The presence of users was welcomed and helped to 'keep alive' many of the issues they raised in the project and workshops.

3   Broader planning forums

One of the aims had been to integrate user input into planning forums so that this would be well established by the end of the project. An attempt to set up a user group which could either nominate members to sit on identified forums or receive and debate information provided by professionals was poorly attended.

The experience suggests that families and professionals can work together on service development within the context of 'special events' but that sustained involvement over a longer period requires a dedicated development worker who can prepare users for meetings, help them develop advocacy and organising skills, and work with the professional network. Equally important was the need for influential individuals within organisations to 'champion' the importance of user input and to facilitate changes in management and organisational structures to support user involvement.

Conclusions

The families' accounts of their lives were often characterised by a long struggle against chronic illness, poverty, poor housing, racism and isolation. Many were frustrated by the barriers to accessing long-term, supportive services geared to meeting the needs of their families. Their interactions with professionals were fraught with anxiety about being 'sectioned' or their children being removed from their care. Access to services tended to occur in response to crises. This meant that earlier support, when the situation was less fraught, did not occur.

Nonetheless, many parents did acknowledge that there were individuals who were doing their best in difficult circumstances. The workshops which brought together families and professionals generated opportunities for inter-agency planning. Positive actions within agencies have also occurred, such as routinely recording the presence of child dependants of adults known to the mental health trust, and the requirement that reference be made to them within discharge plans.

To what extent users will contribute to service development in future is unclear. That they have a right to be heard and an important contribution to make is not in doubt. Changes must be made in the structure, resourcing and culture of all services so that families with long-term needs do not continue to receive services based on the assumption that inadequately resourced, crisis driven responses can alleviate enduring social care and mental health problems.

References

1   Dearden, C. & Becker, S. (1995) *Young Carers: The Facts.* Loughborough University Young Carers Research Group.

2   Aldridge, J. & Becker, S. (1993) Punishing children for caring: The hidden cost of young carers. *Children and Society*, **7**(4) 376-387.

3   Department of Health (1995) Chief Inspector Letter CI(95)12

4   Falkov, A. (Unpublished survey) *'Troubled Lives': School aged children's understanding of parental psychosis.*

5   Marlowe, J. (1996) Helpers, helplessness & self help. In: M. Gopfert, J. Webster & M. Seeman, *Parental Psychiatric Disorder: Distressed Parents and Their Families,* pp101–105. Cambridge University Press.

6   Social Services Inspectorate (1995) *Young Carers: Something to think about.* Report of Four SSI Workshops. London: Department of Health.

7   Elliott, A. (1992) *Hidden children.* Mental health development section, Leeds City Council, Department of Social Services.

8   Office for National Statistics (1996) *Young Carers and their Families.* London.

9   Jenkins, S. & Wingate, C. (1994) Who cares for young carers? *British Medical Journal*, **308**, 733–734.

10 Rickford, F. (1995) Young carers: The ones who get away. *Community Care*, 7–13 Sept.

11 Bilsborrow, S. (1992) *You Grow Up Fast As Well: Young carers on Merseyside.* Carers National Association & Liverpool Personal Social Services Society & Barnardos North West.

12 Hendessi, M. (1996) *Report of the survey of young carers in Hammersmith and Fulham.* Linx Research and Training Consultancy.

13 Wiffen, J. (1995) Young Carers: Back them up – A plea to practitioners. *Community Care*, 26th October.

14 Department of Health (1996) Carers (Recognition & Services) Act 1995: Policy & Practice Guidance. London: HMSO

Chapter Six

Access to services

'So far as contact with the children was concerned, I would certainly stress how important it was to me to feel somewhat in control of how long the visit would be and when it would take place. There was no family room with the relevant facilities to entertain, feed or generally see to the needs of small children. Even a television with video facilities in a private room would have been helpful and enabled a parent to at least sit with children for a while. For some time I was not able to leave the ward without an escort and so was unable to take the children to the cafe for a drink. Even if I could have done this, I felt too unwell to cope with that or did not have the finances to do so – my benefits had been stopped after six weeks in hospital.

'When Hannah and Georgina visited with their foster mother, they at least brought snacks and drinks and she would offer to take them for a walk with me. If I needed the visit to be shorter than arranged, she would agree to this without a fuss and when it was time to for the children to leave she would always be comforting to them and telephone me later to let me know that they had settled down if they left feeling upset. Knowing that their needs were met emotionally and physically made a big difference to me emotionally. In this respect, the foster parents showed an understanding and compassion that even other professionals seemed to overlook completely. Perhaps because it was so simple and basic.'
Heide Lloyd

Individuals with similar problems should receive similar types, levels and quality of help, regardless of differences in racial, cultural, gender and socio-economic circumstances. Service providers must take into account the accessibility and acceptability of the help provided. Ignoring factors such as language, racism, social conditions, gender and religion leads to poor access and inappropriate service provision which fails to address the needs of all members of society.

Racial and ethnic inequalities in mental health and mental health services are increasingly evident but the underlying causes remain poorly understood and controversial.[1] Racial discrimination is indicated by differential rates of unemployment, uptake of social security benefits and wealth generation, all factors which affect mental health and well-being.[2–5] The combination of ethnic minority status and female gender combined with parental responsibility creates a potent combination for those individuals to experience various forms of discrimination and oppression.[6] Their children in turn are at risk of not having their needs adequately met and for cycles of adversity to be perpetuated.[7]

Links between mental illness and poverty are well established.

> *'If welfare benefits are essential for mentally ill people to function effectively in the community, then changes may be necessary to counteract the disincentives within the existing system that reduce the uptake of benefit entitlements. The stigma associated with mental illness and the language used in official advice leaflets may be a disincentive to people claiming their full benefit entitlement; for example, to be eligible for Disability Living Allowance a person with illness must be 'severely mentally impaired with severe behavioural problems...'* [8]

Some fundamental concepts and principles for effective access to services for all individuals include:

● **Availability**

A full and appropriate range of services should be available within each 'locality' or, in the case of specific individuals, regionally (for example, specialist child needs such as autism) and, for very rare cases, nationally (for example, mentally disordered individuals who are a danger to themselves and/or others).

● **Information**

Mentally ill parents and family members need to have sufficient information about what services (primary, specialist or voluntary) are available, and whom they should approach about provision or support. Those who are approached must be able to provide appropriate information and advice about accessing services.

● **Recognition of need**

It is only when service providers recognise the needs of individuals, families and communities that needs can begin to be met. Some individuals may not recognise their mental health needs, or that the difficulties they are experiencing could be alleviated. These issues are of particular importance to children and adolescents (see **Chapter Five**), and individuals in certain communities or cultural groups. For example, certain cultural groups may not believe in mental illness as conceptualised in Western society (see **Culture and mental illness** opposite).

● **Referral**

Transfer from primary to secondary/tertiary care can fail. This may be due to discrimination by primary care workers, inadequate preparation, or inflexibility in accessibility of secondary/tertiary care services.

● **Engagement**

Professionals' inability to engage mentally ill parents and/or their children successfully is an important cause of poor access to services and support. Ethnic and cultural differences between users and practitioners can heighten these difficulties.

- **Utility**

  What is offered must be usable, taking into account language and disability.

- **Acceptability**

  Even when resources are available, the referral has been effective and the individuals concerned have attended, the resource offered may be in a form that is not acceptable to those concerned.

- **Effectiveness**

  Access needs to be to effective treatments.

Culture and mental illness[9–11]

Culture influences how people experience and express distress.

Definitions of what constitutes normal and abnormal behaviour vary widely from culture to culture and within any given group, and are dependent on demographic factors such as age, sex, social class and occupation. Across cultures, differences exist in the definition and meaning of 'normal'/acceptable behaviour and what is regarded as problematic/unacceptable. It is the interpretation of unusual, erratic, disturbing or threatening behaviours which is important, especially if these occur without obvious reason. In some cultures, these behaviours may be seen as bad, meriting punishment, while in others they may be seen as signs of illness requiring treatment.

Practitioners may come into contact with individuals or families whose behaviour(s) may be acceptable, at least sometimes, in their culture of origin, but which could be seen as evidence of mental illness in the UK.

Each culture provides its members with culturally sanctioned ways of accounting for misfortune or expressing distress. In the West, the emphasis is on psychological factors, life events, and the effects of stress, but in many developing countries explanations for mental illness take into account wider social and religious factors. These include spirit possession, witchcraft, the breaking of religious taboos, divine retribution and the capture of the soul by a spirit. These factors will need to be considered if treatment is to be accepted. Taking tablets may not make sense to someone who perceives his or her problems to be rooted in some religious misdemeanour.

Cultural aspects of treatment

For many people from ethnic minority groups, their everyday experience of racism is a major factor shaping their presentation and use of health services. It is vital to find out how a patient seems to members of his or her own culture, and practitioners can benefit from enlisting the help of family members and close friends. Other useful informants include religious officials and traditional healers, together with impartial interpreters when there are language barriers.

When a mental disorder is diagnosed, it is appropriate to recommend Western treatments such as drugs or electro-convulsive therapy. However, an awareness of the individual's own understanding of his/her experiences can help when trying to explain the prescribed treatment. This collaborative approach can enhance trust and facilitate engagement and compliance. If a mental health problem does not exist and the person is exhibiting culturally appropriate behaviour, a traditional healer may be more relevant.

Migration and mental illness

Both the reasons for migration and experiences within the new community contribute to stress and the onset or exacerbation of mental illness. Recent immigrants may experience 'culture shock', isolation and loss, and the absence of close, confiding relationships and social support.

Refugees and asylum seekers may experience post-traumatic stress disorder following persecution, compounded by fear of repatriation. Their children have substantial mental health needs.[12]

Disproportionate representation of minority ethnic groups

Minority ethnic groups are both over- and under-represented within different components of the mental health and childcare systems, and this is associated with mis-, over- and under-diagnosis of mental illness.

●   There are **higher rates for a first diagnosis of schizophrenia** among second-generation British-born African-Caribbean individuals. Currently, African-Caribbean men are up to ten times more likely than white men to be given the diagnosis of schizophrenia.[11,14] Similarly, the rate of schizophrenia in immigrants from West Africa aged 25–35 has been estimated at nearly 30 times that of the native British population.

●   West-Indian immigrants have **higher admission rates** for schizophrenia than people born in Britain (although concerns exist that this may be accounted for in part by over-diagnosis of schizophrenia in this group)[9,11] and they are more often admitted to hospital during crisis, using compulsory orders. While about 8% of white patients in psychiatric hospitals are detained under the Mental Health Act, the figure for black patients is about 25%.[9] Around 60% of black individuals, compared to 10–15% of the rest of the population, in special (high security) hospitals have been transferred there under the Mental Health Act.

●   Irish individuals living in the UK have higher rates of mental illness than any other population. Men from Northern Ireland are more likely to be admitted with a diagnosis of alcoholism than native British men.[9]

●   Lower rates of admission to psychiatric hospitals and lower rates of mental illness generally have been found for people of Asian origin.[15]

These statistics may not reflect the true prevalence of disorders. Factors such as stigmatisation and racism as well as poverty are likely to account for some of the differences in admission rates. Although lower admission rates and disorder may indicate true prevalence, the actual rates may be higher than the recorded rates, indicating under-recognition and treatment. Reduced diagnosis of 'minor' mental illness (depression or anxiety) has been noted in black and ethnic minority groups, and black service users are less often provided with counselling and psychotherapy, or with access to culturally acceptable prevention programmes. A community survey by Nazroo[15] noted that white and South-Asian single mothers had particularly high rates of mental illness with a 10% prevalence of depression.

Various theories have been proposed to explain these differing prevalence rates and access to services including:

- racism, social disadvantage and cultural insensitivity combining to produce inadequate mental health services

- difficulties in adapting to the cultural norms of the host society are perceived as intensely stressful

- dislocation from host community, rejection by host community (circumstances associated with departure)

- mental illness manifesting itself differently in different cultures[10]

- differing cultural interpretations of 'abnormal' behaviour leading to mis-diagnoses and treatments which unwittingly contravene cultural norms.[11]

Women and mental illness

In Western society, women continue to provide the bulk of childcare. A variety of needs and concerns arise from the role of parenthood that can be compounded directly or indirectly by the presence of mental illness:

- **prior to pregnancy and childbirth**, some women who are (or have been) mentally ill will worry about the potential impact of their difficulties on pregnancy itself, childbirth, the care of their child and on the child him/herself

- for some women who develop their illness **following childbirth**, there are anxieties that perhaps they should not have had children; they may blame themselves for not being able to be the parent they had hoped to be.

Women may delay seeking support or treatment for mental health problems or childcare concerns because they:

- blame themselves for their mental health problem; they fear that having a mental illness may be interpreted as evidence of being a 'poor/bad' parent

- fear that expressing concerns about their parenting and asking for help to meet their children's needs may be interpreted as being a 'bad' parent

- worry that as a consequence of 'bad' parenting, their children will be removed from their care.[6]

These delays may lead to crises of the very sort the person wished to avoid (such as a coercive relationship with practitioners, compulsory hospitalisation and/or children needing to be 'looked after').

'Looked after' children

Various studies document the presence of mental illness and substance misuse in the parents of children who are 'looked after'.[16–20] There are high rates of mental health problems in both children who are 'looked after' and their natural parents.

> *'Official statistics do not record how often a diagnosis of mental illness in the mother is involved, but research suggests that it is common. One study found that nearly half the mothers of children who had been in care at least twice had been psychiatric in-patients, as compared to only one in 50 of a matched control group of mothers whose children had not been in care.'*[16]

Isaac *et al.*[17] concluded from their study that:

> *'Parents of children in foster care for the longer period were more likely to have received psychiatric treatment and this was correlated with a high rate of past and current psychiatric disorder in the total sample of parents. Parental psychiatric distress was an important factor in influencing children's admission and discharge from foster care.'*

Black women appear particularly likely to have their children taken into care following diagnosis of mental illness. One study found that 80% of black mothers with children in care were referred for mental health reasons, as compared to only 20% of white mothers.[6]

Addressing inequalities of access and choice

Examples of inequalities of access and choice in service provision for women and their children in the mental health and wider system include:

● There is insufficient and inadequate provision of childcare facilities in out-patient departments, hospital wards and community settings.

● Specialised units for mothers and infants do exist, but they are not readily (geographically) accessible for the majority of people and intake is restricted in terms of parental diagnosis, severity of the illness and the age of child.

● Appointments are made without sufficient regard for parental responsibilities such as children having to be collected from school or playgroup. Failure to attend appointments can be interpreted as evidence of 'poor compliance' with treatment and care plans.

● Mothers' concerns following hospitalisation include: the adequacy of childcare arrangements; the well-being of the children; how a partner is coping with childcare and job and/or the affordability of alternative childcare; and whether the children's needs will outweigh her need to be in hospital. These concerns influence compliance with treatment.

Recognition of these concerns is essential to promote successful the[...] between mothers and practitioners and to meet the family's needs.

- Provision to support children visiting parents in hospital is inadequate and at t[...] unsafe. There may be: unsuitable areas for families to be together in privacy; insu[...] staff to facilitate the visit and ensure safety for all participants; absence of practical facilities for children (such as nappy changing); absence of toys or materials to promote positive experiences for parents and children; and an approach and atmosphere that is not child- and parent-friendly.[6]

- Despite the recognised vulnerability to depression and anxiety in mothers with responsibility for young children, the majority of day centres and community facilities do not have crèches.

Mind's Stress on Women Campaign[6] recommended:

- a government review of services for people with mental health problems and their children

- childcare issues to be explicitly included in all mental health assessments

- training for magistrates involved in child care decision making

- parental suites for those parents admitted to hospital

- accessible, affordable day care for all children who need it.

Practitioners should:

- be realistic and honest in discussion with parents about their children. Information about who is looking after children and how they are coping is vital. Practical plans about communication and contact with children, according to circumstances and safety, can further support parents and children. Considering what explanation to give children is also important

- prepare children and their parents for admission to hospital whenever possible. **Planning how to maintain links with family and community during a period in hospital can reduce the distress of separation**

- ensure that the first 24 hours of a person's admission to hospital are as positive as possible. Initial experiences play an important role in determining the quality of therapeutic relationships with staff and the effectiveness of assessment and treatment

- maintain links with family and community during hospitalisation. The service user is also a mother, an employee, someone who has to pay bills, who has important relationships, who has a property.

Support and treatment must focus on helping the woman as an individual as well as recognising the associated (and sometimes competing) roles and responsibilities such as being a parent, a partner and/or having a job and career. Improving self-esteem and promoting greater self-awareness about current and past experiences are important factors associated with quality of parenting and ability to meet children's needs and ensure their safety.

ss

...ecialisms, it can be difficult to get an accurate
..., especially when a 'hidden' issue (such as family
... is struggling to meet her childcare responsibilities
...health or childcare services. However, if domestic
...v focus to assessment will reduce the chances of
...highlighted the consequences when the focus is too
...fficult to prioritise children's needs or the needs of

relationship

Associations between adult/parental relationship difficulties and mental illness are well
documented. Many mothers have come into contact with the mental health system as a direct
or indirect consequence of violence perpetrated by their (male) partner but family violence
can take many forms and does not necessarily involve physical assault.

High rates of depression and anxiety have been reported in victims of severe domestic
violence. However, there is debate about whether mental illness (such as depression) in a
partner *causes* the relationship difficulty or whether the problematic relationship *results* in
mental illness. The combination of mental illness, low self-esteem and factors associated with
material and social deprivation can create a vulnerability to exploitation. A mentally ill mother
may then become increasingly dependent on a manipulative partner who uses violence as a
means of control to maintain the relationship. In such circumstances, the mother's attempts
to seek help may be actively prevented (threats of or actual violence, threats to 'report' her to
social services). The mother's mental illness may be used as justification for her difficulties in
parenting and her 'failure to protect' the children, rather than addressing the violence and/or
its consequences directly.

Impact on children

Exposure to hostility and discord between parents is an important determinant of emotional
and behavioural problems in children of all ages, especially if the discord is persistent over
time and the child becomes embroiled in hostilities between the adults.

In situations where violence has occurred in families, the presence of mental illness in
a parent/carer may:

● lead to the expression of hostilities towards a child – for example, parental aggression
   as a consequence of psychotic delusions or parental irritability (verbal aggression) related
   to depression

● impair or prevent a parent/carer from taking appropriate steps to ensure adequate
   care and safety of the children when they experience maltreatment by the mentally ill
   person's partner or another adult (inability to protect children from harm); for example,
   a depressed parent who is lacking in energy and is self-preoccupied may also fear
   precipitating further hostility or violence if the perpetrator is challenged.

There are therefore particular challenges which practitioners must address in order to support parent and child victims of domestic violence appropriately.

Even when domestic violence is suspected by professionals, the violence may not be 'named' and the focus may remain on mental health or childcare issues. The role and responsibility of the perpetrator may remain hidden or ignored.

Fears about children being 'removed' can prevent mothers from actively seeking help. For those who do manage to ask for help, the route to rehousing can involve moving with the children to a refuge, followed by temporary accommodation, followed by an offer of permanent accommodation. This process could take more than a year, staying in crowded, often inadequate, temporary accommodation, involving several moves of schools, re-applications for benefits, changes of GP and other professionals trying to support the family.

Assessment and care planning must take account of aggression and violence in families. All staff must be aware of the possibility of 'hidden' or unacknowledged violence. Practitioners must be aware of the cycle whereby domestic violence affects the mental health of a parent whose parenting skills may thus be further impaired and who is then less able to meet the needs of the children. Supporting parents (who are themselves victims) whilst also ensuring appropriate care and protection of children can present practitioners with difficult dilemmas.

Key points for practice

When working with a mentally ill adult, child and family, all issues relating to access to services need to be addressed to enable delivery of an effective, efficient and equitable service. Establishing a holistic approach that is sensitive to cultural, historical, social, developmental, familial and physical needs would include: [21–23]

- awareness of needs at a community, cultural and local level

- awareness of needs of clients, carers and dependants in relation to the illness

- awareness of the effects of racism on people's lives including (mental) health inequalities

- recognition of the effects of living in a hostile environment, including the effects of unemployment, poverty and overcrowding

- understanding of inter-relationships between gender and mental illness

- recognition that needs are not defined solely in terms of psychiatric diagnosis but require assessment across a broad range of separate but related domains

- sensitivity to access difficulties within different communities/groups; this would include providing information about services, preparation for referral and engagement

- basing the formulation of any intervention on an understanding of local and individual need, within the surrounding familial, environmental and cultural context.

References

1   Bhopal, R. (1998) Spectre of racism in health and health care: Lessons from history and the United States. *British Medical Journal*, **316**, 1970–1973.

2   Fergusson, D., Horwood, L. & Lynskey, M. (1997) The effects of unemployment on psychiatric illness during young adulthood. *Psychological Medicine*, **27**, 371–381.

3   Meltzer, H., Gill, B., Petticrew, N. & Hinds, K. (1995) *The prevalence of psychiatric morbidity among adults aged 16-64 living in private households in Great Britain.* OPCS Surveys: Report 1. London: OPCS.

4   Goldberg, D. & Huxle,y P. (1992) *Common Mental Disorders: A bio-social model.* London: Routledge.

5   Weich, S. & Lewis, G. (1998) Poverty, unemployment and common mental disorders: Population based cohort study. *British Medical Journal*, **317**, 115

6   Darton, K., Gorman, J. & Sayce, L. (1994) *Eve Fights Back – The Successes of Mind's Stress on Women Campaign.* London: Mind Publications.

7   Oliver, J. E. (1988) Successive Generations of Child Maltreatment: The Children. *British Journal of Psychiatry*, **153**, 543–553.

8   Slade, M., McCrone, P. & Thornicroft, G. (1995) Uptake of welfare benefits by psychiatric patients. *Psychiatric Bulletin*, **19**, 411–413.

9   Davies, T. & Craig, T. K. J. (1998) (Eds.) *ABC of Mental Health.* London: BMJ Books.

10   Rack P. (1982) *Race, Culture and Mental Disorder.* London: Tavistock.

11   Littlewood, R. & Lipsedge, M. (1989) (2nd Ed) *Aliens and Alienists: Ethnic Minorities and Psychiatry.* London: Routledge.

12   Hodes, M. (1998) Refugee children: May need a lot of psychiatric help. *British Medical Journal*, **316**, 793–794.

13   King, M., Coker, E., Leavey, G., Hoare, A. & Johnson-Sabine, E. Incidence of psychotic illness in London: Comparison of ethnic groups. *British Medical Journal*, **309**, 1115–1119.

14   Harrison, G., Owens, D., Holton A., *et al.* (1988) A prospective study of severe mental illness among Afro-Caribbean patients. *Psychological Medicine*, **18**, 643–657.

15   Nazroo, J. (1997) *Ethnicity and Mental Health: Findings from a community survey.* London: Policy Studies Institute.

16   Rutter, M. & Quinton, D. (1984) Parental psychiatric disorder: Effects on children. *Psychological Medicine*, **14**, 853–880.

17   Isaac, B., Minty, E. B., & Morrison, R. M. (1986) Children in care-the association with mental disorder in parents. *British Journal of Social Work*, **16**, 325–329.

18   Sheppard, M. (1993) Maternal depression and child care: The significance for social work research. *Adoption and Fostering*, **17**, 10–15.

19   Bell, C., Conroy, S. & Gibbons, J. (1995) *Operating the child protection system: A study of child protection practices in English local authorities.* London: HMSO.

20   Cleaver, H., Unell, I. & Aldgate, J. (forthcoming) *Parent's Problems – Children's Needs: Child Protection and Parental Mental Illness, Problem Alcohol and Drug Use and Domestic Violence.* London: Department of Health.

21   Sayce, L. & Sherlock, J. (1994) Good practices in services for women with child-related needs. In: *Women and Mental Health: An information pack of mental health services for women in the United Kingdom.* London: Good Practices in Mental Health.

22   Bhui, K., Christie, Y. & Bhugra, D. (1995) Essential elements in culturally sensitive psychiatric services. *International Journal of Social Psychiatry*, **41**, 242–256.

23   Wilson, M. (1993) *Mental health and Britain's black communities.* London: Kings Fund.

Chapter Seven

Inter-agency service responses

'When I eventually left hospital, it was still several months before Hannah, Georgina and I were living together full-time. My continual anxiety about the effects of my illness and our separation upon them did not resolve for a long time. I had previously been told by a practitioner that after six months of separation the bond between child and parent can be destroyed. I paid to see a child mental health professional who reassured me about the positive relationship I had with Hannah and Georgina. They needed support, especially my support and to be able to talk with me.

'I firmly believe:

- that it is imperative that children have as much access to information about the mental health of a parent as they are able to cope with

- that they should be free to discuss their feelings and ask any questions they wish to ask whenever they wish to do so

- that the simplest of things such as their normal diet, daily routine and contact with friends/family are taken into account

- that their moods are understood and not just reacted to, and

- that during the worst part of a parent's illness, when perhaps they will not be able to have contact with that parent, they are continually reassured and have access to an individual they can confide in and trust with their fears – such as, Will their parent die? Will they ever live together again?

'Hannah and Georgina found it useful when they were with their foster parents to write about things they had been doing and to draw pictures to show me when we did meet. I found it to be a special way of us being able to share with each other our different roles at the time. It gave them something positive to focus on when they were missing me. They also had activities after school and at weekends. They were taken for walks with the foster parents' children, encouraged to visit friends and Georgina attended a playgroup whilst Hannah was at school.

'Hannah and Georgina were very close and strongly emotionally inter-dependent at times and often relied on each other for physical contact – able to show the affection which had been there before I *became ill. I did not interfere with their closeness even after we returned home and gradually we adjusted to me being a full-time parent who was capable of and responsible for setting boundaries again.*

'*They had to re-learn to trust my judgement and authority and I had to recognise that they had grown in ways emotionally that initially I could only guess at. I also had to accept that I had lost almost nine months of their physical and intellectual development which at times made me feel that I did not know my children anymore.*

'*My psychiatrist and, more recently, my CPN have helped me significantly through the therapeutic process to come to terms with my past, cope with present events and everyday life and have with kindness and empathy encouraged me to find ways of coping with the effects of my depression upon my children and myself.*'

Heide Lloyd

Developing integrated services

Separate mental health and social care assessment and intervention systems currently operate for mentally ill adults and for children. This chapter suggests an approach for clarifying how practitioners in specialist adult and children's services can prioritise arrangements for jointly supporting families in which mentally ill adults and dependent children live together. Opportunities for joint working exist at all stages from initial referral to assessment and treatment.

The basic framework outlined in this chapter will require adaptation according to local needs and variations in patterns of service provision. The framework does not address ways in which specialist and primary care services should link. It is an attempt to facilitate greater coherence **within specialist services** as a starting point for developing integrated services for mentally ill parents and their children.

A continuum of need, varying over time and between individual family members is emphasised. The challenge is to assess requirements accurately and to match those needs with relevant support and intervention. **Table 9** opposite summarises the **separate but similar approaches for adult mental health and children's services.**

A service protocol

Referral

Staff should approach referral issues from a **family** perspective (recognising the social context and living circumstances of the referred child or adult). Staff should prioritise referrals according to the degree of need or concern. **The quality of information available in the initial referral is an important determinant of the appropriateness of the initial response.**

Table 9 Descriptions of service responses related to family needs		
Children		**Adults**
	Legislation	
CA89		MHA 1983
Working Together		Code of Practice
	Needs Assessment	
See Wallace *et al.* (**Appendix i**)	Provision	See Wing (**Appendix i**)
Children's services plans		Community Care Plans
In need of support (including from voluntary organisations)		In need of support – mental health, parenting (including from voluntary organisations)
In need of services (including education, primary care, health social care)		In need of services (AMH, primary care, housing and benefits)
In need of protection (SSD, Courts)		In need of protection/containment (in-patient, secure settings, special hospitals)
Child Protection Register		CPA/Supervision Register

Initial response

Staff in each service must respond according to the degree of urgency. Whilst there must be a priority on safety and the needs of the 'core' client/patient, ascertaining the needs of other family members at the same time will facilitate comprehensive assessment and planning of joint working opportunities. Definitions of levels of need or urgency of response are described in **Table 10** below.

Table 10 Descriptions of service responses related to family needs		
Service response	**Child**	**Adult**
Urgent (acute concerns)	Explicit child protection issue (such as physical abuse or neglect).	Acute adult mental health emergency (for example, mental state an overt threat to child or evidence of harm to child; parental inability to ensure child's safety).
Significant	Child's development and /or mental health impaired but no immediate danger to physical health or need for protection from sexual abuse. Impairment contributed to by quality of care experienced.	Parental mental health impacts on social functioning, including parenting. Requires treatment or problems likely to persist, such as quantitative/qualitative extremes in parent-child interaction (see **Chapter Two**).
Concerning	Child's development not markedly impaired but parenting and associated risk factors indicate that it might become impaired if support is not provided.	Parental mental health problem not seriously impairing social functioning including parenting but associated risk factors and stressors indicate situation could deteriorate without support.
Coping	In general, child's development and adjustment progressing well in relation to living with mentally ill parent but child may require short-term support during acute crisis, for example, parental hospitalisation, life (loss) event.	Mentally ill parent managing with childcare responsibilities but may require short-term support during crisis, for example, relapse of illness.

According to the degree of urgency, practitioners must decide whether immediate action is required or whether to undertake further information gathering. **The nature and level of need may be different for adults and children in the same family.** It is therefore important that standard procedures and protocols are available which must be adhered to according to what is found during initial (and subsequent) contacts with family members.

Diagram 3 illustrates in simplified form the processes involved at various stages following receipt of a referral and the associated tasks for practitioners. Whilst the separation between adult mental health and children's services has been highlighted, there are common requirements for staff in all services to meet the needs of their clients/patients. These common requirements provide opportunities to work together to meet the needs of all family members.

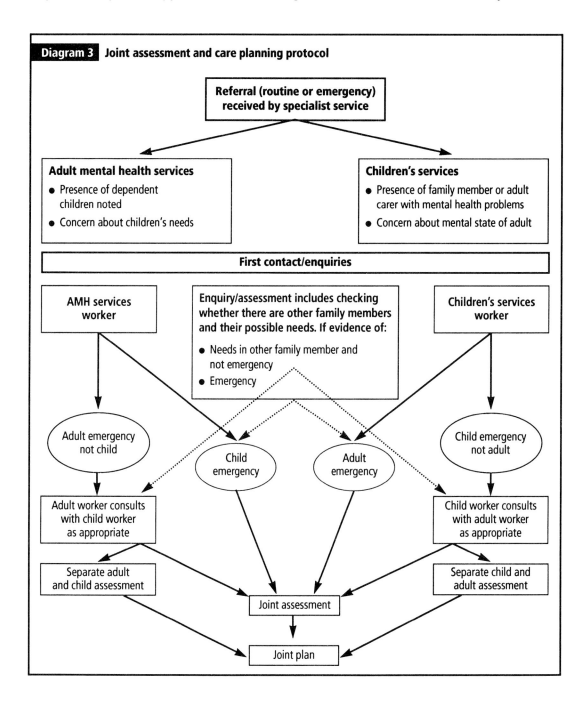

Diagram 3 **Joint assessment and care planning protocol**

This model provides a framework for joint working across adult mental health and children's services. The complementary perspectives of both children and families and mental health workers are essential in order to provide a holistic and comprehensive service. Ultimately, interpreting and managing different levels of concern will depend on the quality of the initial response, information gathering, and subsequent decision making. **All staff will need support, supervision and training to acquire the necessary experience to make comprehensive assessments and good decisions to support and protect mentally ill parents and their children.**

The priority in adult services is for staff to know which of their clients/patients have children. For staff in children's services, finding out about the mental health of the parents of referred children is the priority. **A broader approach to assessment means that the presence and needs of all family members can be considered.**

If the situation is urgent, practitioners must concentrate on the 'core' client/patient in the first instance. For example, workers in adult services must address the needs of an acutely disturbed adult but will also be aware of the presence of children and will consult with colleagues in children's services as appropriate. This may require an urgent joint assessment or there may be options to make arrangements for a joint assessment at a later stage. An adult worker faced with a child emergency should undertake a joint assessment with a member of the children and families team. Similarly, a childcare practitioner faced with an adult mental health emergency should have the support of a colleague from mental health services.

Joint work

Following a referral, working together should not be seen as requiring an automatic joint home visit by a representative from adult mental health and a representative from children's services. A broader interpretation is suggested. For example:

- discussion with colleagues, either directly or by telephone for advice and clarification of concerns

- meeting formally or informally to share uncertainty, clarify roles and plan intervention

- attending each other's meetings (case discussions, ward rounds, CPA review, CP conferences)

- establishing a regular forum for reviewing cases and developing or modifying local protocols.

However, a joint visit can be vital to ensure that the needs and safety of adults and children are considered during a crisis and beyond.

Joint work can take place in a variety of settings and for a variety of reasons:

- facilitating communication between parents and children about mental illness and its implications

- providing explanation about mental illness for parents and children

- supporting treatment and compliance as well as making explicit the range of consequences for parent and child of poor adherence to treatment

- implications of a parent refusing a trial of treatment (medication, admission, therapy) or refusing a parenting assessment

- addressing the role of the mental illness in poor compliance and devising collaborative strategies (adult, child workers and family members)

- opportunities for managerial inter-agency planning and strategy forums.

The overall context

The key domains to consider in assessment are discussed in **Chapter Two** (see pages 74–76). Other considerations include:

Questions for AMH workers

- Are there children? How old? Where are they?

- Who looks after them?

- How are they? Parental concerns? Child professional concerns (health visitor, teachers, social worker, other)?

- Has parent talked with child?

- Has child asked parent questions?

- How is the child managing at school?

- Who helps with childcare if parent is unwell?

Questions for children's services workers

- Does this child's key carer/parent have mental health problems? Is referral necessary or is parent known to AMH service?

- Is there evidence of excessive use of alcohol or illicit drugs?

- What impact is the mental illness having on the children?

- How is the mental illness affecting parenting and the relationship between parent and children?

- What range of supports could assist a parent to meet the child's needs more effectively?

- Has anyone talked with these children about difficulties in their lives?

Staff need to consider the overall context in which children are being brought up and how well parents are able to manage themselves and their children's needs. This context also provides information about what additional resources parents may need to care for their children, taking into account cultural and ethnic factors.

If there are serious concerns about a parent's capacity to meet their children's needs and ensure their safety, not only must the mental state of the parent be assessed but their parenting capacity as well.

The resolution of a parent's mental illness must *not* automatically be assumed to indicate that baseline parenting skills are adequate to meet their child's needs and ensure their safety. Several domains must be assessed:

- the context of the parent-child relationship (for example, the extent of care provided by a mentall ill parent)

- the developmental needs and attainments of the child

- the availability of family and social support.

Important factors related to mental illness include:

- the prognosis (for example, chronic but mild to moderate symptoms may have a more negative effect than a severe but acute episode)

- history of violence and self-harm (for example, use of alcohol and/or illicit drugs)

- co-morbidity and diagnostic uncertainty

- treatment resistance and failed treatment

- compliance.

Compliance and insight

Staff must develop strategies in collaboration with parents to improve compliance and ensure that parents and children can benefit from support and treatment. Talking with parents is essential to ensure they understand:

- reasons for treatment (for example, counselling or use of medication)

- implications of poor compliance (for example, ongoing symptoms, longer episode, difficulties meeting child's needs, potential for other carers to become involved).

Children's services staff must obtain information about medication and side-effects from the mental health keyworkers, psychiatrist or GP. **Where poor compliance occurs, professionals must explore other forms of support and monitor the situation, including provision for children's needs and safety.**

Non-mental-health practitioners have a key role in helping to promote insight into the illness, its implications and improving compliance with all forms of treatment. In so doing, they can contribute towards effective inter-agency partnerships to support mentally ill parents and their children.

Engaging parents and children

In order to provide information, promote understanding and facilitate harmonious relation-ships within families, effective engagement is crucial. Some stages in the process include:

- recognising and acknowledging the presence of children and their individuality

- engaging and forming a relationship with parent/carer and child

- recognising the patient/client as parent

- establishing clarity about practitioner's role

- developing positive practitioner qualities: listening skills, empathy and warmth, respect, honesty

- establishing what parents and children know about the illness

- supplementing existing knowledge with relevant information whilst facilitating more open discussion between parents and children

- enabling children to ask questions and empowering parents to respond confidently.

In general, the earlier that parents and children are actively involved in talking with each other the better. Timing is always important and practitioners must judge, according to circumstances (including children's safety), when to facilitate discussion. However, even in an acute crisis, the provision of an explanation to a child about the actions that professionals will be taking represents good practice and can have lasting benefits for children. Whilst consideration of individual and family needs should occur routinely at the point of first referral or contact, opportunities exist at all stages for joint involvement and intervention.

Children may understand how their parent's mental illness affects themselves and their parent, but not have an intellectual concept of 'mental illness'. Some issues to consider when talking to children are the child's:

- **level of awareness and knowledge** about the parent's illness (nature, cause and resulting behaviours)

- **concepts of the illness** (mind/body/brain/stress/other)

- **feelings about the situation** and changes in circumstances

- **relationships**, particularly changes in relationships with ill parent and other key people in the child's life

- **changing role** at home and effects on schooling as a consequence of parental illness

- **responsibilities** (especially increases) during periods of parental illness

- **view of the future**.

These issues are discussed in more detail in **Chapter Eight** (page 156).

Engaging children and parents according to setting and circumstances

Parent/carer known to practitioner (existing caseload)

Consideration of the social and family context of the ill parent/carer will have provided information about parental concerns regarding children and ways in which mental illness may be affecting the children or the carer's parenting abilities. These conversations will also have enabled practitioners to emphasise the importance of considering the needs of the children.

The majority of parents want to ensure that their children are given appropriate support but may be anxious about:

- being perceived as a 'bad' or inadequate parent

- children being removed from their care

- adverse effects of their illness on children

- talking about mental illness having a 'damaging' effect on children.

Discussion should address these concerns in an honest and open way, emphasising the benefits for the child and parent of talking more openly and considering the possible impacts on children. There should be recognition of the fact that parents do worry a great deal about their children and want the best for them. In some instances, there are serious inabilities to meet children's needs, but in the majority of situations children are not removed. Early consideration of children's needs with provision of support for parents can reduce the likelihood of children needing to be removed from their carers.

Children do worry about their parents but may be anxious about asking questions for fear of upsetting them. They need opportunities to feel safe enough to ask questions, express fears and talk openly with their parents/carers in order to make sense of their experiences. Helping children to express themselves is unlikely to be harm them, but will help them to understand more about their worries or difficulties and to develop more effective coping strategies.

A **first meeting** with children and parent(s) is an important opportunity to establish a positive relationship. The practitioner can then be seen as an important adult within the family's social network. A detailed conversation may not be necessary. It is much more important for the children to be helped to feel part of events by having been spoken with directly.

Some children may not be able to answer questions directly, but will be keen to be a part of any discussion about the parent's illness. Indirect approaches can be helpful, for example asking one family member about another's behaviour or feelings. Such children may subsequently begin to contribute to the conversation once they have seen their parent talking more openly about previously unspoken issues. Sometimes the converse may occur: when a parent, anxious to protect a child, has avoided any discussion, but then hears the child talking about illness-related matters which have been 'overheard', thus demonstrating their capacity to cope with such matters; this often brings great relief to the parent and facilitates further discussion.

Some parents may refuse to talk about their children; whilst trying to respect a parent's wishes. It is important to explore the reasons for refusal – the source of the denial/anger/anxiety. A better understanding of parental fears and dilemmas may facilitate more open discussion.

A parent's persistent refusal to talk about their children, together with denial of any impact on them, and an inability to obtain any information about children from other family, friends or agencies, must be seen as a serious concern, especially if associated with poor insight and compliance and a history of difficulties engaging with other services. Practitioners should consult childcare professionals if there are any concerns about child safety and welfare and where there is evidence of:

- persistent negative views expressed about a child

- ongoing emotional unavailability, unresponsiveness and neglect

- inability to recognise a child's needs and to maintain appropriate parent-child boundaries, including involvement of the child in the parent's symptoms or abnormal thinking

- ongoing use of child to meet parent's own needs

- distorted, confusing or misleading communications with child

- ongoing hostility, irritability and criticism of child

- inconsistent and/or inappropriate expectations of child.

Meeting child and family in crisis

When a crisis occurs (including parental hospitalisation) basic principles still apply; judgements will need to be made about the extent of involving the child balanced against safety requirements. There may be uncertainty about the circumstances which precipitated the referral, or about parental diagnosis. The aim of the meeting will be to gather basic information as part of the assessment. Childcare and safety issues may be a priority. If a disturbed parent/carer is to be admitted to hospital urgently, it is important to ensure the presence of a trusted adult with the children. Once decisions have been taken, an explanation (appropriate to the child's age) should be given about forthcoming actions for parent and child.

The crisis of admission will have an impact on all family members. Improved co-ordination between childcare provision and mental health services can reduce the trauma of separation.[1] Admission provides an opportunity to review family circumstances and to consider the needs of children and the 'patient as parent'.[2–4] Whilst such approaches should be part of routine practice, it is important to note that parents will vary in the extent to which they welcome or block discussion about their children.[5–6] Rather than accepting at face value parental refusal to discuss aspects of parenthood and child welfare, practitioners should endeavour to explore sensitively the reasons underlying reluctance/resistance. If this is unsuccessful, the ill parent should still be kept fully informed about what is happening to the children. Parental fears have been outlined above (see page 147) and such concerns must be routinely and actively addressed if appropriate support for parents and children is to be provided.

To meet children's needs when a parent is hospitalised, staff looking after a parent and those caring for the children should:

- **Be open and honest**

  Children will have an awareness of what is happening including the absence of their parent/carer. They may have observed all that went on or overheard conversations whilst in another room or while hurriedly taken to neighbours, friends or family. Pretending nothing has happened may be especially confusing. They need to be kept informed.

- **Provide explanations**

  A truthful statement/description appropriate to the child's age, but without minute detail is sufficient. It is important to use language which the child can understand. The ill parent could be described as sad, confused, upset, needing a rest, stressed, mixed-up inside and so on. Describing what happens while the parent is in hospital – talking, being looked after, medication and so on – is also helpful.

- **Emphasise that the child is not to blame.** The child should be told this.

- **Help to minimise disruption and maintain daily routines** for children; 'special time' (extra attention) is helpful.

- **Support opportunities for contact**

  Contact (for example, children visiting parents in hospital) according to parental well-being, in an appropriate and safe setting, can reduce children's distress. Other ways of maintaining contact include letters, phone calls, pictures and so on.

- **Recognise changes in behaviour patterns**

  Children will worry, have fears/anxieties, be confused. This may manifest in a wide range of observable behaviours and hidden distress; for example, disrupted sleep or routines, uncharacteristic quietness/inaccessibility, poor appetite, clinginess, bed wetting, demanding or disruptive behaviour, anger, irritability, tearfulness, stomach aches, nightmares.

- **Alert school and teachers** that the child may need extra support/attention/praise.

Parental self-harm

Self-harm is a significant accompaniment to severe mental illness, substance dependence and personality disorder. It has also been shown to have important associations with child maltreatment.[7,8] Attempted suicide is also an important risk factor for those who go on to successfully commit suicide. The phenomenon of 'extended suicide' or homicide-suicide by parents is well described.[9] Given that not all parents who attend hospital Accident and Emergency Departments following an episode of self-harm will be admitted, the presentation provides an important opportunity to review family circumstances and the welfare and safety of children – an opportunity for preventive intervention.

The first stage must be more accurate and systematic recognition of which adults who present following overdose or self-mutilation are parents. Thereafter, routine inquiries about the whereabouts and well-being of the children at the time of crisis, including availability of social support and quality of family relationships, must be made.

This consideration of child safety and the broader needs of children requires routine liaison between staff in Accident and Emergency Departments, AMH teams, GPs and children's services – in short, an effective communication network between acute and community services and across agencies. Appropriate checks as well as provision of support should be part of the Clinical Plan, even if – or *especially* if – the parent is thought not to be sufficiently mentally ill to warrant admission. The association between personality disorder, substance dependence and depression – especially when occurring together in the same individual who has childcare responsibilities – requires active consideration of the needs of dependent children.

When assessing the mental state of a parent who has attempted suicide, good practice requires inquiry not only about prior and ongoing suicidal thoughts and plans but, where there are dependent children, inquiry about homicidal thoughts and plans.[9]

References

1   Ekdahl, M., Rice, E. & Schmidt, W. (1962) Children of parents hospitalised for mental illness. *American Journal of Public Health*, **52** (3) 428–435.

2   Shachnow, J. (1987) Preventive intervention with children of hospitalised psychiatric patients. *American Journal of Orthopsychiatry*, **57**, 66–77.

3   Oppenheimer, R. (1981) At risk: Children of female psychiatric inpatients. *Child Abuse and Neglect*, **5**, 117–122.

4   Castleberry, K. (1988) Helping children adapt to the psychiatric hospitalisation of a parent. *The Psychiatric Hospital*, **19** (4) 155–160.

5   Stormont, F., Craig, T., Atakan, Z., *et al.* (1997) Concerns about the children of psychiatric in-patients – what the parents say. *Psychiatric Bulletin*, **21**, 495–497.

6   Wang, A. & Goldschmidt, V. (1994) Interviews of psychiatric inpatients about their family situation and young children. *Acta Psychiatrica Scandinavica*, **90**, 459–465.

7   Hawton, K., Roberts, J. & Goodwin, G. (1985) The risk of child abuse among mothers who attempt suicide. *British Journal of Psychiatry*, **146**, 486–489.

8   Falkov, A. (1997) *Parental Psychiatric disorder and child maltreatment – Part II: Extent and nature of the association.* Highlight Series No. 149. London: National Children's Bureau.

9   West, D. J. (1965) *Murder followed by suicide.* London: Heinemann.

Chapter Eight

Preventive interventions

The interactions between a parent's mental illness (including its intensity, frequency, duration, severity and pattern), the quality of parenting, the parent-child relationship, the individual attributes and needs of a particular child, together with family factors and broader social/community supports, all will determine the quality of a child's adjustment. The interplay between individual, family and environmental risk factors and protectors will exacerbate or ameliorate difficulty and disorder. **The greater the number of adversities experienced, the more likely it is that vulnerabilities will emerge along with difficulties in successful adaptation** (see **Chapter Two**).

Thus a bright, healthy and attractive child with good social skills is less likely to be adversely affected, especially when the parental illness is mild, of short duration, not associated with parental discord, conflict and disorganisation, not associated with impaired parenting and does not result in family break-up. The presence of a non-ill parent or adult in the family with whom the child has a positive, confiding relationship is an important protective factor, as is the presence of a good social support network.

Aims and principles of prevention

The core aim of preventive intervention is to minimise the impact of mental illness on parents and their children.[1-9] This can be achieved through clear and explicit assessment of needs, including stressors and protective factors (see pages 69–72), and treatment and prevention approaches which involve both children and parents.

Factors which reduce the impact of parental mental illness on children include:

Primary prevention

- Early detection of parental mental illness; for example, screening for postnatal depression.[10]

- Early detection of risk factors for parental mental illness; for example, detection of social isolation and history of adverse childhood experiences in mother.

- Early assessment of children's needs when a parent/carer is mentally ill.

Secondary prevention (parental mental illness *and* evidence of child impairment)

● Broad assessment of risk and protective factors including:
  – illness in parent
  – needs and disorder in child
  – appraisal of whether home situation is (or could be) good enough with support.

● Treatment of illness/disorder in children as well as parents.

● Reduction of risks and stressors.

● Promotion of strengths and protective factors.

Tertiary prevention (parental mental illness *and* long-standing child impairment)

● Broad assessment of risk and protective factors.

● Assessment, treatment and rehabilitation of developmental and psychiatric disorder in child.

● Careful appraisal of childcare circumstances.

● Promotion of strengths and protective factors, especially with enduring difficulty/disorder.

Preventive strategies

Strategies to reduce the impact of parental mental illness on children include:

1 **Reduce child exposure to disturbing parental symptoms** (for example, delusions, socially embarrassing behaviour, deliberate self-harm)

2 **Actively/assertively treat parental mental illness**

  ● Treat early (efficient and effective access and outreach components) to minimise severity and duration of episodes.

  ● Admit to hospital when child exposed to severe symptoms and poor quality social support.

  ● Promote insight into illness and its implications by providing information about diagnosis, prognosis, services.

  ● Ensure compliance with treatment and explore reasons for poor compliance, including cultural issues, side-effects of medication.

  ● Prevent relapse.

3 **Promote positive parenting**

  ● Reduce multiple changes of carers and facilitate continuity in care environments.

  ● Link childcare support with acute mental health services.

  ● Reduce stress associated with parenting by providing access to practical support for parents and children; a balance of home and nursery or home and after-school clubs can alleviate stress associated with parenting but also provides opportunities to sustain parent-child relationships and minimise parenting stress.

● Establish parenting programmes to improve understanding of children's needs and requirements for effective parent-child relationships.

● Prepare for admission to and discharge from hospital, including opportunities for contact between children and their hospitalised parent appropriate for the children's age and parental situation.

● Recognise that the birth and presence of a child can activate painful memories of carer's own childhood experiences.

● Improve parents' capacity to differentiate their own needs from their children's; for example, by enhancing parental ability to:

    – recognise the child as an individual with needs that are different and separate from carer's

    – participate in a reciprocal relationship with the child

    – realistically appraise the child's emotional, physical needs, and respond to children's needs for safety within environment

    – recognise the child's realistic abilities

    – adapt to the child's age-appropriate needs

    – tolerate ambivalent feelings about parental role and responsibilities for children.

● Counsel child and parent to reduce exposure to harmful/distressing symptoms.

4 **Reduce exposure to parental discord**, hostility and criticism and promote expression of praise and warmth.

5 **Educate parents about mental illness** (symptoms, treatment, ways of coping and adapting despite ongoing symptoms) about child development and how mental illness might impact upon children, and the effect of the mental illness on parenting.

6 **Educate children about mental illness and ways of coping effectively**

● Teach them to recognise changes in the relationship with their ill parent which signify onset or recurrence of symptoms (reality testing).

● Reduce guilt and self-blame so that children know they are not the cause of parental illness.

● Provide social skills training to develop competence in relating to peers and approaching relevant adults for help (enhance positive temperament).

● Improve social problem-solving skills and critical thinking (enhance 'reality testing' abilities, assertiveness and communication skills).

● Promote positive self-esteem; provide opportunities for sustained and harmonious relationships with a range of adults and peers, for personal achievement and success in academic, sport and personal interests.

7 Promote open discussion about mental illness within the family

- Help to develop a climate of openness and collaboration within families and between families and services.

- Enable children to ask questions and parents to respond positively by providing age-appropriate explanations.

- Encourage partners or non-ill adults/carers to participate in consultation or therapeutic work.

- Repeat explanations as children develop so that more sophisticated concepts can be incorporated over time.

8 Encourage the development of supportive links and positive expectations for children outside the home

- Therapeutic nurseries for infants, day care for toddlers, after-school clubs for school-age children and adolescents can all reduce exposure to parental symptoms and broaden socialisation experiences and opportunities, especially where social isolation exists in association with or as a consequence of mental illness. (These also provide some respite for parents.)

9 Provide opportunities within school to promote positive relationships (with adults and peers), and for the experience of success (academic, sport, hobbies).

10 Address other factors (such as financial circumstances or housing).

Communicating with families

Talking with children and parents to improve understanding about mental illness enhances adaptation for all family members. Approaches are described here which highlight opportunities for practitioners working in various settings, and examples of initiatives undertaken by practitioners are provided to demonstrate possibilities in daily practice.

Children's understanding of parental mental illness

Feedback from users has highlighted the importance parents and children attach to receiving information about parental mental illness (see **Chapter One**, p16). Christensen[11] interviewed 32 children whose parents had alcohol problems. Aside from conveying a much greater awareness about the effects of parental drinking than their parents recognised, the children also reported that the best place to receive help would be from the service dealing with their parents. They felt that these practitioners would be appropriately knowledgeable about alcoholism and that they would be reassured in knowing that their parents were receiving help, too. A further advantage would be the reduction in stigma that tends to be associated with referral to a children's service. Children have also expressed a wish to be able to meet other children who have had similar experiences.[12] However, despite the clear wish for information to be provided for children, very little work has occurred around children's understanding of parental mental illness as an initial step in developing effective, age-appropriate interventions.

A qualitative, group approach was undertaken by Garley et al.[13] in a small study designed to elicit subjective experiences of children (aged 11–15 years) living with a depressed parent. Analysis of the transcriptions revealed four key themes or areas of particular concern to the children with a number of subthemes:

1   **Understanding the illness**

   ● personal concerns

   ● attributions as to the cause of the illness

   ● quest for information

2   **Recognising the signs**

3   **Impact of hospitalisation** and

4   **Managing the illness**

   ● coping with impact of illness on self

   ● coping with impact on their parent

   ● perceptions of what is helpful for parent

   ● recommendations for other children whose parents are depressed.

The **major personal concern** was actual or feared parental separation. Other concerns included academic and behavioural difficulties at school, fears about becoming mentally ill themselves, and concerns about the cause and prognosis of the parental illness. Various **attributions** were made regarding the cause of parental illness: low self-esteem, child sexual abuse, important bio/environmental factors and stress. All children wished to have more **information** to assist in their struggle to make sense of the parental illness. The capacity to **recognise deterioration** in a parent's mental health was thought to be an important marker for those children who were more able to make sense of their experiences and circumstances in living with a depressed parent.

Where alternative carers for children were available in the family, **parental hospital admission** was felt to be positive, sometimes a relief.

In managing **the impact of the illness on themselves**, participants valued friends as a source of support, regardless of whether or not they confided in them about their parent's illness. Talking within the study group and sharing experiences related to depressed parents was also felt to be positive. Diverting attention/distraction, reading, watching TV and playing sport were other examples of how children coped. In coping with **the impact on parents**, role reversal and descriptions of the burden for the children were extremely common. Excessive responsibilities and loyalty conflicts were frequently described.

With regard to **help for parents**, most children were aware of the chronic, intractable nature of their parent's mood disorder and realised that medication was important as a control, not a cure. Discontinuation of medication was a frequently cited reason for relapse and they attached importance to professional availability to monitor medication.

Explanations about mental illness

Providing an explanation about mental illness for children must occur in the context of the parent/carer-child relationship and at a pace which reflects the level and quality of engagement between family members and practitioners. That children wish to have information about their parent's illness has been clearly demonstrated (see **Chapter One**), as has the willingness of both parents and children to talk about their experiences.[14]

The nature and extent of children's understanding of parental mental illness has also been hypothesized as having an important link with the quality of the child's adaptation.[14] Scherer and colleagues[15] evaluated the subjective perceptions of 57 children regarding their mothers' mental illness and reported that the children's perceptions of their mothers' mental health were significantly related to their psychological functioning. Children who reported their mother as having more psychiatric symptoms had less perceived self-competence and social support.

Working with a small sample of 36 families in which a depressed parent and children (aged 8–15 years) lived together, Beardslee *et al.*[13] compared two preventive interventions designed to:

- increase families' understanding of parental depression

- help parents recognise symptoms of distress and respond appropriately

- prevent depression in the children.

The intervention consisted either of a single lecture and discussion about depression for parents only or provision of six to ten sessions for clinical work involving children, parents and family.

The authors concluded that the results for both groups yielded benefits, but that the more intensive intervention demonstrated the additional advantage of linking information about mental illness to the individual life experiences of all family members and for directly involving children to achieve long-term (preventive) effects.

Talking with children

Issues to consider when talking with children include:

How much does the child know and/or understand about their parent's illness?

- Is the child aware of changes in the parent or the parent-child relationship?

- What does the child think caused the illness?

- Does the child understand that their parent is ill (is their change in behaviour/mood due to an illness?)

How does the child conceptualise their parent's illness?

● Is it an illness, or is it their mother/father being difficult/irritable?

● Is it something to do with the mind/body/brain/stress?

● Does the child see it as something wrong with the brain, or as a response to stress?

How does the child feel about their situation?

● Is the child worried about the current situation (self, parent, parent in hospital, school)?

● Is the child confused?

How does the child perceive their relationships?

● How does the child perceive their parent's feelings about them? (Does this change when mental illness is present?)

● Is the child's relationship with the parent changed as a result of the illness?

● How has the child's relationship with other people (including friends) changed?

What are the consequences of the illness?

● Does the illness affect the child's role within the home and/or school and social activities (taking friends back home, going out and so on)?

● What changes for the child when the parent is mentally ill ?

● Who cares for the child (professionals, family/friends)?

● Is the child in contact with the ill parent – particularly during acute phases?

What, if any, are the responsibilities of the child when their parent is mentally ill?

● Is this role the same as when the parent is well? Does the child take on a caring role? (See information about young carers on page117.)

How does the child think about the future?

● Does the child see the parent getting better, staying the same or getting worse?

● Does the child worry about getting ill themselves?

● Is the child worried about how long the parent will be in hospital?

● Does the child worry about who will look after her/him?

Intervention for individual families

Below is a summary of some opportunities for intervention for individual practitioners and teams. The intention is to demonstrate realistic and practical possibilities within the multiple daily constraints experienced by all staff. Most of these examples represent initiatives which are small in scale and have not been fully evaluated, if at all. However, on page 160 a brief summary of specialist intervention programmes is included where more systematic evaluation has occurred.

Individual/team audit of needs to identify eligible families
This could ascertain, for example:

● the number of ill adults who have dependent children

● the number of parents of referred children who have mental health problems

● the number of children subject to care proceedings whose parents have mental health problems

● the number of young carers in the local area.

Adaptation of clinical/administrative assessment pro formas
For example:

● including section on children and family circumstances in hospital admission and discharge sheets

● incorporating relevant details in CPA and CPR forms.

Development of protocols and procedures to be followed when:

● a crisis occurs involving adult mental health and childcare – identifying and alerting appropriate individuals/services

● routine referral occurs involving mentally ill parent and children – joint procedures, individual responsibilities and so on.

Direct work with children and parents

● 'What's wrong with Mum?' (see Appendix iv)

● 'Children have feelings' (see Appendix vi)

● *Coping at home – A booklet for parents* (see Appendix vii)

● *Jake's Dinosaurs*[17]

● *Robby Rose and Monkey*[18]

● *Troubled Lives*[14]

● Children, Siblings and Spouses in *Helping Families Cope with Mental Illness.*[19]

Crisis card schemes

As part of the growing 'voice' of the user movement regarding mental health services in this country,[20,21] Sutherby and Szmukler describe various crisis cards and self-help initiatives.[22] Crisis cards have been used to record and provide basic/personal information at a time of acute mental health crisis, to provide information about past and/or current treatment, and as an advocacy tool. They also enable advance planning for care in the event of a crisis. Marie Diggins[20] and colleagues in Lewisham Social Services Department extended the use of crisis cards to include hospital and financial planning sheets. This enabled forward planning to occur for those users who also had childcare responsibilities and provided a good opportunity for collaboration between parents and practitioners in making links between mental health and childcare needs. Although usage is increasing, uncertainty remains about the extent of uptake and utilisation within mental health services; this requires further evaluation.

Voluntary sector initiatives

- Newpin[7]
- Young Carer schemes[24] (for example, Willow)
- Mental Health Foundation[25]
- Family Welfare Association[26]
- AACPMI[27]

FAMILI – Families And Mental Illness Initiative[28]

This three-year Joint Finance pilot between Lambeth Healthcare (NHS) Trust and Lambeth Social Services Department began in 1995 and provided funding for a CPN, social worker and part-time administrator to develop a service for families in which mentally ill parents and dependent children were living together. Workers are based in the Health Trust child psychiatry department but much of the work occurs in other settings – in-patient units, community mental health centres, GP surgeries and family homes.

The project began with a survey of staff working in local authority child and adult teams, and a range of acute and community-based AMH settings to ascertain their awareness about family numbers and needs. Some of the results have been mentioned in the **Overview** (see pages 10 and 11). The project has been successful in establishing closer links with other agencies, especially the AMH service. Activities include consultation, supervision, direct clinical work (including joint work with adult CPNs) and teaching. Emphasis has been on promoting children's understanding of parental illness, and facilitating more open dialogue within families about mental illness and its impact on family members.

Specialist intervention programmes

In the UK, one of the first accounts of in-patient provision for mentally ill parents (mothers) and their children (babies) was by Douglas in 1956.[29] Since then, acute provision for mothers and infants has evolved either as single-bed provision within acute adult psychiatric units, or as specialist mother and baby units in selected areas of the country, with varying degrees of outreach provision as part of 'perinatal services'.[30] More detailed descriptions are provided in relevant chapters in Cox & Holden[10] and Brockington.[31]

Several larger-scale, evaluated programmes have been developed over the years, most notably in the USA. These were initially institution-based (in-patient or day programmes) but evolved to community and home-based provision with comparisons of the effectiveness of intervention depending on type, setting, intensity and duration. For the interested reader, more details are provided in the references.[32–35]

Specialist programmes have the following features in common:

- home and community-based, with links between hospital and community

- approaches which recognise both the significance of early intervention and prevention efforts for young children and their families as well as addressing relevant issues across the life-span

- recognition of the public health implications for large numbers of children whose parents are moderately anxious and depressed, not just those of severely mentally ill parents

- addressing eligibility/threshold issues (those who do not require hospital CMH services), those who do not require formal psychiatric services (primary health care, GP, voluntary sector, self-help); creating effective linkages

- a preventive perspective: children's services seen as preventive arm of adult service. If adult service can support/link with this approach to create successful programmes, then it may be possible to reduce the proportion of children who go on to require adult services

- direct work to promote optimal parent-child relationships

- support, assistance and education for parents whilst also providing direct stimulation, enrichment and therapy for (young) children.

For **mothers/carers** the focus is on:

- support in dealing with individual burden (past experiences and current difficulties and dilemmas)

- enhancing personal skills (education/employment, organisation, social interaction, parenting – for example, reciprocal relationship with child, picking up cues from child, responding appropriately)

- enhancing child's capacity to develop competence, control and autonomy

- facilitating the capacity to separate from or engage appropriately with child.

For **children** the focus is on:

- consistent care, predictable events through the day and from day to day

- age-appropriate stimulation

- development of trusting relationship with parent

- safety (physical and emotional)

- improving language development and communication skills, and attention-span

- capacity to express powerful emotions

- cause-and-effect relationships with people and environment

- help in dealing with separation from ill parent.

The following list of good practice points will enhance the quality of support and provision for all family members:

- establish routine, systematic and accessible recording of families with dependent children and mentally ill adults

- acknowledge the child as part of the family in which there is a mentally ill adult

- ensure systematic consideration of parenting burden for mentally ill adults and developmental and mental health needs of children according to age, developmental stage and range of experiences

- determine intervention by systematic and comprehensive gathering of information, objective analysis of information, discussion and consultation with colleagues and relevant practitioners in other services

- link individual personal and family life experiences with up-to-date information, concepts and theoretical approaches

- establish and convey the meaning of 'mental illness' for all family members

- take a proactive, longer-term perspective which provides support or access to support beyond the immediate crisis and recognises the progression in children's developmental needs and the requirement for ongoing adaptation in parental provision for children

- facilitate continuity of relationships – for children with their carers, for parents with their keyworker

- arrange practical support, including for housing, financial/benefit and childcare issues

- support children's interests, develop their strengths and enhance coping capacities

- provide age-appropriate information for both parents and their children

- help child to respond to questions about his/her parents from peers/teachers/other adults

- support children's relationships with non-ill family members, peer group and so on.

References

1   Newton J. (1998) *Preventing Mental Illness.* London: Routledge & Kegan Paul.

2   Berbheim, K. & Lehman A. (1985) *Working with families of the mentally ill.* W W Norton & Co: New York.

3   Goodman, S. & Isaacs, L. (1984) Primary prevention with children of severely disturbed mothers. *Journal of Preventive Psychiatry*, **2**, 387–402.

4   Constantino, J. (1993) Parents, mental illness and the primary health care of infants and young children. *Zero to Three*, **13** (5) 1–39.

5   Browne, K. (1995) Preventing child maltreatment through community nursing. *Journal of Advanced Nursing*, **21**, 57–63.

6   Scott, D. (1992) Early identification of maternal depression as a strategy in the prevention of child abuse. *Child Abuse & Neglect*, **16** (3) 345–358.

7   Cox, A., Pound, A., Mills, M. *et al.* (1991) Evaluation of a home visiting and befriending scheme for young mothers: Newpin. *Journal of the Royal Society of Medicine*, **84**, 217-220.

8   Zelkowitz, P. & Milet, T. (1995) Screening for post-partum depression in a community sample. *Canadian Journal of Psychiatry*, **40**, 80–86.

9   Silverman, M. (1989) Children of Psychiatrically Ill Parents: A prevention Perspective. *Hospital & Community Psychiatry*, **40**, 1257–1265.

10 Cox, J. & Holden, J. (Eds.) (1994) *Perinatal Psychiatry: Use and misuse of the EdinburghPostnatal Depression Scale.* Gaskell London.

11 Christensen, E. (1997) Aspects of a preventive approach to support children of alcoholics. *Child Abuse Review*, **6**, 24–34.

12 Hill, M., Laybourn, A. & Brown, J. (1996) Children whose parents misuse alcohol: A study of services and needs. *Child & Family Social Work*, **1**, 159–167.

13 Garley, D., Gallop, R., Johnston, N. & Pipitone, J. (1997) Children of the mentally ill: A qualitative focus group approach. *Journal of Psychiatry & Mental Health Nursing*, **4**, 97–103

14 Falkov, A. (Unpublished survey) *'Troubled Lives': School aged children's understanding of parental psychosis.*

15 Scherer, D., Melloh, T., Buyck, D. *et al.* (1996) Relation between children's perceptions of maternal mental illness and children's psychological adjustment. *Journal of Clinical Child Psychology*, **25** (2) 156–169.

16 Beardslee, W., Wright, E., Salt, P. *et al.* (1997). Examination of children's responses to two preventive intervention strategies over time. *Journal of the American Academy of Child Adolescent Psychiatry*, **36**, 196–204.

17 Sved Williams, A. (1996) *Jake's Dinosaur.* Produced by Document Services, University of South Australia, Helen Mayo House, Women & children's hospital, Adelaide, South Australia, Australia.

18 Louis, A. (1995) *Robby Rose and Monkey.* Produced by Document Services, University of South Australia, Helen Mayo House, Women & children's hospital, Adelaide, South Australia, Australia.

19 Judge, K. (1994) Children, siblings & spouses. In: H. Lefley & M. Wasow (Eds.) *Helping Families Cope with Mental Illness.* Switzerland: Harwood Academic Publishers.

20 Bhui, K., Aubin, A. & Strathdee, G. (1998) Making a reality of user involvement in community mental health services. *Psychiatric Bulletin*, **22**, 8–11.

21 Crawford, M. & Davies, S. (1998) Involvement of users & carers in the training of psychiatrists: Making it happen. *Psychiatric Bulletin*, **22**, 42–43.

22 Sutherby, K. & Szmukler, G. (1998) Crisis cards and self-help crisis initiatives. *Psychiatric Bulletin*, **22**, 4–7.

23 Diggins, M. (1994) Lewisham SSD crisis card scheme. Personal communication.

24 Stuart, A. Willow Young Carers Scheme. Stringer House, 34 Lupton Street, Leeds, LS10 2QW.

25 Mental Health Foundation

26 Family Welfare Association

27 Australian Association of Children of Parents with Mental Illness (AACPMI) newsletter. Prahran Mission, Mothers Support Program, PO Box 68, Prahran VIC 3181.

28   Falkov, A., Murphy, M. & Antweiler, U. (work in progress) The 'Families And Mental Illness Initiative' (FAMILI), an interagency survey.

29   Douglas, C. (1956) Psychotic Mothers, *Lancet*, **1**, 124–125.

30   Appleby, L. & Dickens, C. (1993) Mothering skills of women with mental illness: Not enough known about the postpartum period. *British Medical Journal*, **306**, 348–349.

31   Brockington, I. (1996) Chapter 11 in *Motherhood and mental health*. Oxford University Press.

32   Grunebaum, H., Weiss, J. Cohler, B., Hartman, C, & Gallant, D. (1982) *Mentally ill mothers and their children* (2nd edition). University of Chicago Press.

33   Musick, J., Clark, R. & Cohler, B. (1981) The Mother's Project: A program for Mentally Ill Mothers of Young Children. In: B. Weissbourd & J. Musick (Eds.) *Infants: Their Social Environments.* Washington, D.C.: National Association for the Education of Young Children.

34   Cohler, B. & Musick, J. (Eds.) *New Directions for Mental Health Services No 24: Intervention Among Psychiatrically Impaired parents and their Young Children.* San Francisco: Jossey-Bass.

35   Feldman, R., Stiffman, A. & Jung, K. (1987) *Children at Risk: In the web of parental mental illness.* London: Rutgers University Press

Appendix i

Key documents

Adult mental health policy and guidance

Department of Health (1990) *Mental Health Act, 1983*. HMSO.

Department of Health (1995) *Mental Health (Patients in the Community) Act*. HMSO.

Department of Health and Welsh Office (1993) *Code of Practice: Mental Health Act, 1983*. HMSO.

Department of Health (1994) *Introduction of Supervision Registers for Mentally Ill People*, HSG(94)5.

Department of Health (1994) *Guidance on the Discharge of Mentally Disordered People and their Continuing Care in the Community*, HSG(94)27.

Department of Health (1995) *Building Bridges: A guide to arrangements for inter-agency working for the care and protection of severely mentally ill people*. HMSO.

Department of Health/SSI (1994) *The Health of the Nation Key Area Handbook: Mental Illness* (2nd edition). HMSO.

Department of Health (1990) *The Care Programme Approach for people with a mental illness referred to the specialist psychiatric services*. HC(90)23/LASSL(90)11.

Department of Health, British Medical Association & Conference of Medical Royal Colleges (1994) *Child Protection: Medical Responsibilities – Guidance for Doctors working with Child Protection Agencies*. (Addendum to *Working Together Under the Children Act*.) London: HMSO.

Department of Health (1990) *The NHS and Community Care Act, 1990*. HMSO.

Department of Health (1995) *Carers (Recognition and Services) Act, 1995*. HMSO.

Local Community Care Plans.

Adult mental health needs assessment

Thornicroft, G., Brewin, J. & Wing, J. (Eds.) (1993) *Measuring Mental Health Needs*. London: HMSO.

Children's services policy and guidance

Department of Health (1989) *The Children Act, 1989*. London: HMSO.

Department of Health (1990) *The Children Act – Principles and Practice in Regulations and Guidance*. London: HMSO.

Home Office, Department of Health, Department of Education and Science, Welsh Office (1991) *Working Together Under the Children Act 1989: A guide to arrangements for inter-agency co-operation for the protection of children from abuse*. London: HMSO.

Department of Health (1995) *Child Protection – Messages from Research*. London: HMSO.

Department of Health (1988) *Protecting Children – A Guide for social workers undertaking a comprehensive guide to assessment*. London: HMSO.

Department of Health/SSI (1995) *Young Carers – Something to think about*.

Department of Health (1995) *The Challenge of Partnership in Child Protection*. London: HMSO.

Local Area Child Protection Committee (ACPC) procedures.

Local children's services plans.

Child mental health needs assessment

NHS Health Advisory Service (1995) *Child and Adolescent Mental Health Services: Together we stand – The commissioning, role and management of child and adolescent mental health services*. London: HMSO.

Department of Health (1995) *A Handbook on Child and Adolescent Mental Health*. London: HMSO.

Wallace, S. A., Crown, J. M., Berger, M. & Cox, A. D. (1997) Child and adolescent mental health. In: A. Stevens & J. Raftery (Eds.) *Health Care Needs Assessment: The epidemiologically based needs assessment reviews*.

Kurtz, Z., Thornes, R. & Wolkind, S. (1994) *Services for the Mental Health of Children and Young People in England – A National Review*. London: Maudsley Hospital and South Thames (West) Regional Health Authority.

Inquiry reports

Boyd, W. (1996) *Report of the Confidential Inquiry into Homicides and Suicides by Mentally ill People*. Royal College of Psychiatrists.

Ritchie, J., Dick, D. & Lingham, R. (1994) *The Report of the Inquiry into the Care and Treatment of Christopher Clunis*. London: HMSO.

The Woodley Team Report (1995) *Report of the Independent Review Panel to East London and the City Health Authority and Newham Council following a homicide in July 1994 by a person suffering with a severe mental illness*. East London & City Housing Association.

Appendix ii

Glossary

Aetiology	Cause(s) of illness or disorder.
Comorbidity	Co-existence in one person of more than one illness or disorder.
Disorder	Persistent dysfunction of body, mind, behaviour or emotions; impairment of health.
Epidemiology	Study of illnesses or disorders identifying their distribution in populations and of variables and factors with which they are associated.
Morbidity	Prevalence of illness, disease or disorder.
Mortality	Death rate.
Prevalence	Frequency with which a symptom or disorder occurs in a defined population.
Prognosis	A prediction of the probable course and outcome of a disorder.
Somatisation	Physical symptoms without physical cause.
Symptom	Perceptible change in bodily function, behaviour or emotion indicative of an illness or disorder.
Syndrome	Pattern of symptoms indicative of a specific illness or disorder.

Appendix iii

Developmental indicators

1 Health and physical development

0–2 YEARS	Have all immunisations been received?

By 6 months, most babies can...
- hold head upright and steady
- roll over
- transfer objects from one hand to the other

By 12 months, most babies can...
- sit unsupported for at least one minute
- rise to sitting positions from lying down
- pull themselves up to a standing position
- walk around while holding onto furniture or with support

If child is not sitting or standing unsupported for one minute, discuss concerns with child health professional.

By 24 months, most children can...
- walk as a primary means of mobility
- pick up small objects with thumb and index finger
- run safely, stopping and starting with ease and avoiding obstacles
- climb – for example, onto furniture to look out of window, or to open doors and so on

3–5 YEARS

By age 4, most children can...
- walk down stairs with alternating feet and without assistance
- open doors that require only pushing or pulling
- stand and walk on tiptoe
- use scissors to cut paper
- screw and unscrew lid of jar

By age 5, most children can...
- grip strongly with either hand
- climb with proficiency
- copy a square
- thread beads onto a string

6–8 YEARS

By age 8, most children can...
- hop forward on one foot with ease
- throw ball in a specific direction
- catch a ball
- unlock key-lock
- draw with pencil and ruler

9–12 YEARS

By age 12, most children can...	ride a bicycle without training wheels, without falling cut out geometric shapes with scissors

13–16 YEARS

By age 16, most children can...	complete complex tasks requiring manual dexterity engage in complex physical activity (such as sport)

2 Education and cognitive development (including language)

0–2 YEARS

By 6 months, most babies can...	smile responsively show interest in colourful toys follow adult activities with eyes reach for toys
By 12 months, most babies can...	babble – vocalisations contain most vowels and many consonants (in a way that sounds like speech) reach for out-of-reach toys give toys to adults on request imitate waving, banging on table (if you bang on table, baby will copy, for example) and adult playful vocalisation
By 24 months, most children can...	demonstrate an understanding of the meaning of 'no' produce spontaneous speech of at least six words enjoy picture books – recognising fine detail in pictures pretend/imitate adults – such as making a cup of tea point to simple objects when directed, for example, 'look at the light'/ 'show me the light'

3–5 YEARS

Children are able to listen to teacher for at least 2–10 minutes (depending on age)

By age 3, most children will...	know several nursery rhymes to repeat and (sometimes) sing listen eagerly to stories and demand favourites over and over again imitate drawing a straight line be able to put four small blocks one on top of another
By age 5, most children will...	be able to draw a recognisable person with head, arms, trunk and fingers be able to draw a house with windows, roof, chimney know the names of all the main colours ask frequent questions (why, when, how...) be able to concentrate sitting for 15 minutes

6–8 YEARS

By age 8, most children can...	read simple stories aloud dress themselves if asked **NB:** Once a child is attending school, the progress made and evidence of any special educational needs will be the best indicators

3 Emotional and behavioural development

0–2 YEARS

By 6 months, most babies will...	laugh aloud in play smile spontaneously cry easily when frustrated stop fussing when touched or picked up by main carer co-operate with feeding
By 12 months, most babies will...	be predominantly happy in mood comply with simple requests try to assist being dressed
By age 2, most children are...	attached to special toys, or objects using language more frequently to express emotion easily distracted when angry able to engage in simple negotiation

By age 5, most children...	recognise happiness/anger/fear and so on in others have become more self-assured enjoy jokes and show a sense of humour often ask questions as to why, how, and the meaning of words are tender and protective towards animals and younger children are usually happy

By 6–8 years, most children...	laugh or smile appropriately in response to positive statements become sensitive about sex – curiosity should lessen if questions are answered show modesty cope with new situations without excessive anxiety

By 9–12 years, most children...	control anger or hurt feelings when denied own way look to the future and start to plan things Around the age of 10, girls start becoming more mature than boys Around the age of 11, shyness increases

By 13–16 years, most children...	feel secure to express themselves within the company of their carers

4 Family and peer relationships

0–2 YEARS

By 6 months, most babies will...	look at face of caregiver smile or vocalise to make social contact make eye contact with carer and others
By 12 months, most babies will...	reach out for and show a preference for familiar person/caregiver show affection for caregiver uses caregiver as a resource in a social way take an interest in other children

By 24 months, most children will...	be demanding of carer's attention defend own possessions play near peers readily
By age 5, most children will...	be able to addresses at least two familiar people by name show an interest in the activity of others show affection for younger siblings engage in simple and informal peer group games
By age 8, most children will...	show a preference for some friends over others make own friends comfort other people when they are upset dislike being alone and want companionship become more resentful of parental authority
By 9–12 years, most children...	know likes/dislikes of others can cope with staying overnight at a friend's house go places with friends co-operate with rules of play and teamwork engage in team games engage increasingly in girlfriend/boyfriend talk
By 13–16 years most children...	converse with others on topics of mutual interest, initiate social small talk when they meet acquaintances have a group of friends Emerging sexual relationships are more common

5 Self-care and competence

0–2 YEARS

By 6 months most babies will...	open mouth when food is presented
By 12 months, most babies can...	feed self a biscuit or other appropriate food demonstrate an understanding that hot things are dangerous
By age 2, most children can...	drink from cup without spilling indicate toilet needs
By age 3, most children can...	dress self apart from laces, ties and buttons brush teeth without assistance use a knife and fork
By age 5, most children can...	eat skillfully in culturally appropriate manner care for all toileting needs without assistance

By 6–8 years most, children will...	be able to dress in anticipation of changes in the weather demonstrate an interest in changing clothes when they are wet and muddy
By 9–12 years, most children can...	care for minor cuts on their own wash and clean themselves unsupervised
By 13–16 years, most children can...	take medicine on their own (with parental awareness) perform chores show an awareness of healthy diet, need for dental care manage menstruation (girls) cook simple food wash sufficiently and frequently to be socially acceptable travel without an adult (if safe and if there are opportunities to do so)

6 Social presentation

By 3–5 years, most children will...	say please when asking for something comfort parents/carers/peers when they are distressed share toys or possessions with others
By 6–8 years most children will...	greet people in socially appropriate way, begin to consider needs and wishes of others participate in conversation with peers and adults
By 9–12 years most, children will...	cover mouth and nose when coughing or sneezing refrain from publicly commenting on others' physical attributes
By 13–16 years, most children can...	care for all physical and self-presentation on own apologise for their own mistakes

7 Identity

Between 0–2 years, most children develop...	a sense of trust and security a sense of separateness an ability to respond to their own name
Between 3–5 years most children develop...	a sense of autonomy – child views self as an individual in their own right although still dependent on carers a sense of initiative – this is a period of vigorous reality testing, imagination, and imitation of adult behaviour
Between 6–8 years most children develop...	an awareness of self as an individual and part of a family, with increasing awareness of cultural and racial identity confidence for self-expression an ability to see self as individual but also part of peer group
Between 9–12 years, most children develop...	an increasing establishment of cultural identity an awareness of race and racism
Between 13–16 years, most children...	have hobbies of their own have begun the adolescent clarification of their identity and role

Appendix iv

'What's Wrong With Mum?'

by Briege Rooney, Senior Social Worker,
Newbury Social Services Department

Background

This story was designed to help two boys aged six and eight understand why they couldn't live with their mother. She had a diagnosis of depression and 'borderline personality disorder'. This story could help school-age children who are struggling to understand parental mental illness. In the case of Michael and Thomas (not their real names), the boys' mother was in hospital and they were voluntarily placed by her in local authority care.

Mother (a single parent) saw the story before her children and she approved. She was present (along with the boys' keyworker) when we read it with them. It led to a family discussion about their mother's symptoms which the boys had noticed and how her illness affected her and the family. This enabled more accurate identification of areas of confusion. The boys were subsequently able to attend play therapy sessions. 'Muddles' was the term one of the boys used and one both could understand. Overall, they did seem to benefit from the story, the discussion it provoked, and neither the carers nor the mother reported any adverse affects.

'What's Wrong With Mum?'

A story for Michael and Thomas

'Our mum is not well. She has an illness which means that sometimes she does not feel very well. When mum isn't feeling well it is because she has 'muddles in her head'. 'Muddles in the head' make people feel all jumbled up and confused. They can also make people feel sad. Sometimes mum feels sad. When mum is feeling sad, she is sometimes silent and quiet. Sometimes mum worries about things too much. All of these things can make mum feel very tired and 'muddled'.

People who have 'muddles' in the head need lots of help to sort them out. There are special nurses and doctors to help mum. Mum sometimes goes to a 'special hospital' to have a rest, and to let the special doctors and nurses help her to sort out the 'muddles' in her head. They do this by talking to mum, and by mum talking to them. This is called 'talking treatments'. Sometimes mum is also given special medicine to help with her 'muddles'. This medicine can make mum feel very tired and she needs to rest a lot.

When mums (or dads) become ill with 'muddles' in the head, it is never the fault of the children. Children do not cause mums to have 'muddles' in their head. No-one is sure how or why people get 'muddles' in the head.

Although mum has 'muddles' in her head, she still knows that she loves Michael and Thomas very much. However, because the 'muddles' make mum feel sad, confused and unwell, it means that she cannot look after Michael and Thomas the way that she would like to. That is why Michael and Thomas are being looked after at 'Woodlands'.

The special doctors and nurses will help mum get well again. However, they do not know how long it will be until the 'muddles' in mum's head get better. A special nurse called Sue will come to see mum at her house to check how mum is, and how her 'muddles' are. The special nurse Sue also makes sure that mum has enough medicine. Briege also visits mum to see how she is and to try to work out when mum will be well enough to look after Michael and Thomas again. At the moment, mum is well enough to look after Michael and Thomas on Saturday nights.

It is good for children to have someone to talk to when they have a mum who has 'muddles' in her head. This can be a friend or relative, a carer at 'Woodlands', Briege, the school nurse or a teacher.

Mum is being well looked after and we all hope that one day her 'muddles' will get better.

Appendix v

Resources and further reading

Books and reviews

General

Cleaver, H., Unell, I. & Aldgate, J. (forthcoming) *Parent's Problems – Children's Needs: Child Protection and Parental Mental Illness, Problem Alcohol and Drug Use and Domestic Violence.* London: Deptartment of Health.

Davies, T. & Craig, T. K. J. (Eds.) (1998) *ABC of mental health.* London: BMJ Books.

Gopfert, M., Webster, J. & Seeman M. V. (1996) *Parental Psychiatric Disorder: Distressed Parents and Their Families.* Cambridge University Press.

Lefley, H. & Wasow, M. (Eds.) (1994) *Helping Families Cope With Mental Illness.* Harwood Academic Publishers.

Penfold, P. & Walker, G. (1984) *Women and the psychiatric paradox.* Milton Keynes: Open University Press.

Perris, C., Arrindel, W. & Eisemann, M. (Eds.) (1994) *Parenting and psychopathology.* Chichester: John Wiley & Sons.

Reder, P. & Lucey, C. (Eds.) (1995) *Assessment of Parenting: Psychiatric and psychological contributions.* London: Routledge.

Dinner, S. (1989) *Nothing to be ashamed of: Growing up with mental Illness in your family.* New York: Lothrop, Lee & Shepard.

Weir, A. & Douglas, A. (forthcoming) *Child Protection and Adult Mental Health: Conflict of interest?* Oxford: Butterworth-Heinemann.

Leaflets

Department of Health (1997) *Fostering good mental health in young people.* Intended primarily for foster carers, residential workers and social workers working with children and young people. It aims to encourage greater awareness about the mental health needs of children and young people. Obtainable from: Department of Health Publications, PO Box 410, Wetherby, West Yorkshire LS23 7LN (Fax: 0990 210266).

Australian Association of Children of Parents with Mental Illness (AACPMI) Newsletter available from: Prahran Mission, Mothers Support Program, PO Box 68, Prahran 3181, Victoria, Australia.

The National Children's Bureau Highlight series, produced by the library and information centre, 8 Wakley Street, London EC1V 7QE. (Tel: 0171 843 6000).

Child mental health

Rutter, M., Taylor, E. & Hersov (Eds.) (1994) Child and Adolescent Psychiatry: *Modern Approaches.* Oxford: Blackwell Scientific Publications.

Child abuse

Cicchetti, D. & Carlson, V. (Eds.) (1991) *Child Maltreatment: Theory and research on the causes and consequences of child abuse and neglect.* Cambridge University Press.

Domestic violence

Mezey, G. & Bewley, S. (1997) Domestic violence and pregnancy: Risk is greatest after delivery. *British Medical Journal,* **314**, 12–95.

O'Hara, M. (1995) *Children and domestic violence.* Highlight Series No. 139. London: National Children's Bureau.

Richardson, J. & Feder, G. (1995) Domestic violence against women: Needs action from doctors and the health service. *British Medical Journal,* **311**, 964–965.

Schizophrenia

Barrowclough, C., Tarrier, N. (1992) *Families of schizophrenic patients: Cognitive behavioural intervention.* London: Chapman and Hall.

Kuipers, L., Leff, J. & Lam, D. (1997) *Family work for schizophrenia: A practical guide.* London: Gaskell.

Tylee, A. (1994) Guidelines for schizophrenia management. *Hospital Update,* **23** (supplement, psychiatry seminar).

Wilkinson, G. & Kendrick, T. (1996) *A carer's guide to schizophrenia.* London: Royal Society of Medicine Press.

Depression

Clinical Resource and Audit Group (1995) *Depressive Illness: A critical review of current practice and the way forward – consensus statement.* Edinburgh: Scottish Office.

Craig, T. (1996) Adversity and depression. *International Review of Psychiatry,* **8**, 341–353.

Down on the farm? Coping with depression in rural areas; a farmer's guide. Available from: Health Literature Helpline (Tel: 0800 555 777).

The experience of grief. Available from: National Association of Bereavement Services, 20 Norton Folgate, London E1 6DB (Tel: 0171 247 1080).

Personality Disorder

Dolan, B. & Coid, J. (Eds.) (1993) *Psychopathic and antisocial personality disorders: Treatment and research issues.* London: Gaskell.

Tyrer, P. & Stein, G. (Eds.) (1993) *Personality disorder reviewed.* London: Gaskell.

Drug and alcohol dependence

Chick, J. & Cantwell, R. (Eds.) (1994) *Seminars in alcohol and drug abuse.* London: Gaskell.

Department of Health (1991) *Drug misuse and dependence: Guidelines on clinical management.* London: HMSO.

World Health Organisation (1993) *Alcohol action plan for Europe.* Copenhagen: WHO.

UK Alcohol Forum (1997) *Guidelines for the management of alcohol problems in primary care and general psychiatry.* High Wycombe: UK AF.

Prevention of mental illness

Kendrick, T., Tylee, A. & Freeling, P. (Eds.) (1996) *The prevention of mental illness in primary care.* Cambridge University Press.

Newton, J. (1988) *Preventing Mental Illness.* London: Routledge & Kegan Paul.

Williams, R. & Morgan, G. (1994) *Suicide prevention: The challenge confronted.* London: HMSO.

Training materials

Bouras, N. & Holt, G. (1997, 2nd ed.) *Mental Health in Learning Disabilities: A training pack for staff working with people who have a dual diagnosis of mental health needs and learning disabilities.* Brighton: Pavilion Publishing.

The emotional effects of childbirth. A distance learning course for midwives, health visitors and others who care for women around the time of childbirth. The Marce Society.

Learning materials on Mental Health – An Introduction (1996). University of Manchester & Department of Health.

Turning Points: A resource pack for communicating with children. Produced by the NSPCC.

Parker, R., Ward, H., Jackson, S., Aldgate, J. & Wedge, P. (1991) (Eds.) *Looking after children: Assessing outcomes in childcare.* London: HMSO.

DH Training pack: 'Letting through Light' (forthcoming).

Making an impact: Children and domestic violence – a training resource. (1998) Produced by The Department of Health, School for Policy Studies, Bristol University, NSPCC and Barnardos.

A training pack on black people and mental health (1998). REU publications (CI (98)13).

Organisations

Mental Health

Good Practices in Mental Health
380–384 Harrow Road
London W9 2HU
Tel: 0171 289 2034

Assists those involved in mental health services (users, providers or purchasers) to come together to debate and reflect on service provision.

Hearing Voices Network
c/o creative support
16 Tariff Street
Manchester M1 2EP
Tel: 0161 228 3896

A voluntary organisation which assists in setting up self help groups for those who have experienced hearing voices.

Mental Health Foundation
20–21 Cornwall Terrace
Regents Park
London NW1 4QL
Tel: 0171 535 7480

Mind (National Association for Mental Health)
Granta House
15–17 Broadway
Stratford
London E15 4BQ
Tel: 0181 519 2122
Info-Line: (0181) 522 1728 and 0345 660 163

Provides a national information and legal service as well as local groups across the country offering various support services in the community.

National Schizophrenia Fellowship (NSF)
28 Castle Street
Kingston-upon-Thames
Surrey KT1 1SS
Tel: 0181 547 3937

Provides advice service, a network of self-help groups and projects across the country and publishes a useful leaflet for patients and families: *What is schizophrenia?*

Royal College of Psychiatrists
17 Belgrave Square
London SW1X 8PG
Tel: 0171 235 2351

The professional organisation for psychiatrists in the UK and Ireland which publishes leaflets and factsheets on common mental mental health problems in adults and children. Also involved in public campaigns (Defeat Depression) and tackling stigma.

Saneline
199–205 Old Marylebone Rd
London NW1 5QP
Tel: 0171 724 8000 and 0345 678000

A national mental health helpline offering emotional support and practical information to anyone coping with mental illness (sufferers, carers, family member or professional).

Schizophrenia A National Emergency (SANE)
199–205 Old Marylebone Road
London NWI 5Q1

Survivors Speak Out
34 Osnaburgh Street
London NW1 3ND
Tel: 0171 916 6991

An information network to improve contact between groups and individuals who are psychiatric system survivors.

The Samaritans
10 The Grove
Slough SL1 1QP
Tel: 01753 532 713

Confidential 24-hour emotional support
to those in crisis and at risk of harming
themselves.

United Kingdom Advocacy Network (UKAN)
Premier House
14 Cross Burgess Street
Sheffield S1 2HG
Tel: 0114 275 3131

A network of user-led groups involved in
advocacy, patient councils and service
planning.

Depression

Depression Alliance
PO Box 1022
London SE1 7GR
Tel: 0171 721 7672

A national charity run by people who have
suffered from depression to provide information, support and understanding to people
who are depressed and their carers.

The Manic Depression Fellowship
8–10 High Street
Kingston-upon-Thames KT1 1EY
Tel: 0181 974 6550

Has active local groups in many areas which
provide support, advice and information for
those with manic depression, their families,
friends and carers.

Postnatal Depression

Association for Postnatal Illness
7 Gowan Ave
London SW6 6RH
Tel: 0171 731 4867

Stillbirth and Neonatal Death Society (SANDS)
28 Portland Place
London W1N 4DE
Tel: 0171 436 7940

Provides support for parents affected by
the stillbirth or other perinatal or neonatal
death of a child.

The National Childbirth Association
Alexandra House
Oldham Terrace
London W3 6NH
Tel: 0181 992 8637

Substance misuse

Al-Anon Family Groups
61 Great Dover Street
London SE1 4YF
Tel: 0171 403 0888

Provides support and opportunity for
relatives and friends of alcoholics
to share their experience.

Alcoholics Anonymous
PO Box 1
Stonebow House
Stonebow
York YO1 2NJ
Tel: 01904 644026

Drinkline
Weddel House
13–14 West Smithfield
London EC1A 9DL
Tel: 0171 332 0202 or 0345 320202

Offers information, advice and support
to people concerned about their own or
someone else's drinking.

Drugline Ltd
9A Brockley Cross
London SE4 2AB
Tel: 0181 692 4975

Greater London Association of Alcohol Services (GLAAS)
30–31 Great Sutton Street
London EC1V 0DX
Tel: 0171 253 6221

Provides information and advice for and on behalf of the numerous alcohol projects in and around London, including advice to people with drinking problems and to professional workers.

Institute for the Study of Drug Dependence
Waterbridge House
32–36 Loman Street
London SE1 0EE
Tel: 0171 928 1211

Collects and disseminates information on all aspects of drug misuse.

Children

Carers National Association
20-25 Glasshouse Yard
London EC1A 4JS
Tel: 0171 490 8818

Childline
Royal Mail Building
Studd Street
London N1 0QW
Tel: 0171 239 1000

Children's Legal Centre
20 Compton Terrace
London N1 2UN
Tel: 0171 359 9392

Family Rights Group
The Print House
18 Ashwin Street
London E8 3DL
Tel: 0171 923 2628

Provides advice and support to families involved with social services in child protection and court proceedings or contact or support issues involving children.

Family Welfare Association (FWA)
501–505 Kingsland Road
London E8 4AU
Tel: 0181 690 4422

Provides a range of informal drop-in centres and other community services in partnership with health authorities and GP practices. FWA in Lewisham developing services for mentally ill parents and children in partnership with health trust and social services.

National Alliance for the Mentally Ill (NAMI)
Facts for Families: Children of parents with mental illness.
http://www.nami.org
http://www.aacap.org

Newpin
Sutherland House
35 Sutherland Square
Walworth
London SE17 3EE
Tel: 0171 703 6326

Provides opportunities to deal with life patterns associated with depression in parents and abuse in children.

Relate National Marriage Guidance
Tel: 01788 573241

Offer marital and couple counselling.

The Network
PO Box 558
London SW2 2EL

Young Minds
22a Boston Place
London NW1 6ER
Tel: 0171 724 7262

Produce useful series of leaflets in children's mental health.

Mental health services for minority ethnic groups

African Caribbean Mental Health Association (ACMHA)
35–37 Electric Avenue
Brixton
London SW9 8JP
Tel: 0171 737 3603

Provides advice, counselling and psychotherapy for individuals, families, and groups.

Chinese Mental Health Association
Oxford House
Derbyshire Street
London E2 6HB
Tel: 0171 613 1008

Fanon Centre
Brixton
London
Tel: 0171 737 2888

A drop-in and advice centre for mentally ill people of African Caribbean origin. It has support groups for women, homeless people and families.

Horn Of Africa Community Group
Sands End Community Centre
59–61 Broughton Road
London SW6 2LE
Tel: 0171 610 6099

Ipamo ('A place of healing')
Tel: 0171 737 4585.

Developing alternatives to hospital admission for black people with mental health problems.

Medical Foundation for the Care of Victims of Torture
96–98 Grafton Road
London NW5 3EJ
Tel: 0171 482 0219

Provides survivors of torture with medical treatment, social assistance and psychotherapeutic support.

Nafsiyat Inter-Cultural Therapy Centre
278 Seven Sisters Road
London N4 2HY
Tel: 0171 263 4130

Refugee Support Centre
7 South Lambeth Road
London SW9 1RH
Tel: 0171 820 3606

The Advocacy Project
91 Upper Parliament Street
Liverpool L8 7LB
Tel: 0151 709 9442

Aims to raise awareness of health and social care professionals and voluntary sector workers about the needs of black people with mental health problems.

Vietnamese Mental Health Project
Tel: 0171 7336179

Provides support for Vietnamese refugees and their families.

Children

have

FEELINGS

by

Harriet Hampster   AND

Ashley Brown Mouse

1

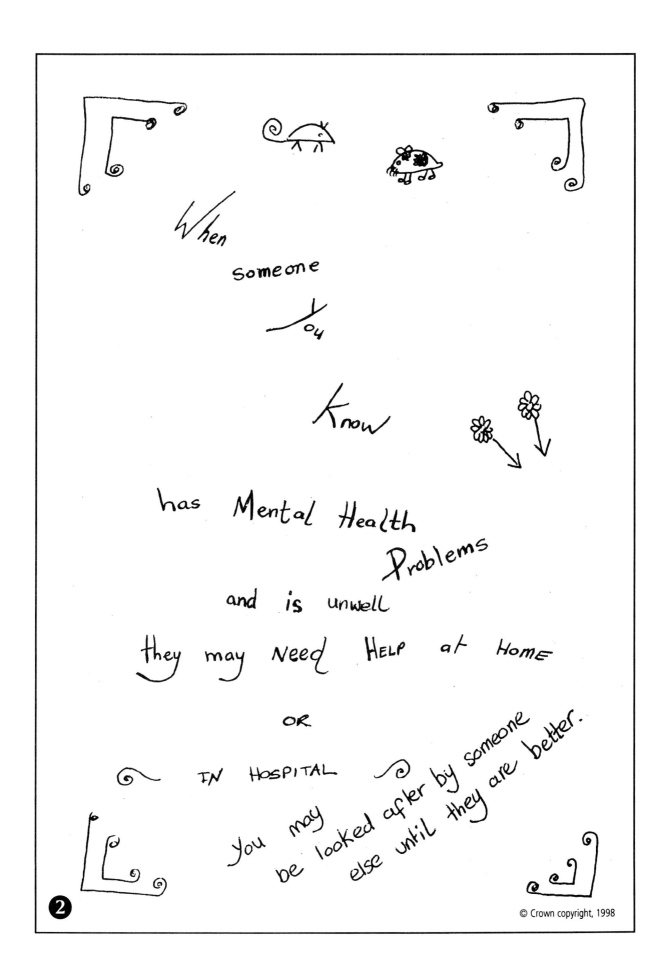

When someone you know has Mental Health Problems and is unwell they may Need HELP at HOME OR IN HOSPITAL you may be looked after by someone else until they are better.

❷

When someone is ill it can be scary....

When it is someone you love it can be very, very, upsetting and maybe you feel very sad inside.

IF IT IS THE PERSON WHO LOOKS AFTER YOU MOST YOU MAY FEEL ANGRY WITH THEM you may feel so cross that you want to shout or stamp or break something.

IF IT IS YOUR MUMMY OR DADDY OR ANOTHER SPECIAL PERSON IN YOUR LIFE YOU MAY EVEN THINK THEY DON'T LOVE YOU ANY MORE AND YOU may even think that it is all your fault.

❸

When someone has a mental health problem it is not easy to see what is wrong with them.

They may not look different but they may act in a different way.

They may want to be alone and not be very cuddly.

They may forget things – like putting on their shoes or making your tea or taking the dog for a walk.

They may seem sad a lot and cry a lot without knowing why.

They may shout a lot.

They may go not want to see outside or see their friends.

They may seem very muddled up.

They may seem to be asking around a lot more than usual.

"mummy why are you going out without your coat?" when it is raining."

4

© Crown copyright, 1998

Ashley Brown Mouse said that when his mummy was ill inside her head she slept a lot in hospital in her bed. He thought she was going to die.

when someone is ill they can feel very tired and need to sleep and be looked after. They may need to be looked after in hospital by nurses and doctors until they feel better and can come home again.

THIS does not mean that they are going to die. It does not mean that they do not love you any more — deep down inside they love you as much as they always have.

It is not your fault that they are ill.

5

Harriet Hampster said that when her daddy was ill she felt like crying but she stopped herself because someone told her not to cry and that everything was OK. Harriet did not feel like everything was ok because she missed her daddy so much and she felt lonely inside herself. Harriet did not tell the person caring for her that she felt like that.

You can cry if you want to

IT's OK

It is ok to cry

Crying can make you feel a bit better or even a lot better — It is NATURAL and NORMAL

6

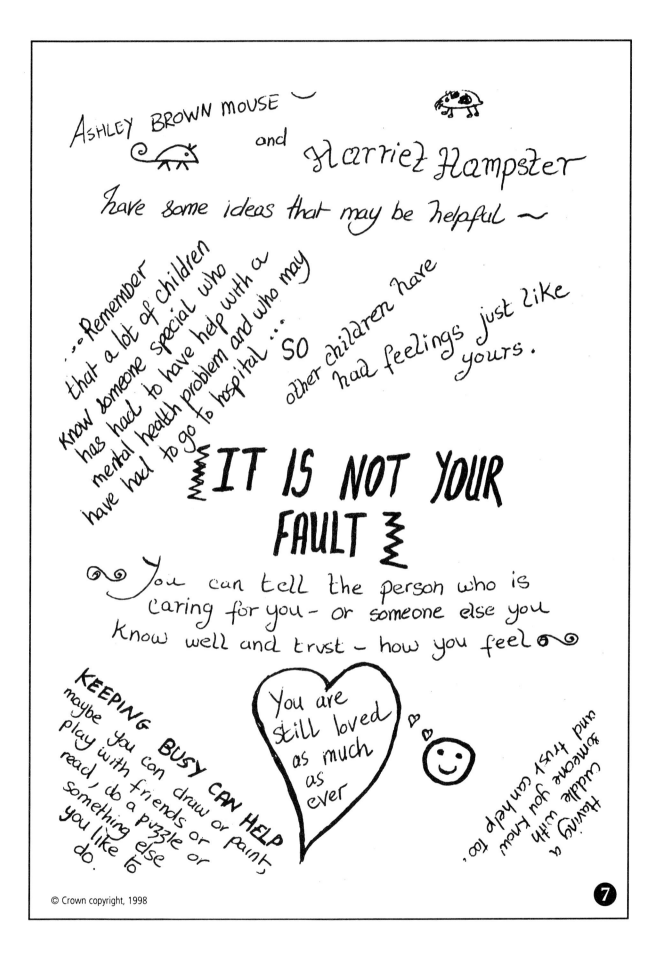

ASHLEY BROWN MOUSE and Harriet Hampster have some ideas that may be helpful ~

...Remember that a lot of children know someone special who has had to have help with a mental health problem and who may) have had to go to hospital... SO other children have had feelings just like yours.

IT IS NOT YOUR FAULT

You can tell the person who is caring for you - or someone else you know well and trust - how you feel

KEEPING BUSY CAN HELP maybe you can draw or paint, play with friends or read, do a puzzle or something else you like to do.

You are still loved as much as ever

Having a cuddle with someone you trust and someone you know can help too.

7

compiled by
Heide, Hannah and Georgina Lloyd
and based on personal
experience.

Hopefully, this booklet will be helpful to children trying to cope with their own feelings when a parent or main carer is unwell with mental illhealth

8

COPING

at Home

FOR PARENTS

by Heide Lloyd

When a person with mental health difficulties tries to cope at home, that is demanding enough. When there are children to care for also it can sometimes seem impossible to cope at all.

Sometimes there is not even a real opportunity to begin to manage an illness, let alone the time to recover enough from the worst stages of illness, before having to take on all of the responsibilities of the parenting role again.

No matter how much a parent loves their children or how well they coped with parenting before becoming ill, the devastating effects of illness upon the parent and children in the family can make home life very difficult.

If you find yourself in this situation you may well feel exhausted, emotionally and physically, and at times feel completely overwhelmed by your responsibilities. Even when relatives and friends are supportive you may still feel isolated and very alone in the world. At times like this it can seem as though no-one really cares about you or the demands placed upon you.

Reassuring children and resettling them into your normal homelife routine can feel daunting. Meeting up with friends again or simply facing school crowds can seem almost impossible and provoke considerable anxiety.

2

COPING AT HOME • *Crossing Bridges* © Crown copyright, 1998.

Many people worry that if they have mental health problems, their children will be removed from their care. This worry stopes them from asking for help when they need it. It is much better to ask for help early rather than let a crisis build up.

It may help to consider the following:

● Not everyone knows how ill you have been or what your illness is.

● You do not have to share details of your illness with others if you do not wish to.

● Having mental health problems does not make you socially unacceptable.

● Your illness, if you allow yourself to be helped by properly qualified professionals, can be treated and the quality of your life improved accordingly.

● Your value as an individual human being has not been reduced because you have suffered from, or are suffering from, a mental health illness.

● You can obtain more specific information about your illness from your GP, CPN, counsellor, psychologist, psychiatrist or a support organisation related to your illness. Telephone numbers for support organisations can be obtained from a booklet produced by Social Services or from a mental health expert who is treating you.

3

COPING AT HOME • *Crossing Bridges* © Crown copyright, 1998.

- You still have the right to be taken seriously in your concerns for your own health and safety and for the health and safety of your children.

- It can be very helpful to talk to your children about your illness, explaining it in ways they can understand. If they ask you questions about your illness, try to answer as honestly as you can. Sometimes children have their own worries and fears. If you can encourage them to share these with you, you may be able to put many of their fears to rest.

Discussing worries about social issues and how you and your children are coping is something you can do with your social worker, CPN or anyone else in your mental health team. If you are not sure who any of these people are you can ask your GP for a name and contact number of someone who is part of your mental health team.

If you have been staying in hospital you can check with your primary nurse as to when your next appointment is and with whom. You can also ask for the telephone number of someone you can contact should you need some support once you are at home. Discussing any practical problems you

4

COPING AT HOME • *Crossing Bridges* © Crown copyright, 1998.

may have, or any fears and anxieties you are experiencing, relating to your hospital discharge and return home can also be reassuring. It is not unusual to be very fearful of returning home and caring for dependant children immediately after hospital discharge.

Other things you can do which may help to reduce stress build-up:

● You could decide to make certain that you have enough food at home to cover meals for at least two days in the event that you should feel too tired or unwell to cope with shopping.

● It may be a good idea to have a few convenience meals to hand for you and your children which can help to make meal preparation less stressful and demanding.

● Preparing for the following day in advance can be helpful. Laying out clothes for yourself and your children, setting out breakfast items as far as is possible and preparing lunch boxes for children and storing them in the fridge overnight can make getting out of bed slightly less difficult. It also helps to regain feelings of being in control so that the start of the day does not seem quite so overwhelming.

5

COPING AT HOME • *Crossing Bridges* © Crown copyright, 1998.

● Structuring your days in advance is not a failing of abilities. It is a constructive step towards managing, and not being managed by, your illness.

● If you are experiencing problems in coping with going to shops, to school with the children, or simply getting out of your home, you can discuss this with a member of your mental health team. Talking about real anxieties can help to reduce the fear and you may discover new ways of coping which could help you. Sometimes stress management courses are run by psychiatric hospitals or local voluntary or self-help groups. You can find out about these courses from social services, your GP or your local psychiatric hospital.

● If you are about to be discharged from hospital and are aware that you do not have enough money to buy food and other essentials for your return home you can discuss this with your social worker, your primary nurse, the DSS or the ward financial manager. If you are experiencing debt or benefit allowance problems you can also contact a local voluntary advice centre for help and advice.

6

COPING AT HOME • *Crossing Bridges* © Crown copyright, 1998.

● Having time in the day to yourself to relax
or to sleep is not a crime. You may be coping
with many thoughts, feelings and demands upon
your time, physically and emotionally. Learning
or relearning to value yourself and your time is
an important part of your life.

**After time you will find other ways of helping
yourself to cope with home and family life, friends
and social situations and many other aspects of
your life.**

7